R. Gupta's®

B.ARCH. NATA

Knowledge Bank

Practice Test Papers

Contains actual NATA questions with answers. Original Sketches, Memory Drawings, 2D/3D Compositions, Perspectives, Colour Drawings prepared by Students Aspiring for NATA Entrance, Coloured Photos of Famous National and International Buildings

Ashok Goel (Architect)
B. Arch. from SPA, New Delhi
Dip. (German), University of Delhi
P.G. Dip., (Journalism)
Fellow Indian Institute of Architects

2021
EDITION

Ramesh Publishing House, New Delhi

Published by: O.P. Gupta for Ramesh Publishing House

Admin. Office: 12-H, New Daryaganj Road, Opp. Officers' Mess,
New Delhi-110002 ✆ 23261567, 23275224, 23275124

E-mail: info@rameshpublishinghouse.com
Website: www.rameshpublishinghouse.com

Showroom:
- Balaji Market, Nai Sarak, Delhi-6 ✆ 23253720, 23282525
- 4457, Nai Sarak, Delhi-6, ✆ 23918938

Book Code: R-1817

ISBN: 978-93-88642-89-7

HSN Code: 49011010

PREFACE

More than fifty per cent of the total development expenditure in India is in the construction sector. The last decade is distinguished by the commencement of several mega projects, both in the public and private sectors. The new policy of the Government has opened up opportunities for large scale investment in the Indian economy by multinational companies as well as their Indian equivalents. These considerable investments by International and Indian funding agencies have brought and will continue to bring unprecedented activities in the construction sector. There is hence, a dire need and urgency to produce professionals, Architects, Construction Managers, Urban Planners, Interior Designers, as our country needs large number of trained man-power to undertake the developmental works speedily. India has become a major center for investments in the field of Realestate and Infra-structural Development.

Number of schools/institutions of architecture with their annual intake are thus being increased every year and they all are governed by Council of Architecture (COA), New Delhi, for their quality education. COA has been constituted by the Government of India under the provisions of the Architects' Act 1972 enacted by the Parliament of India.

Presently the number of schools/colleges offering five years **B. Arch.** Degree course in the country are more than 465 (as on 1 January, 2020) and admission to the course in all schools/colleges of architecture is compulsorily through aptitude tests. The syllabus and pattern of the tests are prescribed by Council of Architecture, New Delhi and it is being conducted by some State Boards and National Testing Agency, New Delhi. **NATA** is conducted by the COA.

Today there are several helpbooks available in the market for mathematics and science subjects but very few for architecture aptitude tests covering the syllabus of **NATA**. Through this book **B.ARCH. NATA KNOWLEDGE BANK,** sincere efforts have been made to provide help especially for those candidates who have no access for personal coaching. It took many years to complete this handbook and hundreds of students were interacted before putting this handbook into final shape.

These **B.ARCH. NATA KNOWLEDGE BANK,** prepare potential entrants for success in obtaining merit in the aptitude test. Full care has been taken to cover the entire syllabus of NATA.

I am indebted to all those architects and students whose work has direct or indirect bearing in preparing this handbook. Council of Architecture, New Delhi need a special mention in this respect. I also wish to express my sincere thanks to architect Arjun Kamal and architect Aditya Kamal who have contributed for bringing out this handbook.

-Ar. Ashok Goel
10A/14 Shakti Nagar, Delhi - 110007
Mobile: 9213102764, 9582240087

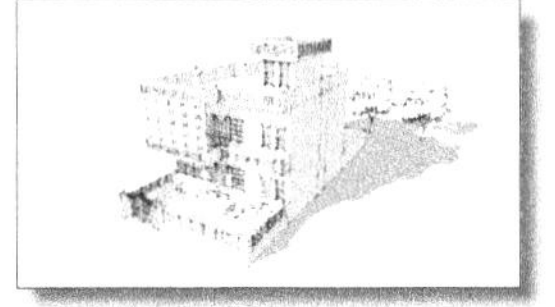

CONTENTS

SHORTAGE OF ARCHITECTS

UK
Population = 6,22,62,000
No. of Architects = 33,000
1 Architect per 1887 persons

United States
Population = 30,87,45,538
No. of Architects = 2,33,000
1 Architect per 1325 persons

India
Population = 1,21,01,93,422
No. of Architects = 49,500 (approx.)
1 Architect per 24,448 persons
You Require 6 lakh 41 thousand architects as per British Standards.
You require 9 lakh 13 thousand architects as per American Standards
If you take the average of UK and USA then you require approximately 7.5 lakh architects in India.
Therefore estimated shortage of architects = 7 Lakhs.

WHAT IS ARCHITECTURE?

The word architecture can have many meanings. Depending on the context, architecture can refer to:
1. Any man-made building or structure
2. A man-made building or structure that is important, large, or highly creative
3. A carefully designed object, such as a chair, a spoon, or a tea kettle
4. A design for a city, town, park, or landscape
5. The art or science of designing and building buildings, structures, objects, and outdoor paces
6. A building style or method
7. A plan for organizing space

The introduction of variety of building materials coupled with their ability to support a particular form and size of a building has added to the wealth of the knowledge that Indians already possessed. With expanding global economies, rising incomes, mass migration of people from rural to urban areas as a result of mass transport systems available, the demand on architecture has increased manifolds.

A wider definition may comprise all design activity, from the macro-level (urban design, landscape architecture) to the microlevel (construction details and furniture). It is the process and product of planning, designing and constructing form, space and ambience that reflect functional, technical, social, environmental, and aesthetic considerations. It requires the creative manipulation and coordination of material, technology, light and shadow. Architecture also encompasses the pragmatic aspects of realizing buildings and structures, including scheduling, cost estimating and construction administration. As documentation produced by architects, typically drawings, plans and technical specifications, architecture defines the structure and/or behaviour of a building or any other kind of system that is to be or has been constructed. While the production of architectural thought requires an understanding of Art, Culture, humanities, context and identity; complexities of physical and social contexts etc. that shape architecture and help in the creation of "Creative Innovations" the implementation of the architectural thought requires sound technical knowledge in the field of structures, building construction, Illumination, Acoustics, Services etc essential for the implementation and execution of the project. In addition, in the digital world, architects today should be well equipped with the knowledge of computers. The responsibilities assigned to an architect require him to be an effective manager. An architect has to be both a team player and a leader. Not only is he required to deal with his clients and ensure the best out of his design team, but also included in his list of activities is to co-ordinate between various design and technical consultants and supervise work at site. In effect, an architect is a project planner and manager.

B.ARCH. DEGREE PROGRAMME

The goal of B.Arch. degree programme is therefore, to build a broad and balanced foundation for this knowledge and these abilities. The potential variety of an architect's practice is mirrored in the educational programme. The architecture students are trained by getting exposed to live problems, situations and circumstances. Teaching, throughout the course of five years, is based on an inter-disciplinary approach which in addition to classroom learning through lectures, slide talks, discussions, assignments, comprehension tests, etc. entails numerous site visits and on-the-spot studies. Students are encouraged to make their own observations of facts, to analyze and to evaluate them so that they may learn to reckon the relevance and applicability of investigative studies to the program requirements of creative course work in architectural design.

B. ARCH. COURSE

The concept and direction of architectural design, however takes shape gradually through the development of the 10-semester course. Beginning with an introduction to the theory and application of Basic Design, exercises in critical appreciation and creativity culminate in a research and/or design thesis in which a student gets an opportunity to handle all phases of architectural design. This attempt ranges from the choice of the subject of thesis, case/prototype/library studies, analysis, identification/statement of the problem and the objectives to the formulation of client's, architect's brief and hence to the planning and design solution. Job Opportunities As professional experts in the field of building design and construction, architects use their unique creative skills to advise individuals, property owners and developers, community groups, local authorities and commercial organizations. Generally architects work with architectural firms, in entrepreneurial ventures. But they are not limited to working only at traditional architectural firms. They also work as corporate and public architects. Corporate architects are employed within the retail, office, manufacturing, medical and hospitality industries, and there are numerous job choices available at such companies, ranging from entry-level planners to high level executives. Public architects work for government agencies. The government recruits architects to serve on capital projects planning, design and construction programs. Besides these, some public institutes and agencies that function at the state level are: Public Works Departments, State housing boards, municipal corporations, cooperative societies. A number of research institutes such as the CBRI is involved in research and development in this field. Researches are conducted to invent new methods and techniques of construction, so that the cost of construction may be minimized. Researches are also conducted to invent new equipment and good quality construction material. In terms of other career options, architects can serve as writers, critics and educators.

Council of Architecture

The Council of Architecture (COA) has been constituted by the Government of India under the provisions of the Architects Act, 1972, enacted by the Parliament of India, which came into force on 1st September, 1972. The Act provides for registration of Architects, standards of education, recognized qualifications and standards of practice to be complied with by the practicing architects. The Council of Architecture is charged with the responsibility to regulate the education and practice of profession throughout India besides maintaining the register of architects. For this purpose, the Government of India has framed Rules and Council of Architecture has framed Regulations as provided for in the Architects Act, with the approval of Government of India.

ARCHITECT

Any person desirous of carrying on the profession of 'Architect' must have registered himself with Council of Architecture. For the purpose of registration, one must possess the requisite qualification as appended to the Architects Act, after having undergone the education in accordance with the Council of Architecture (Minimum Standards of Architectural Education) Regulations, 1983. The registration with Council of Architecture entitles a person to practice the profession of architecture, provided he holds a Certificate of Registration with up-to-date renewals. The registration also entitles a person to use the title and style of Architect. The title and style of architect can also be used by a firm of architects, of which all partners are registered with COA. Limited Companies, Private/Public Companies, societies and other juridical persons are not entitled to use the title and style of architect nor are they entitled to practice the profession of architecture. If any person falsely claims to be registered or misuses title and style of architect, such acts tantamount to committing of a criminal offence, which is punishable under section 36 or 37 (2) of the Architects Act, 1972.

APTITUDE TEST

In terms of Regulations of the Council of Architecture, the conduct of aptitude test is mandatory for admissions to the 5-year B. Arch. course by all colleges or institutions where Architectural Education is given, leading to grant of Recognised Qualification by authorities. Such Colleges or Institutions include a University, its department, its constituent college and its affiliated college; a deemed to be University; institutions established by Act of Parliament; and National Institutes of Technology and institution for higher education declared to be a University.

No admission shall be made under the Minority Institution/Management/Non-Resident Indian/Person of Indian Origin or any another Quota unless a candidate is subjected to the aptitude test in architecture. A separate aptitude test in Architecture should be conducted and such test should not be combined with the tests for admissions to Engineering, Pharmacy, Medicine and other disciplines. Similarly, admission counselling are to be conducted independently.

The candidates admitted to 1st year of a 5-year course without appearing in the aptitude test in architecture and who have been granted B.Arch. degree or other qualifications shall not be deemed to have attained recognised qualification listed in the schedule of qualifications appended to the Architects Act, 1972. Such candidates will not be eligible for registration as an architect with the Council of Architecture.

About NATA

The National Aptitude Test in Architecture (NATA) conducted by Council of Architecture is mandatory for admission to first year B.Arch. course for all architectural institutions in the country, including NITs, IITs, Government Institutions, Government aided Institutions, Universities, Deemed Universities and Private Universities established by a Central or State Legislature and other private institutions. It shall be mandatory for every architectural institution imparting 5-year B.Arch. degree course in the country to join the NATA and to admit students on the basis of valid NATA marks in the said course.

What Is NATA?

The National Aptitude Test in Architecture (NATA) measures the aptitude of the applicant for specific field of study, i.e., Architecture. The test measures drawing and observation skills, sense of proportion, aesthetic sensitivity and critical thinking ability, that have been acquired over a long period of time, and that are related to specific field of study, i.e., Architecture.

Who should take NATA and Why?

Prospective applicants desirous of taking admission to First year of undergraduate course in Architecture (Bachelor of Architecture) in India take NATA. NATA scores are used by admissions authorities of different Government, Govt. Aided and unaided schools/colleges of Architecture, to provide common measure for comparing the qualifications of applicants for admission in addition to their scholastic performance in 10+2 or equivalent examination.

Who Accepts It?

All schools/colleges of Architecture, Government, Government aided, University Departments, private unaided, including colleges affiliated to self-financed Deemed Universities and Private Universities, or any department of Architecture within a college, requires that its applicants take the NATA.

Weightage [NATA] The following shall be the weightage:

Architectural Aptitude 50% (Maximum)

Qualifying Examination 50% (Maximum)

Competent Authority and Conduct of Aptitude Test

The admissions shall be carried out by the Competent authority i.e., the Government or University, or such authorities/institution concerned [School/College of Architecture]/Association or Federation of Institutions [Schools or College of Architecture], as approved by the Government/University, based on the marks obtained in NATA and the qualifying examinations as mentioned above, in the ratio of 50:50.

All architectural institutions in the country shall be required to submit a list of students admitted in the B.Arch. degree course, mentioning the total NATA score and total marks in qualifying examination, to the CoA.

National Aptitude Test in Architecture (NATA) is being conducted by COA since 2006, in terms of the provisions of CoA (Minimum Standards of Architectural Education) Regulations, 1983, published in the Gazette of India. It is implied that a separate aptitude test in Architecture should be conducted and such test should not be combined with the tests for admissions to Engineering, Pharmacy, Medicine and other disciplines. Being the competent authority for fixing norms and standards for architectural institutions, COA has the necessary expertise to hold a Common Aptitude Test in Architecture, at national level to provide a single window system for appearing in aptitude test and to facilitate institutions, students and public at large for admission to First year of 5 year B.Arch. Degree Course at all recognized Institutions all over country.

In order to further strengthen the conduct of the test and to attract more number of bright aspirants into studying Architecture, COA has decided to conduct NATA for admission to B.Arch., as a one-day online examination all over the country, which will comprise of two parts: Part A comprises of Multiple Choice Questions (MCQs) to be answered online and Part B is paper based drawing. This would surely be a step towards producing competent architects to serve the society and to build the nation in coming decades, especially in view of the Govt. of India mission of Smart Cities.

Application has to be filled up ONLINE at the NATA portal. Candidates need to visit the portal and CLICK the requisite link, and thereafter will be directed to the actual application form. The form is interactive in nature and the fields required to be filled up are categorized in different sub-sections.

A candidate applying for NATA has to pay requisite fee as application fee, through ONLINE mode.

Qualifying marks for **NATA** would be based on the following rules:

1. A minimum of 32 marks out of 125 marks must be secured in Part A (approximately 25%)
2. A minimum of 18 marks out of 75 marks must be secured in Part B (approximately 25%)
3. Overall qualifying marks (out of 200) would be based on post-exam statistics and at the discretion of the Council.

A Candidate will not qualify in NATA unless he/she satisfy all three conditions mentioned above.

भारत का राजपत्र

The Gazette of India

EXTRAORDINARY

भाग III—खण्ड 4

PART III—Section 4

प्राधिकार से प्रकाशित

PUBLISHED BY AUTHORITY

सं. 63]	नई दिल्ली, बुधवार, फरवरी 13, 2019/माघ 24, 1940
No. 63]	NEW DELHI, WEDNESDAY, FEBRUARY 13, 2019/MAGHA 24, 1940

COUNCIL OF ARCHITECTURE

(STATUTORY AUTHORITY CONSTITUTED UNDER THE ARCHITECTS ACT, 1972)

NOTIFICATION

New Delhi, the 12th February, 2019

F. No. CA/12/2019/Regulations.—In exercise of powers conferred by clauses (e), (g), (h), and (j) of sub-section (2) of Section 45 read with Section 21 of the Architects Act, 1972 (20 of 1972), the Council of Architecture, with the approval of the Central Government, hereby makes the following Regulations further to amend the Council of Architecture (Minimum Standards of Architectural Education) Regulations, 1983, the same having been published in the Gazette of India, Part-III-Section-4 dated the 26th March, 1983, namely:-

1. (1) These Regulations may be called the Council of Architecture (Minimum Standards of Architectural Education) (Amendment) Regulations, 2019.

   (2) They shall come into force from the date of this publication in the Official Gazette.

2. In the Council of Architecture (Minimum Standards of Architectural Education) Regulations, 1983, in Regulation 4, for sub-regulation (1), the following sub-regulation shall be substituted, namely:-

   "(1) No candidate shall be admitted to architecture course unless she/ he has passed an examination at the end of the 10+2 scheme of examination with at least 50% aggregate marks in Physics, Chemistry & Mathematics and also at least 50% marks in aggregate of the 10+2 level examination or passed 10+3 Diploma Examination with Mathematics as compulsory subject with at least 50% marks in aggregate."

Footnote : The principal Regulations were published in the Gazette of India, Part III, Section 4, dated the 26th March, 1983 and subsequently amended and published in the Gazette of India (i) dated the 27th August, 1983, (ii) dated the 7th January, 2006, (iii) dated the 29th May, 2017.

RAJ KUMAR OBEROI, Registrar

[ADVT.III/4/Exty. /539/18]

JEE (B.ARCH./B.PLAN.)

Joint Entrance Examination **(JEE)** MAIN is being conducted TWICE by the **NATIONAL TESTING AGENCY (NTA)** from 2019 onwards. This Examination was being conducted by the Central Board of Secondary Education (CBSE) till 2018.

Subject combinations for each paper, type of questions in each paper and mode of examination is given in the table below:

B. Arch: Mathematics—Part I and Aptitude Test-Part II in "Computer Based Test (CBT)" mode only and Drawing Test –Part III in "Pen & Paper Based" (offline) mode to be attempted on drawing sheet of A4 size.			
• Subject wise distribution of Questions, Total Number of Questions and Marks	**Subject** Mathematics-Part I Aptitude Test-Part II Drawing Test–Part III **Total**	**No of Questions** (20+5*) 50 02 **77**	**Marks** 100 200 100 **400**
*20 questions will be MCQs and 5 questions will have answer to be filled as numerical value.			
• (a) Marking Scheme for MCQs	Correct Answer Incorrect Answer/Multiple Answer Unanswered /Marked for Review	Four mark (+4) Minus one mark (-1) No mark (0)	
(b) Marking Scheme for questions for which answer is a Numerical value	Correct Answer Incorrect Answer Unanswered / Marked for Review	Four mark (+4) No mark (0) No mark (0)	
(c) Marking Scheme for Drawing Test –Part III	Two questions to be evaluated out of 100 marks.		
• Method of determining merit	Conversion of raw score in Mathematics, Aptitude Test, Drawing Test and Total into NTA Scores. Overall merit shall be prepared by merging NTA Scores of all shifts of all days.		
B. Planning : Mathematics- Part I, Aptitude Test-Part II and Planning Based Questions Part III in "Computer Based Test (CBT)" mode only			
• Subject wise distribution of Questions, Total Number of Questions and Marks	**Subject** Mathematics-Part I Aptitude Test-Part II Planning Based Objective Type MCQs –Part III **Total**	**No of Questions** (20+5*) 50 25 **100**	**Marks** 100 200 100 **400**
• *20 questions will be MCQs and 5 questions will have answer to be filled as numerical value.			
Marking Scheme for MCQs	Correct Answer Incorrect Answer/Multiple Answer Unanswered /Marked for Review	Four mark (+4) Minus one mark (-1) No mark (0)	
• Marking Scheme for questions for which answer is a Numerical value	Correct Answer Incorrect Answer Unanswered / Marked for Review	Four mark (+4) No mark (0) No mark (0)	
• Method of determining merit	Conversion of raw score in Mathematics, Aptitude Test, Planning Based Test and Total into NTA Scores. Overall merit shall be prepared by merging NTA Scores of all shifts of all days.		

PAPER	SUBJECTS	TYPE OF QUESTIONS	Mode of Examination
B.E./B.Tech.	Mathematics, Physics & Chemistry	Objective Type - Multiple Choice Questions (MCQs) & Questions for which answer is a numerical value, with equal weightage to Mathematics, Physics & Chemistry	"Computer Based Test (CBT)" mode only
B. Arch.	Mathematics – Part I	Objective Type - Multiple Choice Questions (MCQs) & Questions for which answer is a numerical value	"Computer Based Test (CBT)" mode only
	Aptitude Test – Part II	Objective Type - Multiple Choice Questions (MCQs)	
	Drawing Test – Part III	Questions to test drawing aptitude	"Pen & Paper Based" (offline) mode to be attempted on Drawing sheet
B. Planning	Mathematics – Part I	Objective Type - Multiple Choice Questions (MCQs) & Questions for which answer is a numerical value	"Computer Based Test (CBT)" mode only
	Aptitude Test – Part II	Objective Type - Multiple Choice Questions (MCQs)	
	Planning Based Questions - Part III	Objective Type - Multiple Choice Questions (MCQs)	

NATA 2020
NATIONAL APTITUDE TEST IN ARCHITECTURE

Schedule of Examination

Date & Time of Examination	Subject and Marks of Examination	
First NATA Examination		
19.04.2020(Sunday) 10.00 a.m. to 1.15 pm (3 hours and 15 minutes) (Grand Total of 200 marks)	FIRST 135 minutes –Part A (PAPER BASED) **TOTAL 125 Marks** (10.00 am to 12.15 pm) Drawings in A4 Size paper 3 Questions carrying 35 marks, 35 marks & 55 marks, respectively	
	Intermission Period of 15 minutes (12.15 pm to 12.30 pm)	
	LAST 45 minutes-Part B (ONLINE) **TOTAL 75 Marks** (12.30 am to 1.15 pm) PCM (MCQ) 15 Questions X 1.5 mark each General Aptitude & (MCQ) 35 Questions X 1.5 marks each Logical Reasoning	
Second NATA Examination		
31.05.2020 (Sunday) 10.00 a.m. to 1.15 pm (3 hours and 15 minutes) (Grand Total of 200 marks)	FIRST 135 minutes-Part A (PAPER BASED) **TOTAL 125 Marks** (10.00 am to 12.15 pm) Drawings in A4 Size paper 3 Questions carrying 35 marks, 35 marks & 55 marks, respectively	
	Intermission Period of 15 minutes (12.15 pm to 12.30 pm)	
	LAST 45 minutes-Part B (ONLINE) **TOTAL 75 Marks** (12.30 am to 1.15 pm) PCM (MCQ) 15 Questions X 1.5 mark each General Aptitude & (MCQ) 35 Questions X 1.5 marks each Logical Reasoning	

Pattern of Questions and Mode of Answering

Part A is to be answered on A4 size drawing sheets and Part B comprises of Multiple Choice Questions (MCQ) to be answered online. Syllabus for NATA-2020 is given on NATA website. Questions and all instructions will be available only in English medium.

ENTRANCE COACHING

GLOBAL ACADEMY OF VAASTU AND DESIGN

Global Academy of Vaastu and Design is an initiative of team of Architects to impart comprehensive guidance and assistance for reparation of B. Architecture Entrance examinations. Global Academy of Vaastu and Design is dedicated to provide education to each and every student who is interested in cracking entrance exams of prominent Architecture institutes.

Ashok Goel

B. Arch. from SPA, New Delhi.

Dip. (German), P.G. Dip. (Journalism)

Ashok Goel at the age of 16 gave programmes on television (Delhi Doordarshan). Later, wrote plays for Urdu service All India Radio. Participated in Akashvaani programmes (All India Radio). Got distinction in Geometrical and Mechanical Drawing (now known as Engineering Graphics) in higher secondary exam. Studied at famous BITS Pilani for one year. Thereafter he was selected for B.Arch. in School of Planning and Architecture, New Delhi after a very tough entrance exam. Published his first book "Home Decoration Guide" at the age of 25. He was the first Indian architect who wrote book on Interior Decoration in Hindi. Mr. J.R. Bhalla, president of Council of Architecture wrote the preface of his book. At the age of 26, prepared his next book, 51 House Designs. Mr. A.P. Kanvinde, famous architect, wrote the preface of this book. Within years, next book "Modern House Plans" co-authored by his architect wife Mrs. Madhu Mohan was published by Pustak Mahal, publishers of famous Rapidex English Speaking Course. All the books were widely acclaimed by famous newspapers and magazines including Navabharat Times, Hindustan, Grihashobha, Dainik Tribune, Patriot, Architect's Trade Journal, Rashtradoot, Navjeevan, Nai Duniya, Blitz, Dharmyug, Manorama, The Indian Architect, Swatantra Bharat, Chic Magazine, Surya India Magazine, etc. More than 200,000 of his books have been sold out. Contributed articles on architecture, interiors, planning and other socio-economic topics in various newspapers, magazines and journals including Indian Express, Hindustan Times, Sarita, Mukta, Grihashobha, Blitz, Tribune, Navbharat Times, Hindi Hindustan, Surya India, Patriot, Architect's Trade Journal, The Indian Architect, Morning Echo, etc. Shared stage with various dignitaries like filmstar Sunil Dutt, politicians Sri Sushil Kumar Shinde, Sri Jagdish Tytler, Sri Kapil Sibal, Sri Ajay Makan, Sri Shakeel Ahmed, Sri Kulanand Bharti and Mr. Arvind Kejriwal. Designed, decorated and supervised a large number of showrooms, houses and factories. Founder director of Academy of Interior Decoration imparting knowledge of interior decoration through correspondence for the last 3 decades. Expert in preparing study material for architecture entrance exams. Now providing guidance to the students aspiring for joining architecture degree course. Registered with Council of Architecture, Fellow member of I.I.A.

Our Strength

We provide our students the winning edge to stay ahead of the competition because of innovative techniques based on collective experience

-- Extensive and best course material for Architecture Entrance Exams
-- Ability to create environment that stimulates out of the box thinking
-- Our academic expertise offers students unique shortcut and time saving techniques for NATA entrance
-- Core faculties consist of team of well-known architects and educationists:

Honorary Advisors :

1. Aditya Kamal

B. Arch from IP University.
M. Arch. From DCR University, Haryana
Author of books on House Design
Associate Professor in a leading Architecture College

2. Arjun Kamal

B. Arch. from Faculty of Architecture and Ekistics,
Jamia Millia Islamia, New Delhi
M. Arch. (Landscape Architecture), MDU
Assistant Professor in a leading Architecture College
Contributed articles in architectural magazines and journals

USEFUL TIPS TO SCORE HIGH MARKS

How to score more marks in NATA ?

* Don't start your preparations after you finish your XII boards - The earlier you start, better for you. Plan your time well for NATA preparation if you are also preparing for other entrance exams along with NATA. Use your time effectively with a time table. Draw two to three sketches daily.

* If you draw well, then half the battle is won. Good sketching is very essential, the questions are framed on topics like effects of light and shadow, sense of perspective drawing, understanding scale and proportions, memory drawing, composing 3-Dimensional elements etc. Therefore, developing these skills are very important.

* **Be Creative** - Creativity is very important. Many people have tried to define creativity in their own ways but there is no single universally accepted definition. It is difficult to summarise it, however, "creativity" is the ability to come up with new, original ideas which are unconventional. It is the breaking away from the stereotype, routine, accepted set of thoughts and possessing a deeper insight to problem solving.

* Speed is very very important. Understand that your drawing and creative skills are useless if you are not able to present your thoughts in the exam in the limited amount of time. You stand to lose marks for the questions you fail to answer or which are left incomplete, it doesn't matter how good you are at your work, if you do not complete the task.

* Go through all **previous papers** of NATA. Solve at least 10 - 20 past papers within the given time limit. Find out a comfortable sequence for answering the paper.

* Do practice in **A3 size sketch books**, because if you can make large sketches in given time then you would be able to make sketches in A4 size as that is normally the standard size of answer sheets in the examinations.

* **G.K. books are not suitable** for NATA exams. Be more aware of the construction work happening around you. Observe the materials, observe the construction methods, observe the scaffolding and shuttering, observe the beams and columns, observe the doors and windows, staircases and verandahs. Increase your observation power. Try to find out about famous architects and their works and how they have contributed to the field of architecture. Read books / magazines and develop a genuine passion for your field. Read the newspapers regularly.

* Find your own deep and compelling reason to successfully clear **NATA.** Motivate yourself. Work with enthusiasm and you will be surprised at your ideas and creations.

* Students normally waste a lot of time in erasing and re-drawing. Always draw with a light hand first, doing mainly the outlining without the details. When you are satisfied with the proportions and the rough outline, finalize your drawing.

* Practice more with dry colours, since they are convenient to use and take less time in exams. Use good quality colours like Faber-Castell or Staedtler.

HOW TO PREPARE FOR
NATA ENTRANCE EXAM?
(NATIONAL APTITUDE TEST IN ARCHITECTURE)

If you wish to become an Architect, you have to appear for NATA exam. You can appear for this entrance exam to B.Arch – Bachelor or Architecture course, provided you have Physics, Chemistry and Mathematics as a subject at 12th level.

NATA is a very interesting exam. Only thing required is you have to prepare in right direction. NATA exam is divided into two parts. First Part is (Part-A) Drawing Test (125 marks; 135 min.). Second Part is (Part-B: 75 marks; 45 min.). In Part B, 15 Qs. from PCM (1.5 mark each) and 35 Qs. from General Aptitude and Logical Reasoning (1.5 mark each). This (Part-B) will be online test for total of 75 marks.)

FOR PART B — PCM, GENERAL APTITUDE & LOGICAL REASONING TEST

There will be 15 questions of PCM and 35 questions of General Aptitude and Logical Reasoning Test. It is MCQ based test wherein for each question, four answer options are given. Only one option Is correct and correct response will yield 1.5 marks. There is no negative marking, but wrong answering will be penalized in case of tie breaking.

For details of the syllabus, visit website of NATA.

Prepare following for the general aptitude (aesthetic sensitivity) test :-

1. Analytical Reasoning
2. Architectural Awareness (Questions about Architecture, famous building etc.)
3. Identifying commonly used material and objects based on their texture
4. Visualising three dimensional objects through two dimensional drawing
5. Visualising different sides of three dimensional objects
6. Mental ability.
7. Imaginative Comprehension and expression.

You do not have to remember each and every building of the world. Just see photos of famous buildings. Regarding building materials, try to see and identify every building material used in your house. Like Glazed Tiles, Mosaic Tiles, Wood, Bricks, Steel, Aluminium, Concrete, Marble, Kota Stone, Granite, Galvanised Pipes, Linoleum flooring, Vinyl flooring, Wooden flooring, Terrazzo, Vitrified flooring, etc.

FOR PART A:- For Part-A: Drawing Test Prepare following:-

1. Learn to sketch given object proportionately and rendering it in a visually appealing manner
2. Light and Shadow on object and its surrounding
3. Perspective Drawing
4. You should be able to combine three dimensional object to form stable structure and depict in sketching.
5. Sense of Scale and Proportion
6. Colour composition, Sense of Colour
7. Memory Drawing
8. You should be able to sketch two dimensional composition using given shape and form.

Just try to draw things in proportion. Observe all day to day objects and try to figure out how tall/big it is from other objects. Also keep a small folding scale with you and try to measure everyday objects. Remember size of most day to day objects like length of Tube Light, Height of Dining Table. By practice you can really achieve best results. Practice about light and shadow, by observing different objects in natural settings. Observe how the shadow is cast on surroundings. Just try to remember three primary colours. Red, Yellow and Blue. By mixing any two you will get secondary colour. Observe colours in day to day surroundings. In any good book Drawing book you will find many samples of Colour compositions, Memory drawing examples, Object Drawing samples, Rendering methods and basic perspective learning.

There are mainly TWO methods of Perspective Drawing.

1. One point perspective   2.   Two point perspective

One point perspective is mainly used for drawing interiors of rooms. Visualise you are sitting in last row of Cinema Hall or a Bus or a Train compartment and looking towards other end. Whatever you see, and the lines you see (all lines converging in one point) that is one point perspective. Two point perspective is as if you are standing on a junction of two roads. You are facing a building from a corner and can see two sides of the building abutting on two roads. Whatever you see can be sketched in Two Point Perspective.

You should be able to combine three dimensional object to form stable structure. In this question NATA will ask you to create some stable structure from the objects named in the NATA QUESTION PAPER. These objects can be wooden logs, wooden planks, pet bottles, balls, cones, cubes etc.

NATA
Practice Test Papers

NATA 2017 DRAWING PAPER

1. One late afternoon, you along with your family members were enjoying a boat ride along a river and viewed a spectacular sunset. You noticed that the boat was moving from south to north and all of you were facing north. Suddenly, your youngest brother shouted and told everybody to see the river bank on your right side. You saw a series of high-rise apartment buildings interspersed with trees. But, in the middle, there was a beautiful river ghat, a garden and a small white mosque adjacent to it. Lots of birds were flying around and sitting on its golden dome. In the concrete jungle, the small structure seemed to be a nice relief. Develop a coloured sketch (use dry colour) of what you experienced.

2. You are waiting in a railway platform for catching a local train. Some people are also waiting there with small and big luggage. Few people are sitting on wooden benches. There is a small food shop. You saw that the roof above is sloped. Standing at the entry point of the platform you noticed that the train is coming and has reached almost midway of the length of the platform. Draw a pencil sketch of what you experienced.

NATA 2018 DRAWING PAPER

1. You are sitting at a table in front of a tea stall in the early morning sipping a hot cup of tea while your companion is reading a newspaper. The tea stall is located in a park and you are observing a man walking his dog and the beautiful garden landscape around you. Sketch the scenario described above and render light and shade using drawing pencils.

2. Using all the three shapes given below, create a visually pleasing composition. The shapes are to be used in the same size as illustrated below and they can be repeated, rotated, overlapped, interlocked and mirrored to create the composition. Use not more than 20 nos. of the shapes (all put together) and colour the composition using not more than 3 colours from analogous colour scheme.

NATA 2019 DRAWING PAPER

1. It is raining and you are looking out of a window from your living room. The window is a wooden panel window with horizontal grills. You can see a playground with play equipment. Some children are playing in the rain and some kids are playing with paper boats in puddles. Beyond the playground there is a tea shop and a hospital. Draw the view using your imagination.

2. Draw a composition with five geometric shapes such as circle, triangle, square, rectangle and hexagon. Each of the shapes is to be used at least once. The composition is to be coloured using a medium of your choice.

NATA Practice Paper - 1

Directions: In each given problem, Out of the five figures (a), (b), (c), (d) and (e), four are similar in a certain way. However, one figure is not like the other four. Choose the figure which is different from the rest.

1.

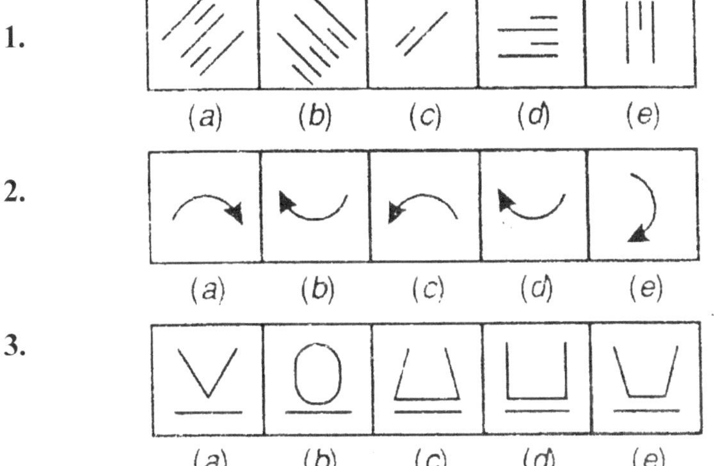

2.

3.

DIRECTIONS: The 3-D Problem figure shows an object. Identify the correct front view amongst the answer figures, looking in the direction of the arrow.

4.

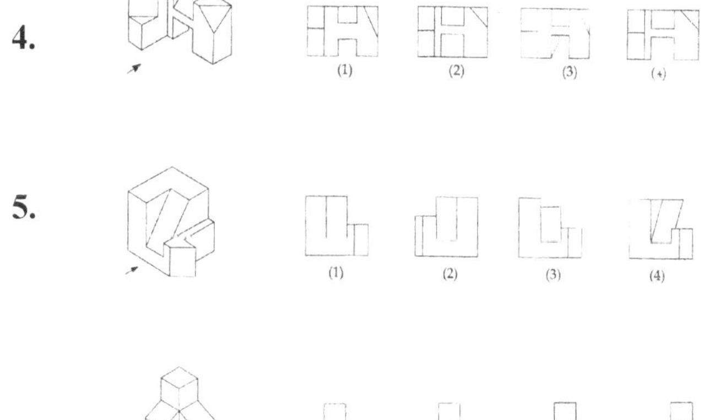

5.

6.

7.

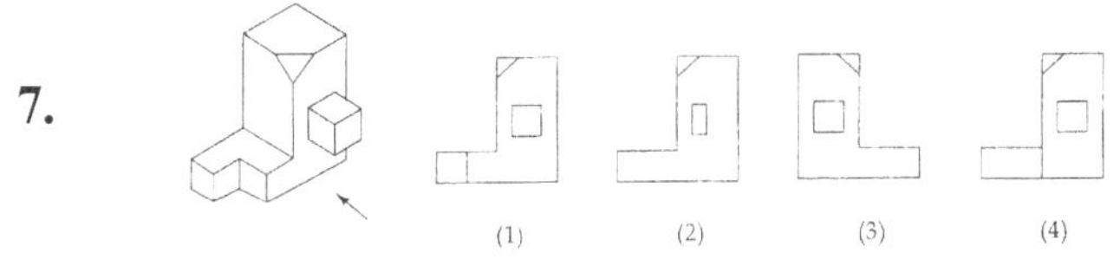

NATA Practice Paper - 1

Directions: Find the total number of inclined surfaces of the object given below in the problem figure.

Problem Figure

8. 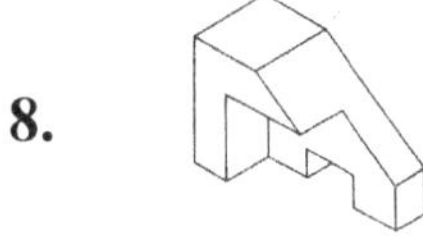   (1) 1   (2) 3   (3) 2   (4) 4

9. 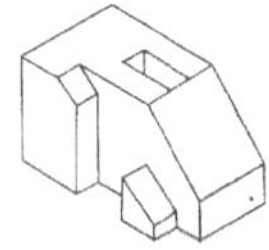   (1) 1   (2) 4   (3) 2   (4) 3

10. 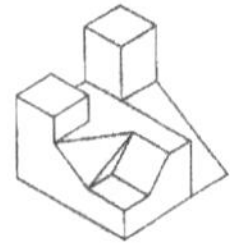   (1) 2   (2) 9   (3) 7   (4) 3

11. 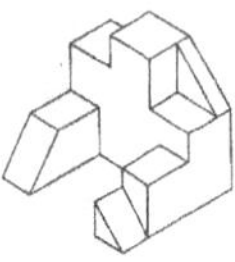   (1) 1   (2) 2   (3) 3   (4) 5

DIRECTIONS: In each one of the following problems, a transparent sheet with a pattern is given. Figure out from the four alternatives as to how the pattern would appear when the transparent sheet is folded at the dotted line.

Transparent Sheet   **Response Figures**

12. 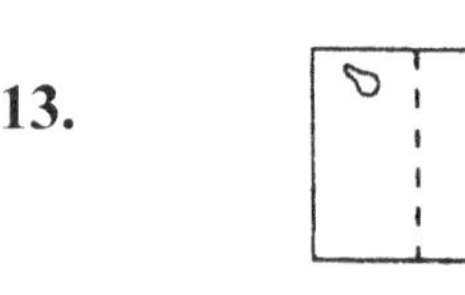
    A   B   C   D

13. 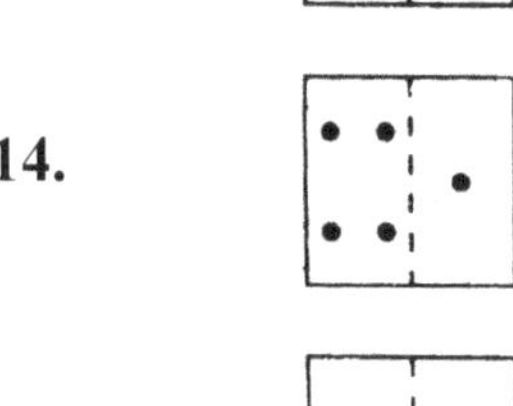
    A   B   C   D

14. 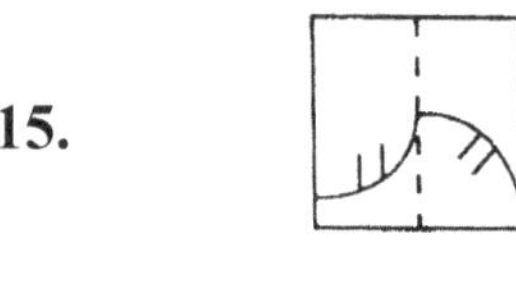 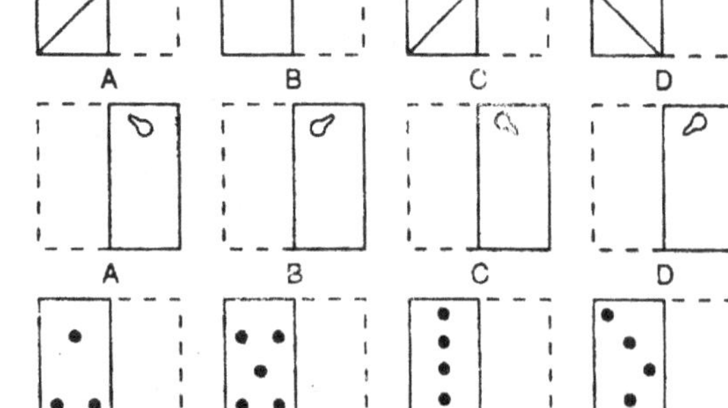
    A   B   C   D

15. 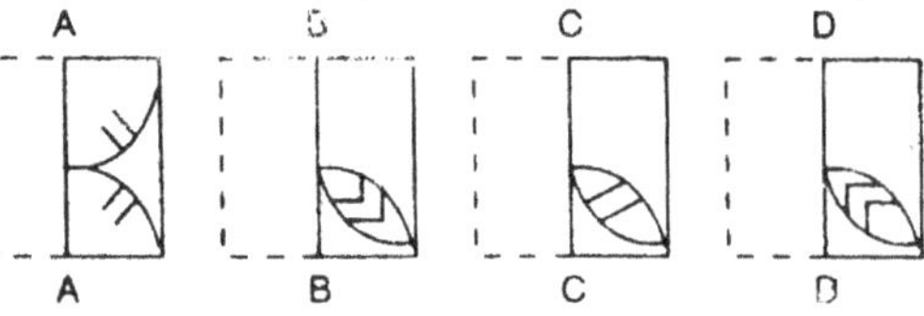
    A   B   C   D

NATA Practice Paper - 1

Directions: Identify the correct top view of the given 3D figure.

16   (1)   (2)   (3)   (4)

17.   (1)   (2)   (3)   (4)

18.   (1)   (2)   (3)   (4)

19.   (1)   (2)   (3)   (4)

20. Which of the following is not a building bye-law?
a) Min. front setback
b) Max. number of windows
c) Max. height
d) Minimum side and rear setback

21. Depending upon its use, which of the following is a building type?
a) Residential and educational
b) Institutional and business
c) Assembly and industrial
d) All of these

22. The portion of a building above and below the ground are referred to as
a) Sub-structure and super-structure
b) Foundation and walls
c) Base and column
d) Floor and roof

23. The lowest part of a structure below the ground level which is in direct contact with ground and transmits all load to soil is known as
a) Plinth
b) Base
c) Foundation
d) None of these

24. The difference of two numbers is 5 and the difference of their square is 135. The sum of the numbers is :
(a) 27   (b) 25   (c) 30   (d) 32

25. The sum of two numbers is 29 and the difference of their squares is 145. The difference between the numbers is :
(a) 13   (b) 5   (c) 8   (d) 11

26. The difference of two numbers is 8 and 1/8th of their sum is 35. The numbers are :
(a) 132, 140   (b) 128, 136   (c) 124, 132   (d) 136, 144

NATA Practice Paper - 1

Directions - A paper is folded as shown in the given figures and some holes are made. When opened, how will it appear? Select from the four given answer figures.

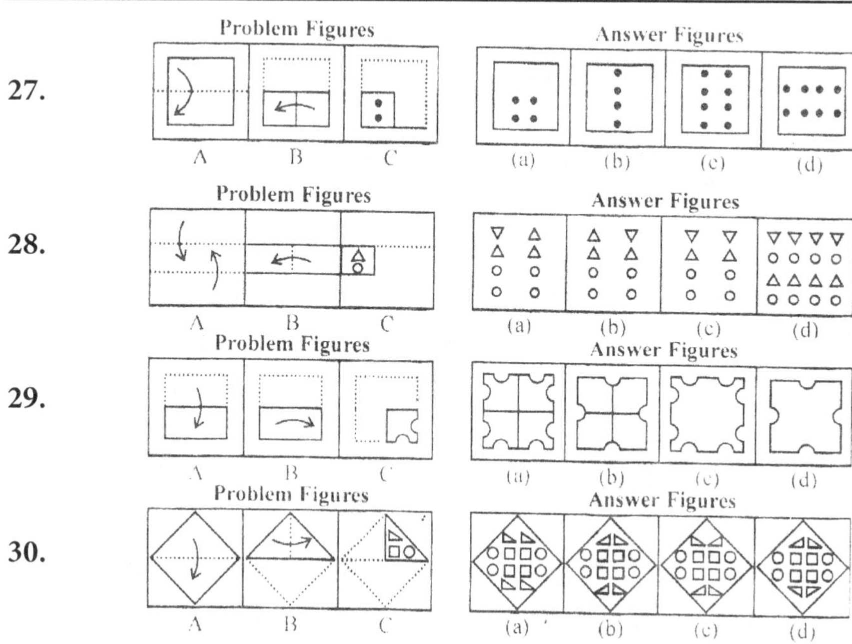

27.
28.
29.
30.

DIRECTIONS: Choose the word which is most nearly the SAME in meaning as the word printed.

31. exhort
   a) threaten   c) encourage
   b) show   d) alert

32. sustains
   a) supports   b) defends
   c) comforts   d) holds

33. emanate
   a) express   b) originate
   c) invent   d) enter

DIRECTIONS: Choose the word which is most OPPOSITE in meaning as the word printed.

34. enrich
   a) poor   b) courage
   c) diminish   d) poison

35. acquired
   a) grabbed   b) freed
   c) stopped   d) lost

NATA Practice Paper - 1

36. Identify this building:

1) Lotus Temple
2) Sydney Opera House
3) SECC Conference Centre
4) Parthenon, Greece

37. Identify this building:

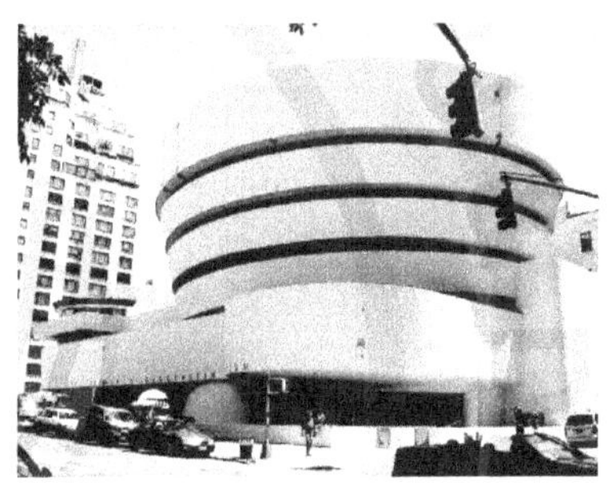

1) Belgium Embassy
2) Guggenheim museum
3) Dhaka Assembly
4) Bombay Stock Exchange

38. A cone has the following:-
a) one vertex, 2 surfaces
b) 0 vertex, 2 surfaces
c) 2 vertex, 1 surface
d) 2 vertex, 2 surfaces

39. A triangular pyramid has the following:-
a) 4 triangular surfaces
b) 3 triangular surfaces
c) 4 triangular surfaces and 4 vertex
d) both (a) & (c)

40. A pentagonal pyramid has:-
a) 10 surfaces
b) 5 surfaces
c) 7 surfaces
d) 6 surfaces

NATA Practice Paper - 2

Directions: In each given problem, Out of the five figures (a), (b), (c), (d) and (e), four are similar in a certain way. However, one figure is not like the other four. Choose the figure which is different from the rest.

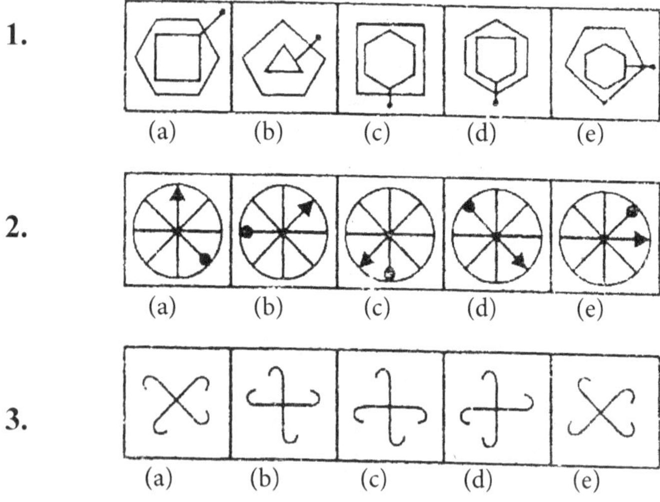

Directions: The 3-D Problem figure shows an object. Identify the correct front view amongst the answer figures, looking in the direction of the arrow.

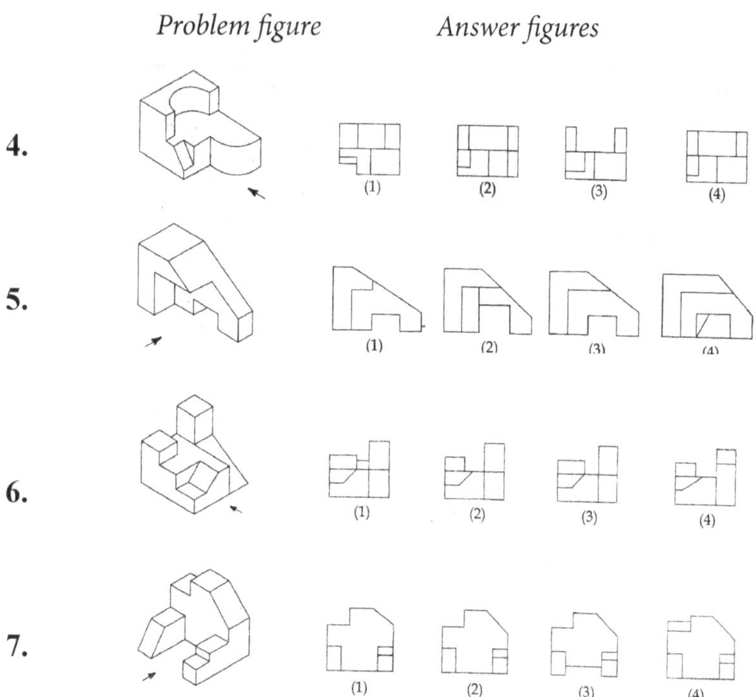

NATA Practice Paper - 2

Directions: Find the total number of inclined surfaces of the object given below in the problem figure.

---

8. 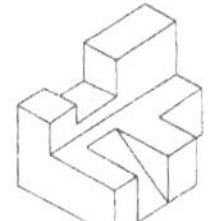   (1) 1   (2) 3   (3) 2   (4) 4

9. 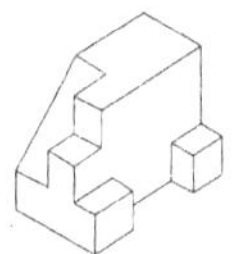   (1) 1   (2) 4   (3) 2   (4) 3

10. 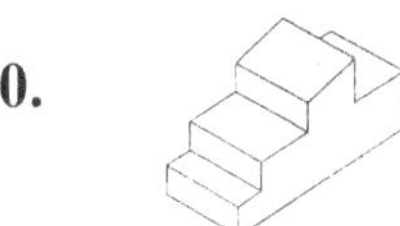   (1) 2   (2) 1   (3) 0   (4) 3

11. 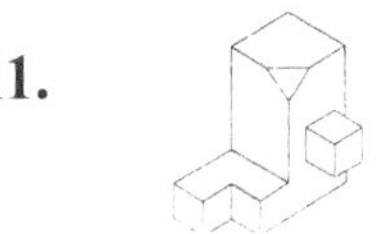   (1) 1   (2) 2   (3) 3   (4) 5

DIRECTIONS: In each one of the following problems, a transparent sheet with a pattern is given. Figure out from the four alternatives as to how the pattern would appear when the transparent sheet is folded at the dotted line.

Transparent Sheet   Response Figures

12.  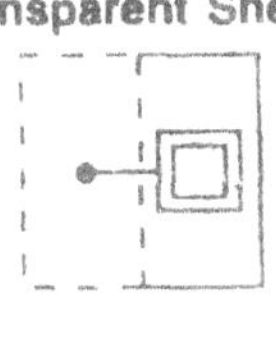   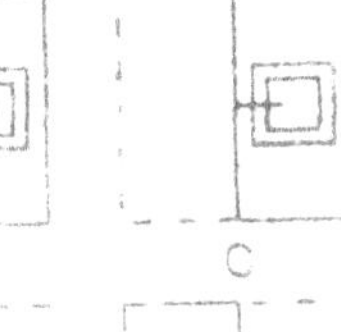 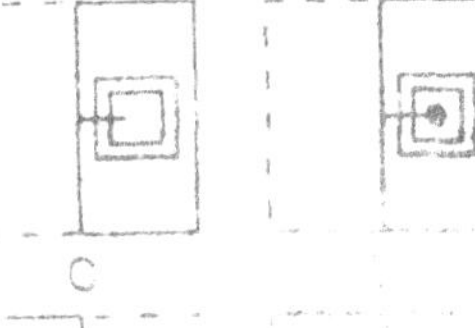

13. 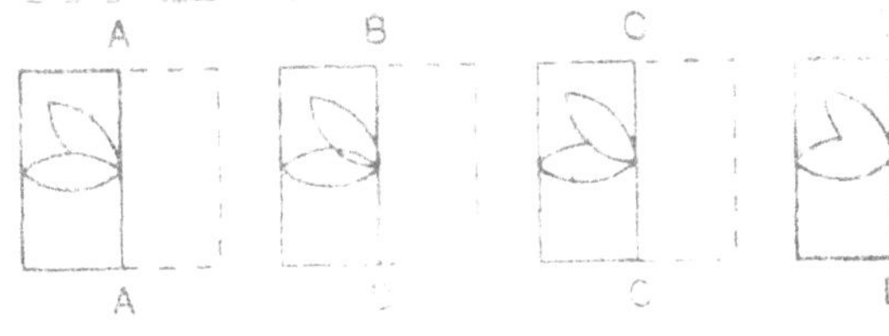

14. 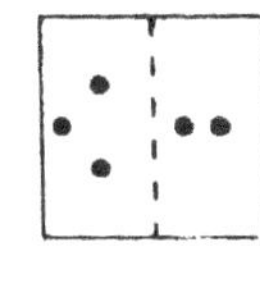 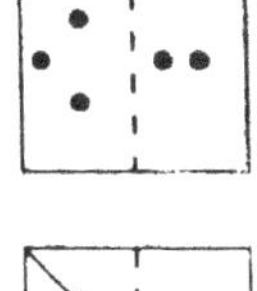 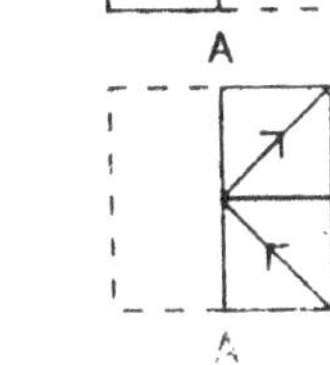 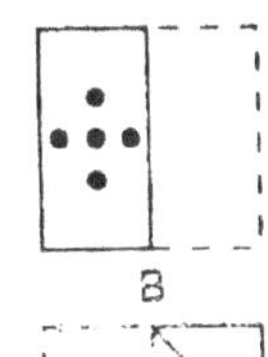 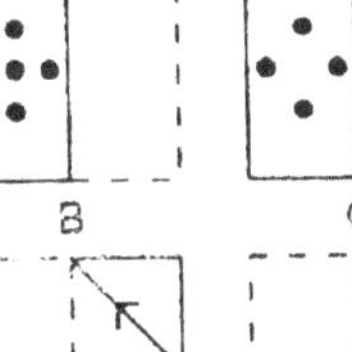

15. 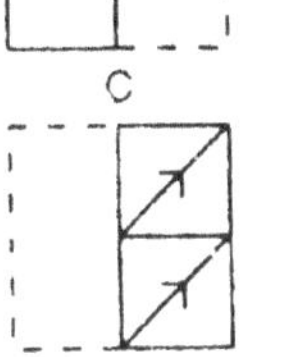 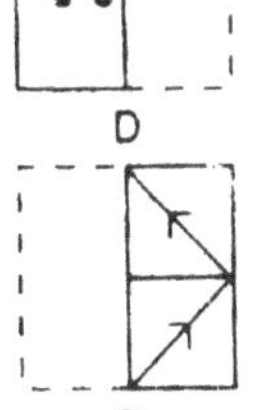

NATA Practice Paper - 2

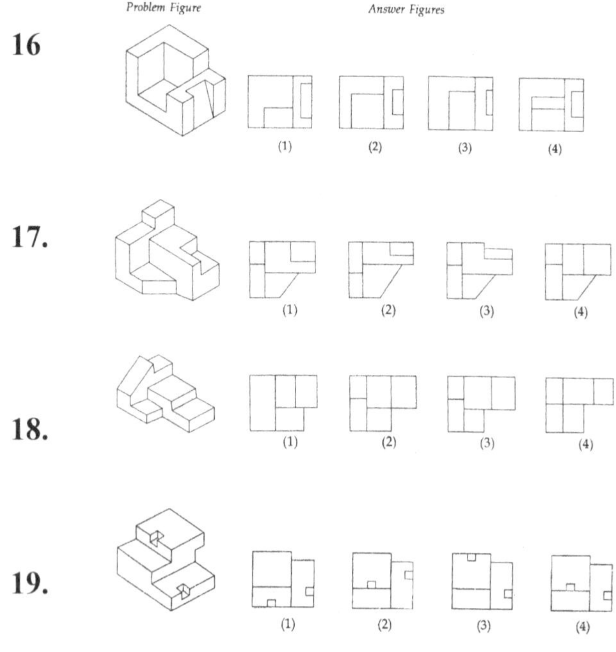

16

17.

18.

19.

20. Bonding of building units (bricks/stone/concrete) in horizontal and vertical joints is known as
a) Brick masonry   b) Stone masonry
c) Concrete block masonry   d)All of these

21. Non-load bearing walls are also known as
a) Glass walls
b) Light walls
c) Partition walls
d) Super walls

22. A column is a
a) Vertical load-bearing member
b) Horizontal load-bearing member
c) Lateral load-bearing member
d) Non-load bearing member

23. Frame and shutter of a door/window is
a) Fixed and movable
b) Fixed and fixed
c) Movable and fixed
d) Movable and movable

24. The sum of two numbers is 100 and their difference is 37. The difference of their squares is
(a) 37   (b) 100   (c) 63   (d) 3700

25. The ratio between two numbers is 3 : 4 and their sum is 420. The greater of the two numbers is :
(a) 175   (b) 200   (c) 240   (d) 315

26. The difference between the squares of two consecutive numbers is 35. The numbers are :
(a) 14, 15   (b) 15, 16   (c) 17, 18   (d) 18, 19

NATA Practice Paper - 2

Directions - A paper is folded as shown in the given figures and some holes are made. When opened, how will it appear? Select from the four given answer figures.

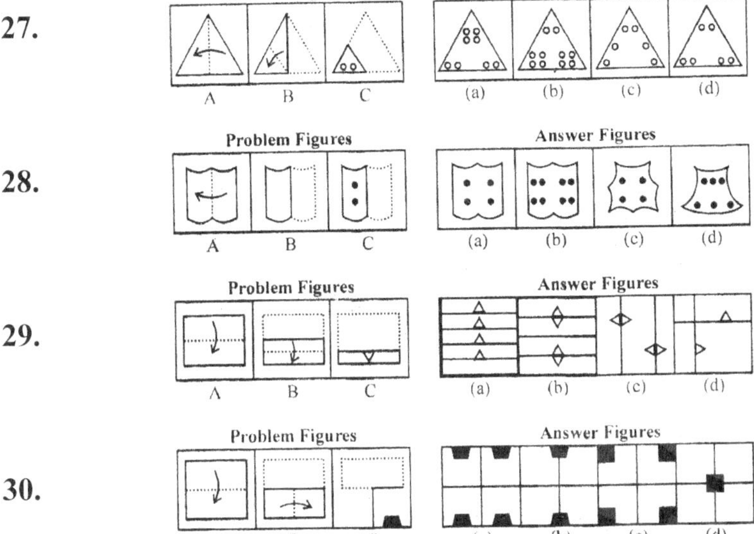

27.
28.
29.
30.

Directions - Choose the word or group of words which is MOST/NEARLY THE SAME in meaning as the word given in bold.

31. APING
   a) criticizing   b) observing
   c) imitating   d) visualizing

32. ENTHRALLED
   a) immensely pleased   b) Greatly distracted
   c) eagerly awaited   d) virtually encouraged

33. SHOCKED
   a) paralysed   b) surprised
   c) amused   d) pained

Directions - Choose the word which is MOST OPPOSITE in meaning as the word given in bold.

34. EXTENSIVE
   a) Meagre   b) Intensive   c) Immense   d) Ardent

35. OPENED
   a) shut   b) disappeared   c) vanished   d) concluded

NATA Practice Paper - 2

<table>
<tr><td>

36. Identify this building:

1) Gateway of India
2) India Gate
3) Arc de Triomphe, Paris
4) Delhi Gate

</td><td></td></tr>
</table>

<table>
<tr><td>

37. Identify this building:

1) Golden gate bridge
2) Laxman Jhula
3) Sydney Harbour Bridge
4) Howrah Bridge

</td><td></td></tr>
</table>

38. A hexagonal prism has:-
a) 8 surfaces
b) 6 surfaces
c) 18 sides and 8 surfaces
d) both (a) & (c)

39. A octagonal pyramid has:-
a) 8 triangular surfaces
b) 9 triangular surfaces
c) 9 surfaces
d) both (a) & (c)

40. A pentagonal pyramid has:-
a) 5 triangular surfaces
b) 9 triangular surfaces
c) 6 surfaces
d) both (a) & (c)

NATA Practice Paper - 3

Directions: In each given problem, Out of the five figures (a), (b), (c), (d) and (e), four are similar in a certain way. However, one figure is not like the other four. Choose the figure which is different from the rest.

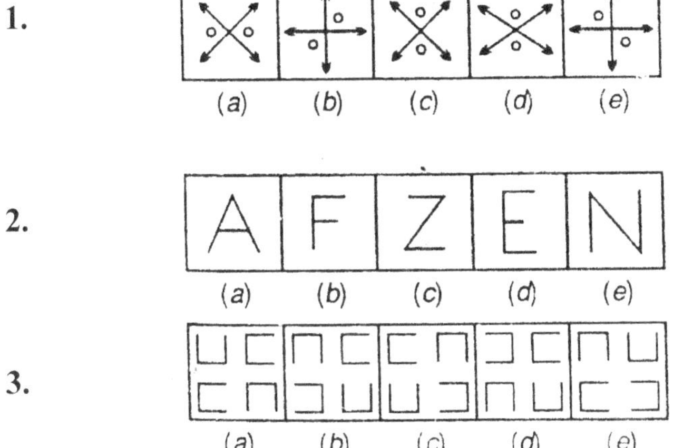

1.

    (a)   (b)   (c)   (d)   (e)

2.

    (a)   (b)   (c)   (d)   (e)

3.

    (a)   (b)   (c)   (d)   (e)

DIRECTIONS: *The 3-D Problem figure shows an object. Identify the correct front view amongst the answer figures, looking in the direction of the arrow.*

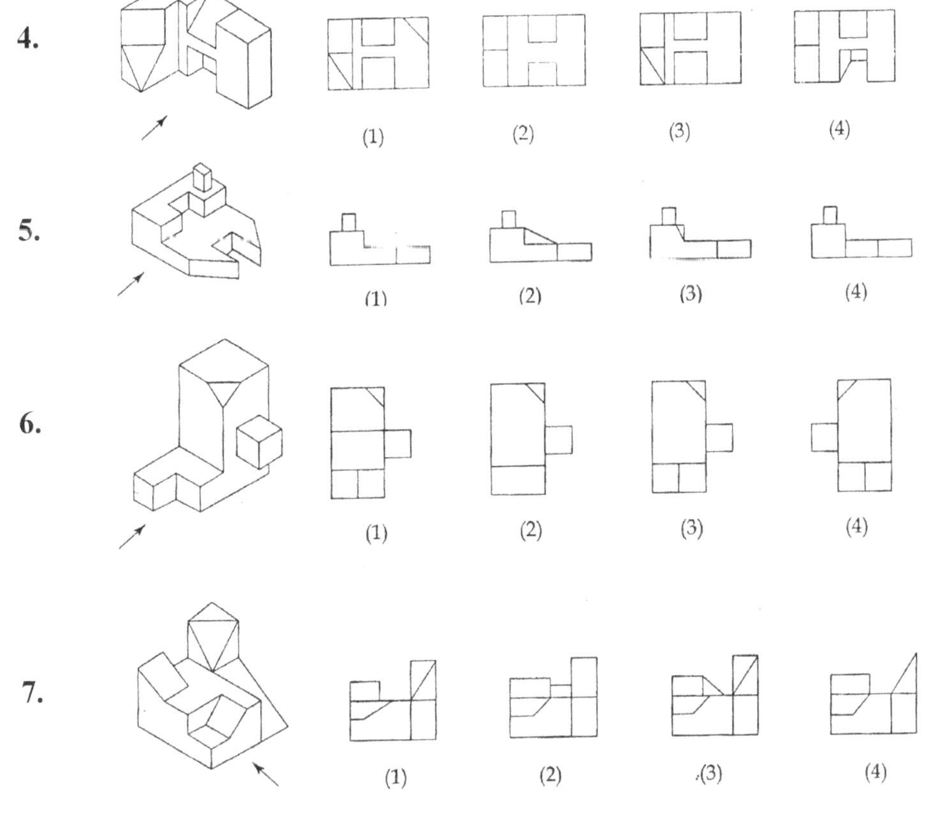

4.

    (1)   (2)   (3)   (4)

5.

    (1)   (2)   (3)   (4)

6.

    (1)   (2)   (3)   (4)

7.

    (1)   (2)   (3)   (4)

NATA Practice Paper - 3

Problem Figure

8. 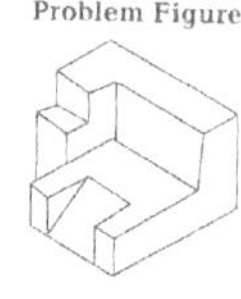   (1) 1   (2) 3   (3) 2   (4) 4

Problem Figure

9. 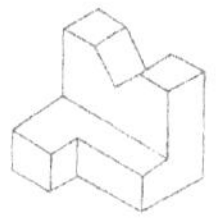   (1) 1   (2) 4   (3) 2   (4) 3

Problem Figure

10. 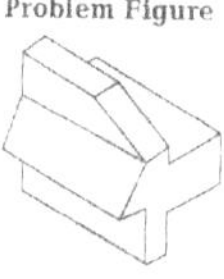   (1) 2   (2) 0   (3) 7   (4) 3

Problem Figure

11.    (1) 1   (2) 2   (3) 3   (4) 5

DIRECTIONS: In each one of the following problems, a transparent sheet with a pattern is given. Figure out from the four alternatives as to how the pattern would appear when the transparent sheet is folded at the dotted line.

Transparent sheet   *Answer figures*

12. 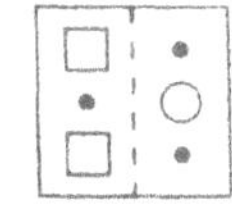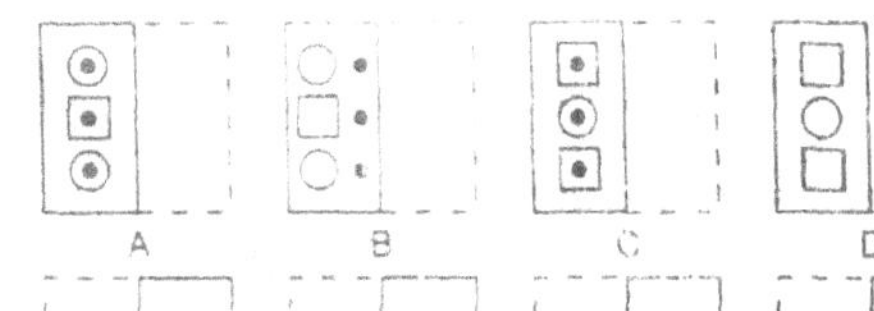

13. 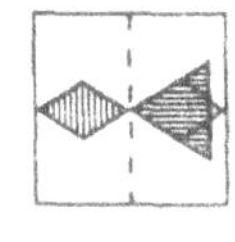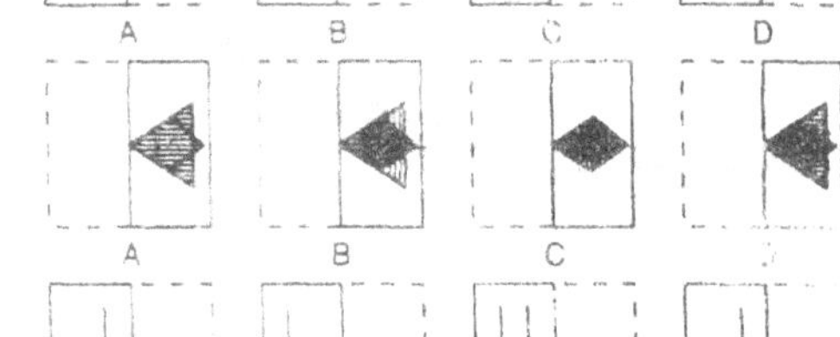

14. 

15. 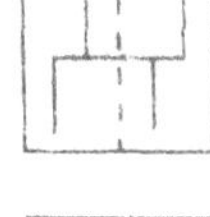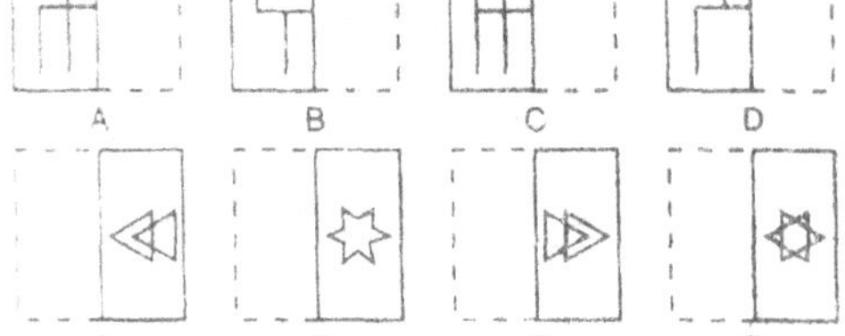

NATA Practice Paper - 3

Directions: Identify the correct top view of the given 3D figure.

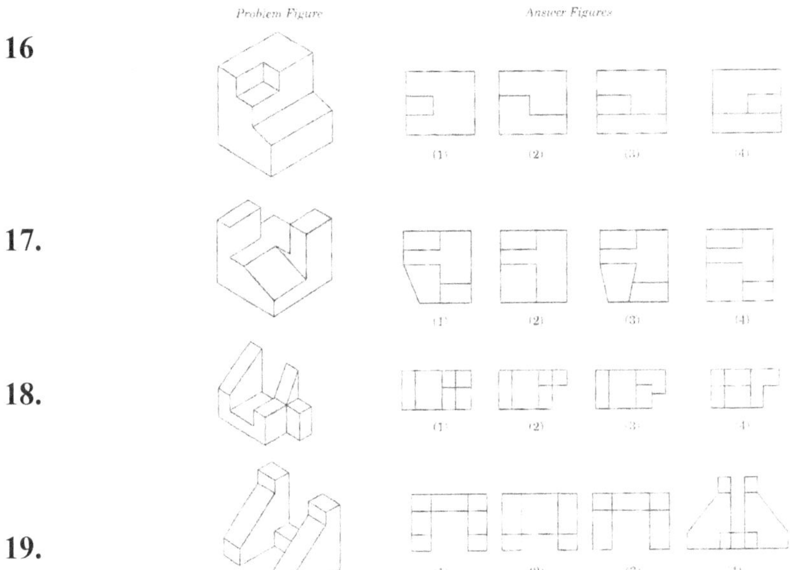

20. **A damp-proof course or D.P.C. to prevent penetration of moisture can be done using**
    a) Bitumen/tar-felt
    b) Plastic sheets
    c) Cement concrete
    d) All of these

21. **A lift specially designed for use by fire-service personnel in the event of fire is known as**
    a) Firing lift   b) Fireman's lift
    c) V.I.P. lift   d) Restricted entry lift

22. **Total covered area of all floors divided by plot area**
    a) BAR – (Best area ratio)
    b) FAR – (Floor area ratio)
    c) PAR – (Plinth area ratio)
    d) UAR – (Use area \ratio)

23. **Parititon walls are interior non-load bearing walls which in height are**
    a) one storey   b) part storey
    c) one storey or part storey
    d) None of these

24. **Five years ago, Vijay's age was one third of the age of Subhash and now Vijay's age is 17 years. What is the present age of Subhash?**
    (a) 9 years   (b) 36 years   (c) 41 years   (d) 51 years

25. **The difference between the ages of two persons is 10 years. 15 years ago, the elder one was twice as old as the younger one. The present age of the elder person is:**
    (a) 25 years   (b) 35 years   (c) 45 years   (d) 55 years

26. **Geeta is twice as old as Sita was two years ago. If the difference between their ages be 2 years, how old is Geeta today?**
    (a) 6 years   (b) 8 years   (c) 10 years   (d) 12 years

NATA Practice Paper - 3

> **Directions -** A paper is folded as shown in the given figures and some holes are made. When opened, how will it appear? Select from the four given answer figures.

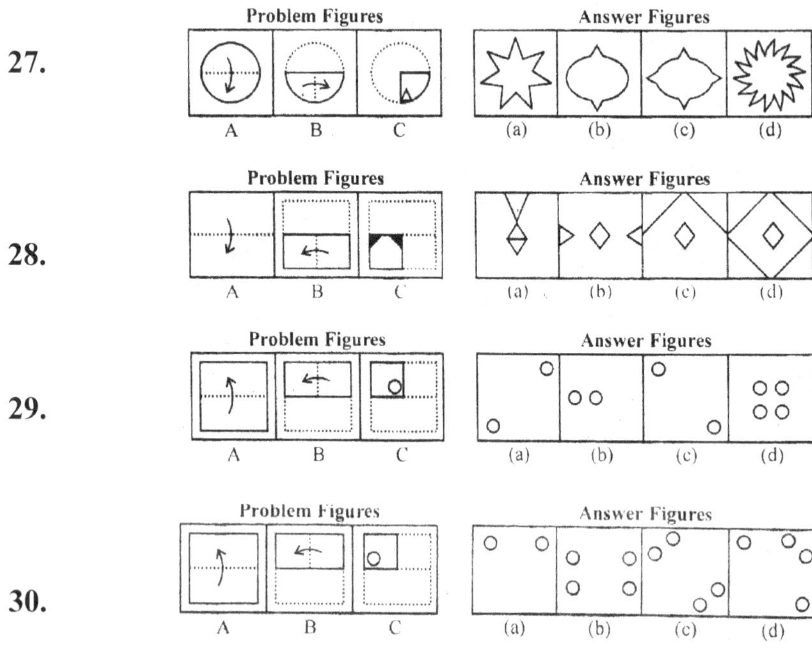

27.

28.

29.

30.

DIRECTIONS: Choose the word which is most nearly the SAME in meaning as the word printed

31. Apart from
    a) in addition to   b) at a long distance
    c) separated from   d) Inspite of
    e) as against

32. Revolutionize
    a) Affect adversely   b) Develop gradually
    c) Illuminate completely   d) Change drastically

DIRECTIONS: Choose the word which is most OPPOSITE in meaning as the word printed

33. Pleasant
    a) Admirable   b) Disgusting   c) Nice   d) Indecent

34. Strange
    a) Familiar   b) Unseen   c) Illfamed   d) Novel

35. Continuted
    a) Irregular   b) Destroyed   c) Reckoned   d) Suspended

NATA Practice Paper - 3

36. Identify this building:

1) Leaning Tower of Pisa
2) Petronas Towers, Malaysia
3) Burj Khalifa, Dubai
4) Empire State Building, New York

37. Identify this building:

1) Niagra Falls
2) The Falling Waters
3) Raj Ghat
4) Rajiv Gandhi Memorial

38. A octagonal prism has:-
a) 10 surfaces
b) 8 surfaces
c) 24 sides and 10 surfaces
d) both (a) & (c)

39. A square pyramid has:-
a) 4 triangular surfaces
b) 5 triangular surfaces
c) 5 surfaces
d) both (a) & (c)

40. A pentagonal pyramid has:-
a) 5 triangular surfaces
b) 6 triangular surfaces
c) 6 surfaces
d) both (a) & (c)

NATA Practice Paper - 4

Directions: In each given problem, Out of the five figures (a), (b), (c), (d) and (e), four are similar in a certain way. However, one figure is not like the other four. Choose the figure which is different from the rest.

1. 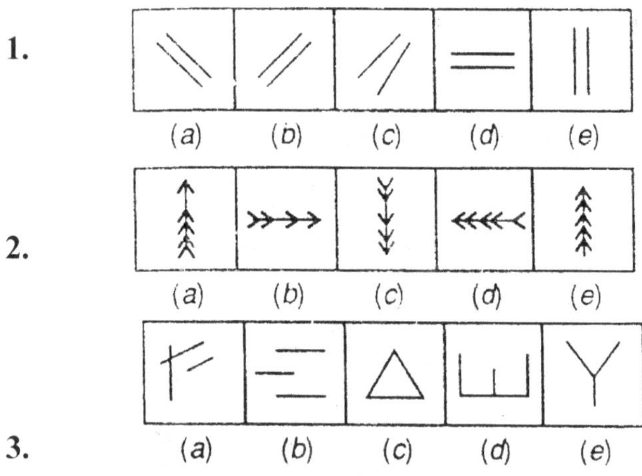

2.

3. 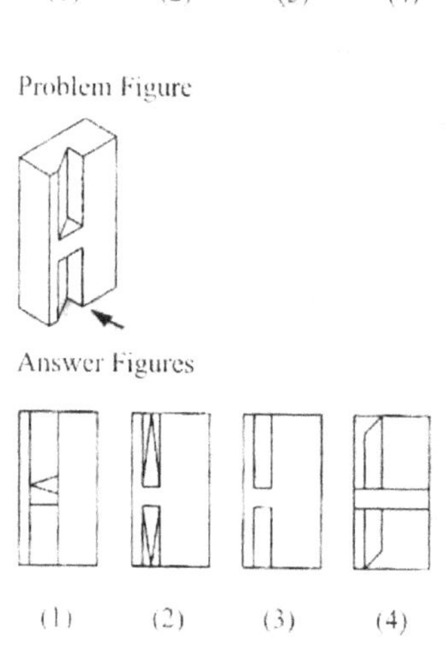

DIRECTIONS: The 3-D Problem figure shows an object. Identify the correct front view amongst the answer figures, looking in the direction of the arrow.

4.

5.

6. 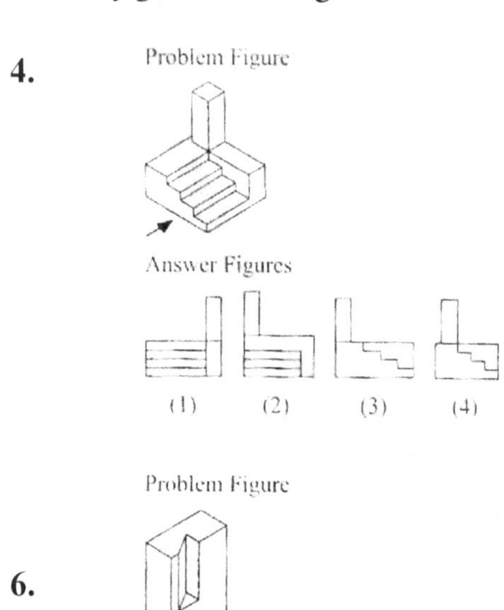

7. 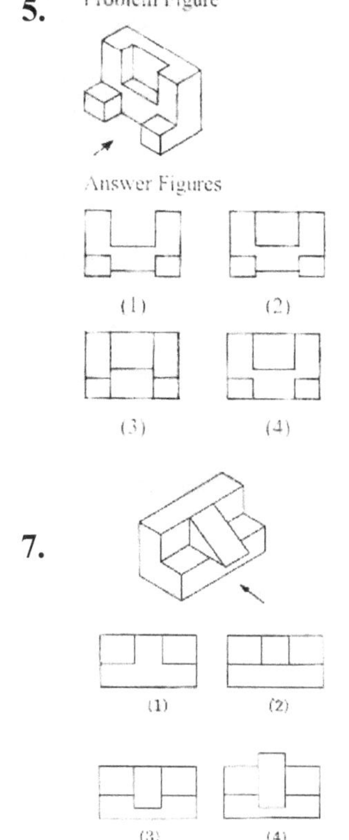

NATA Practice Paper - 4

Directions: Find the total number of inclined surfaces of the object given below in the problem figure.

8.

Problem Figure

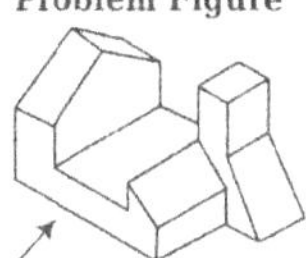

(1) 1   (2) 3   (3) 2   (4) 4

9.

Problem Figure

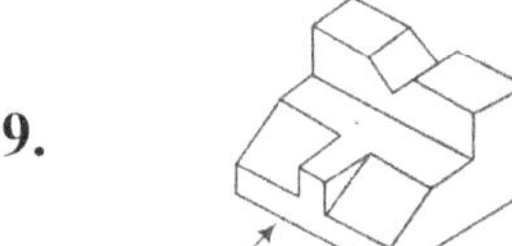

(1) 1   (2) 4   (3) 2   (4) 3

10.

Problem Figure

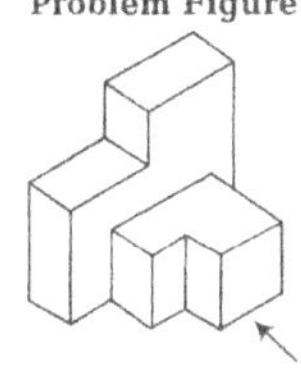

(1) 2   (2) 0   (3) 7   (4) 3

11.

Problem Figure

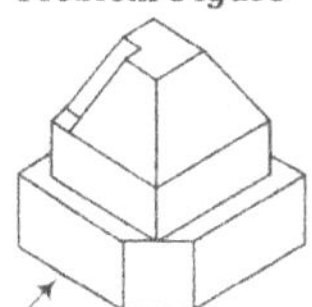

(1) 1   (2) 7   (3) 3   (4) 5

DIRECTIONS: In each one of the following problems, a transparent sheet with a pattern is given. Figure out from the four alternatives as to how the pattern would appear when the transparent sheet is folded at the dotted line.

Transparent sheet   *Answer figures*

12.

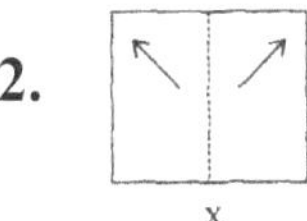 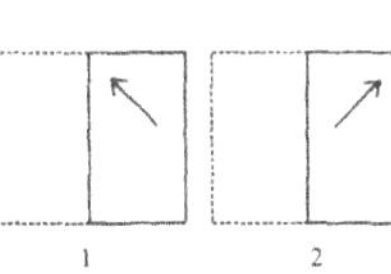 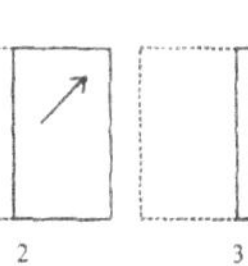 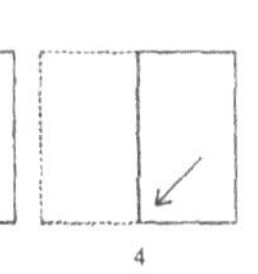

13.

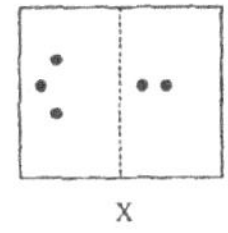 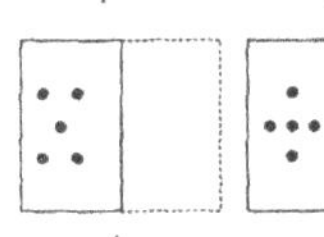 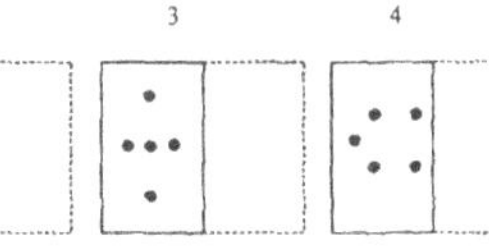

14.

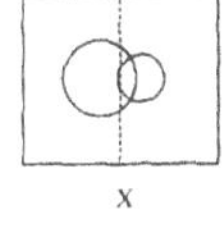 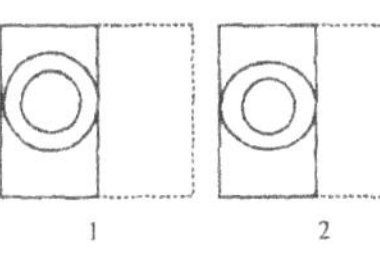 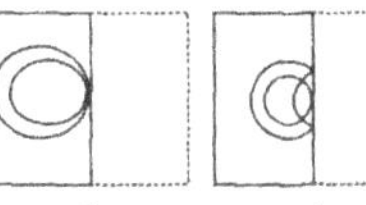

15.

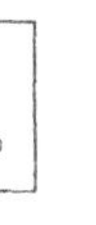 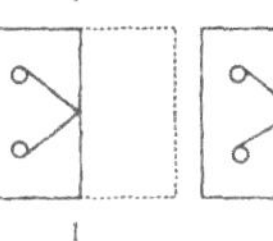 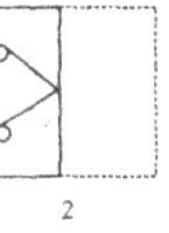 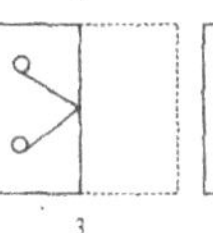 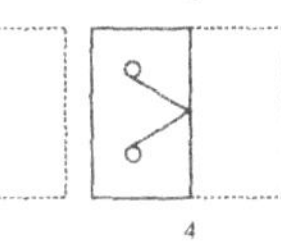

NATA Practice Paper - 4

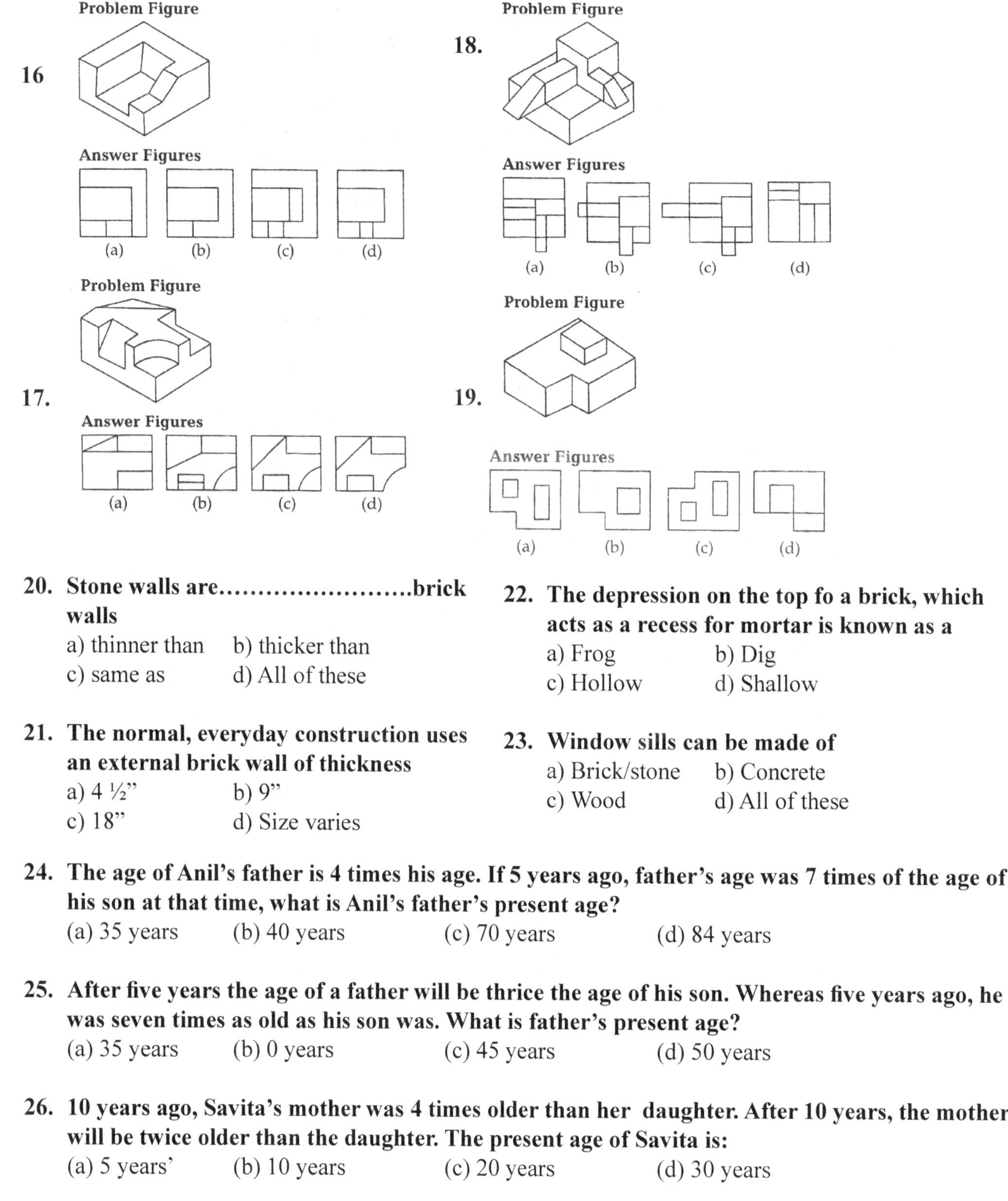

20. **Stone walls are.........................brick walls**
    a) thinner than   b) thicker than
    c) same as   d) All of these

21. **The normal, everyday construction uses an external brick wall of thickness**
    a) 4 ½"   b) 9"
    c) 18"   d) Size varies

22. **The depression on the top fo a brick, which acts as a recess for mortar is known as a**
    a) Frog   b) Dig
    c) Hollow   d) Shallow

23. **Window sills can be made of**
    a) Brick/stone   b) Concrete
    c) Wood   d) All of these

24. **The age of Anil's father is 4 times his age. If 5 years ago, father's age was 7 times of the age of his son at that time, what is Anil's father's present age?**
    (a) 35 years   (b) 40 years   (c) 70 years   (d) 84 years

25. **After five years the age of a father will be thrice the age of his son. Whereas five years ago, he was seven times as old as his son was. What is father's present age?**
    (a) 35 years   (b) 0 years   (c) 45 years   (d) 50 years

26. **10 years ago, Savita's mother was 4 times older than her daughter. After 10 years, the mother will be twice older than the daughter. The present age of Savita is:**
    (a) 5 years'   (b) 10 years   (c) 20 years   (d) 30 years

NATA Practice Paper - 4

Directions - A paper is folded as shown in the given figures and some holes are made. When opened, how will it appear? Select from the four given answer figures.

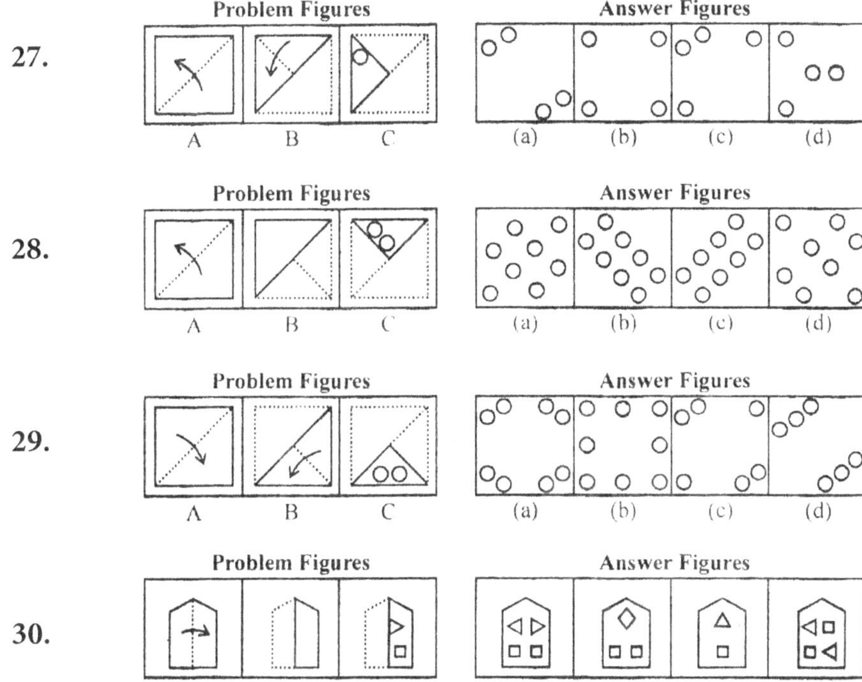

Directions - Choose the word or group of words which is MOST/NEARLY THE SAME in meaning as the word given in bold.

31. REST
   a) remainder   b) relax   c) respite   d) break

32. EXPLORATION
   a) execution   b) cultivation   c) foundation   d) discovery

33. TURNED
   a) rotated   b) twisted   c) spinned   d) revolved

Directions - Choose the word which is MOST OPPOSITE in meaning as the word given in bold.

34. DENSE
   a) crowded   b) dark   c) sparse   d) transparent

35. BARREN
   a) uncultivated   b) fertile   c) forest   d) unlevelled

NATA Practice Paper - 4

36. Identify this building:

1) Town Hall of Calcutta
2) Shanghai Museum
3) Parthenon
4) British Museum, London

37. Identify this:

1) Pyramids, Gujarat
2) Sphinx, Egypt
3) Parthenon
4) Gomateswara

38. A tetrahedron has the following:-
a) one vertex, 2 surfaces
b) four equal triangular surfaces
c) 4 vertex,4 surfaces
d) both (b) and (c)

39. A triangular prism has the following:-
a) 4 triangular surfaces
b) 3 triangular surfaces
c) 4 triangular surfaces and 4 vertex
d) none of the above

40. A square pyramid has:-
a) 10 surfaces
b) 5 surfaces
c) 7 surfaces
d) 6 surfaces

NATA Practice Paper - 5

Directions: In each given problem, Out of the five figures (a), (b), (c), (d) and (e), four are similar in a certain way. However, one figure is not like the other four. Choose the figure which is different from the rest.

1.

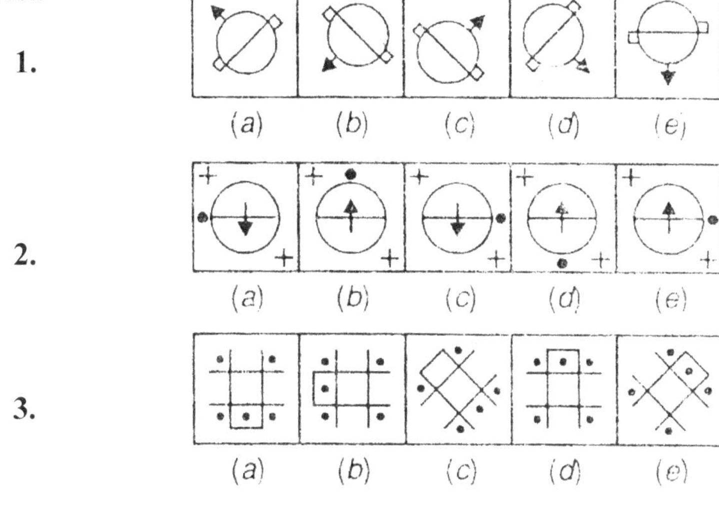

2.

3.

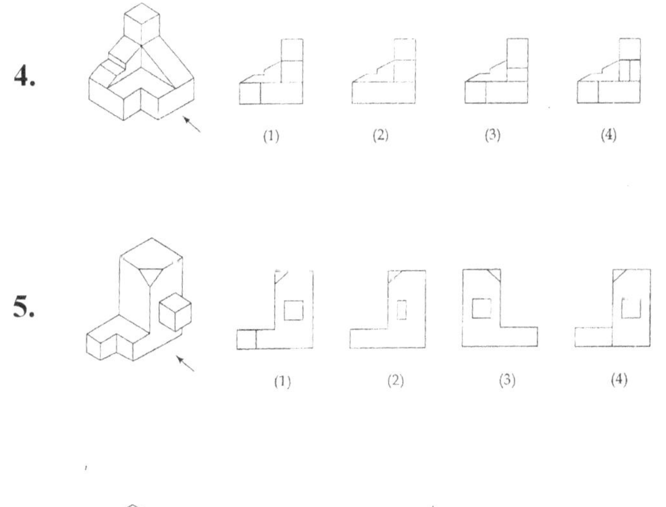

DIRECTIONS: The 3-D Problem figure shows an object. Identify the correct front view amongst the answer figures, looking in the direction of the arrow.

4.

5.

6.

7.

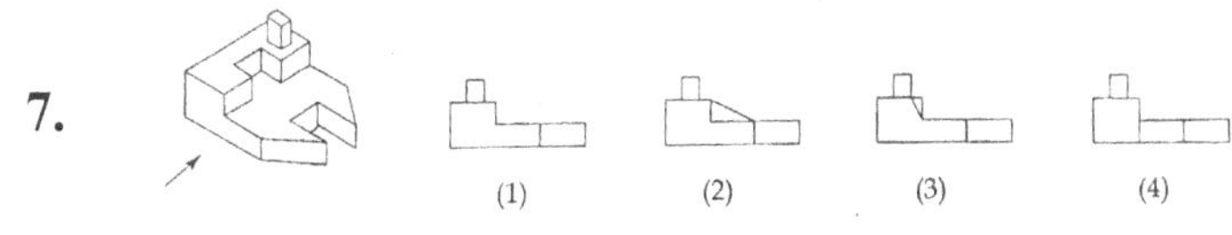

NATA Practice Paper - 5

Directions: Find the total number of inclined surfaces of the object given below in the problem figure.

---

8. 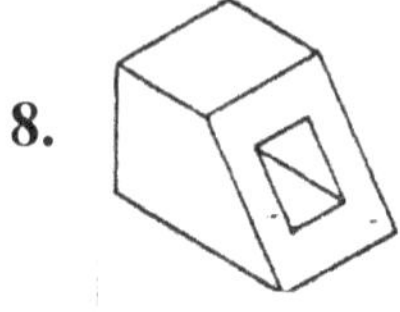   (1) 1   (2) 3   (3) 2   (4) 4

9. 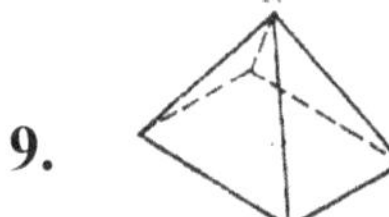   (1) 1   (2) 4   (3) 2   (4) 3

10. 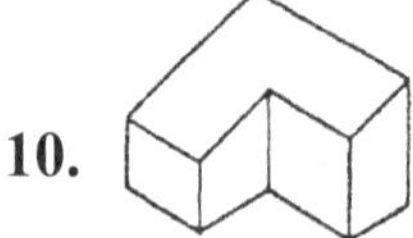   (1) 2   (2) 1   (3) 7   (4) 3

11.    (1) 1   (2) 2   (3) 3   (4) 5

DIRECTIONS: In each one of the following problems, a transparent sheet with a pattern is given. Figure out from the four alternatives as to how the pattern would appear when the transparent sheet is folded at the dotted line.

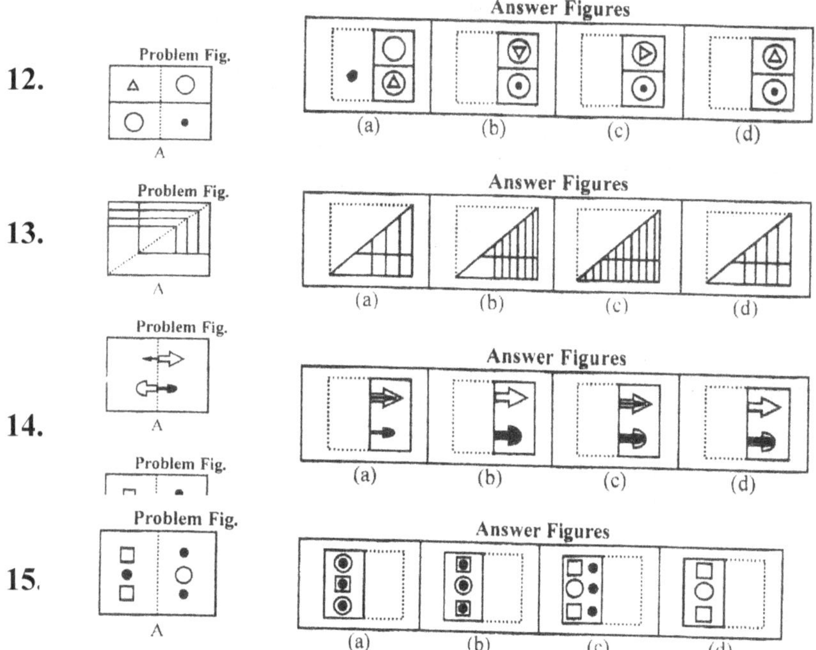

NATA Practice Paper - 5

Directions: Identify the correct top view of the given 3D figure.

16.

Problem Figure

Answer Figures

(a)   (b)   (c)   (d)

17.

Problem Figure

Answer Figures

(a)   (b)   (c)   (d)

18.

Problem Figure

Answer Figures

(a)   (b)   (c)   (d)

19.

Problem Figure

Answer Figures

(a)   (b)   (c)   (d)

---

20. A load-bearing wall that carries load in addition to its own weight is also known as
a) Non-structural wall   b) structural wall
c) both a and b   d) None of these

21. A covered entry supported on pillars or otherwise for vehicular or pedestrian approach is a
a) Nave   b) Arcade
c) Porch/portico   d) Gateway

22. Cavity walls help in
a) preventing transmission of dampness
b) heat and sound insulation
c) economising the budget
d) Both a and b

23. The temporary rigid structure having platform raised up for mason to work and hoist building material to various heights is called
a) scoring   b) scaffolding
c) pinning   d) travelling

24. In a school 1/6 of the girls and 1/7 of the boys took part in NCC camp. Total number of students in NCC camp are:
a) 700   b) 800   c) data inadequate   d) none

25. On a sports day if 30 children were made to stand in columns, 16 columns could be formed. If 24 children were made to sit in the column how many columns will be formed?
a) 45   b) 20   c) 12   d) None

26. A student was asked to multiply a number by 32. By mistake he multiplied the number by 23 and get the answer which was 27 less than the correct one. What is the correct answer?
a) 66   b) 69   c) 96   d) None

NATA Practice Paper - 5

> **DIRECTIONS :** One set is called problem figures and the other is answer figures. Problem figures form some kind of series. Select one figure from the answer figure which will continue the same series as given in problem figures.

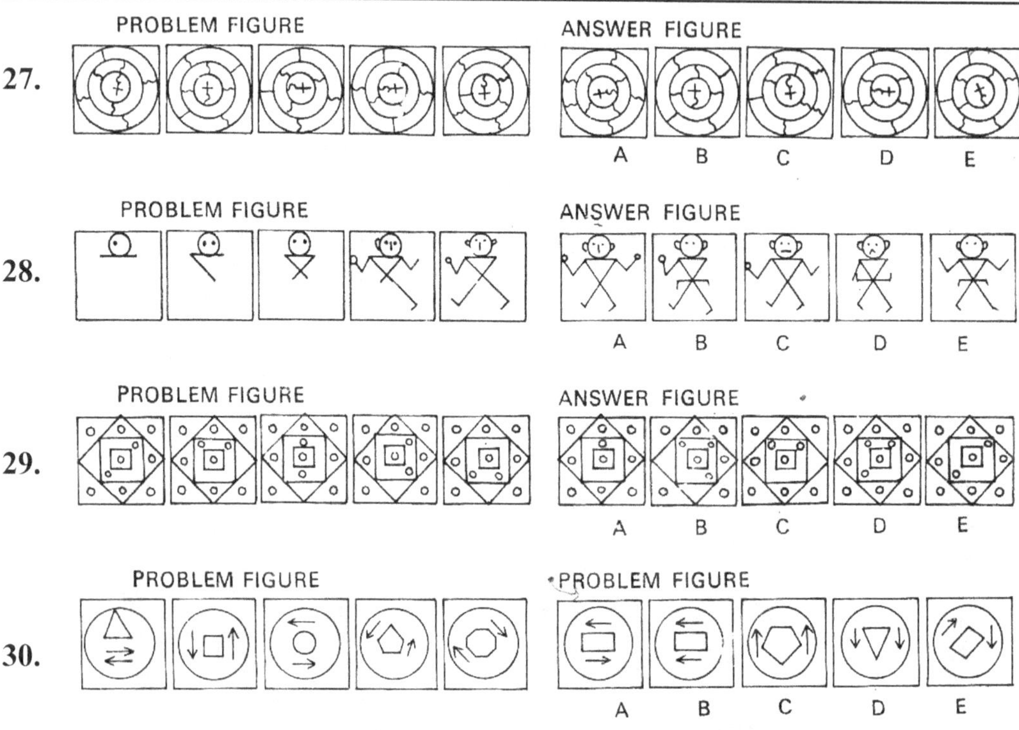

DIRECTIONS : Select one word from the answer words which will continue the same analogy.

31. Ship : Sea :: Camel : ?
    a) Land   b) Desert   c) Mountain   d) Forest

32. Annihilation : Fire :: Cataclysm : ?
    a) Earthquake   b) Steam   c) Emergency d) Disaster

33. Ocean : Water :: Glacier : ?
    a) Mountain   b) Cave   c) Ice   d) Refrigerator

34. Peat : Lignite :: Bituminous:?
    a) Granite   b) Basalt   c) Anthracite d) Coke

35. Mirror : Reflection :: Water : ?
    a) Conduction   b) Reflection c) Refraction d) Immersion

NATA Practice Paper - 5

36. Colosseum of Rome is

1) Battlefield
2) Fort Ruins
3) Amphitheatre
4) Museum Ruins

37. Identify this

1) Rajasthani Mountains
2) The Pyramids at Giza, Egypt
3) Buddhist Burial Mounds, Sarnath
4) Hall of Nations, New Delhi

38. A tetrahedron has the following:-
a) one vertex, 2 surfaces
b) four equal triangular surfaces
c) 4 vertex,4 surfaces
d) both (b) and (c)

39. A pentagonal prism has the following:-
a) 4 surfaces
b) 7 surfaces
c) 15 surfaces and 15 sides
d) both (a) & (c)

40. A cylinder has:-
a) 10 surfaces
b) 5 surfaces
c) 3 surfaces
d) 6 surfaces

NATA Practice Paper - 6

Directions: In each given problem, Out of the five figures (a), (b), (c), (d) and (e), four are similar in a certain way. However, one figure is not like the other four. Choose the figure which is different from the rest.

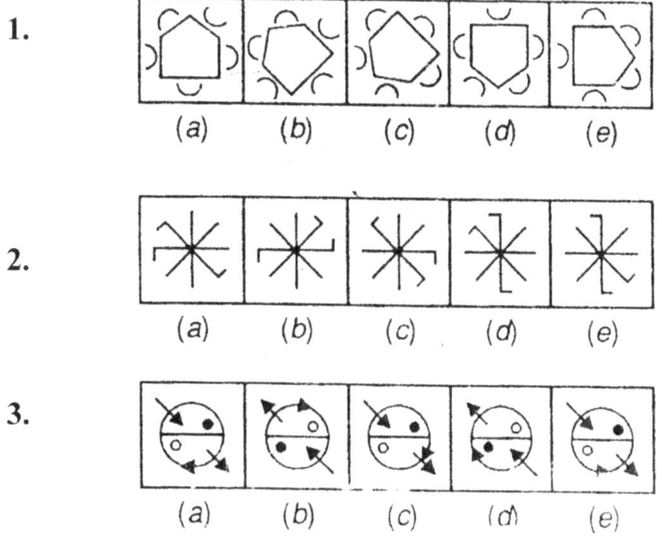

DIRECTIONS: *The 3-D Problem figure shows an object. Identify the correct front view amongst the answer figures, looking in the direction of the arrow.*

NATA Practice Paper - 6

Directions: Find the total number of inclined surfaces of the object given below in the problem figure.

---

8. 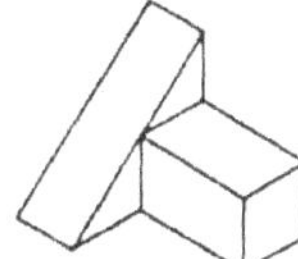   (1) 1   (2) 3   (3) 2   (4) 4

9. 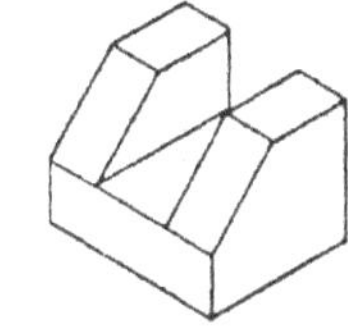   (1) 1   (2) 4   (3) 2   (4) 3

10. 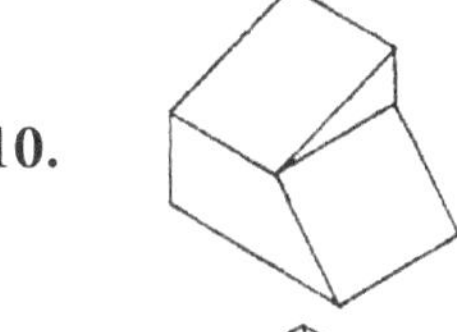   (1) 2   (2) 1   (3) 7   (4) 3

11. 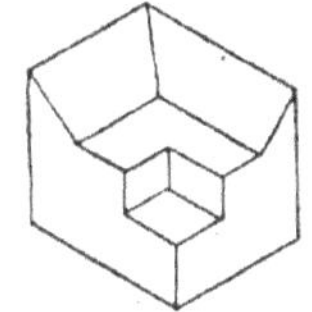   (1) 1   (2) 2   (3) 3   (4) 5

DIRECTIONS: In each one of the following problems, a transparent sheet with a pattern is given. Figure out from the four alternatives as to how the pattern would appear when the transparent sheet is folded at the dotted line.

12. 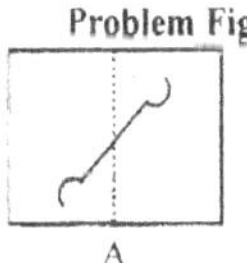 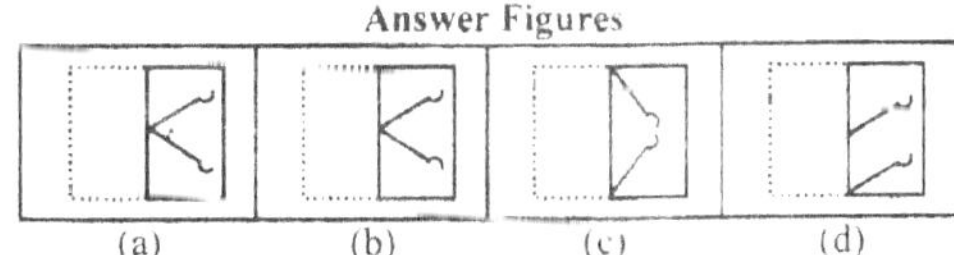

13. 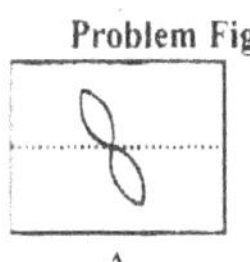 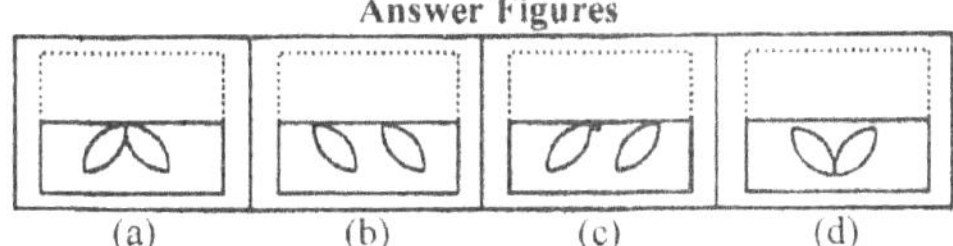

14. 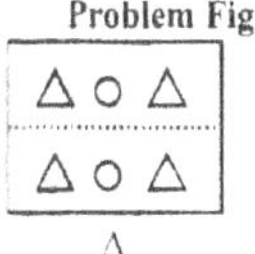 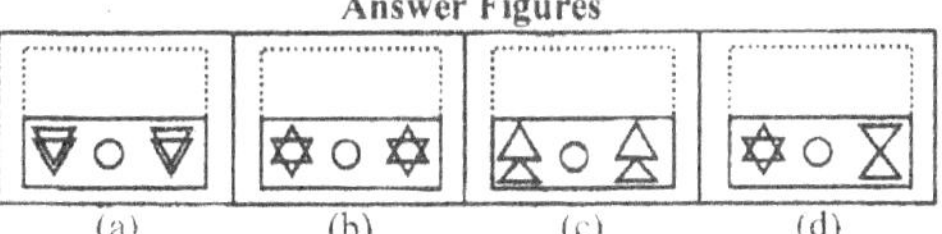

15. 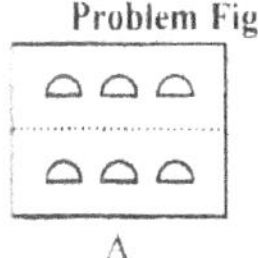 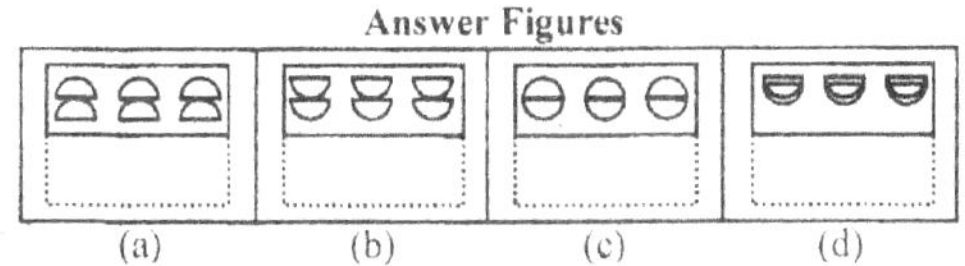

NATA Practice Paper - 6

Directions: Identify the correct top view of the given 3D figure.

16.

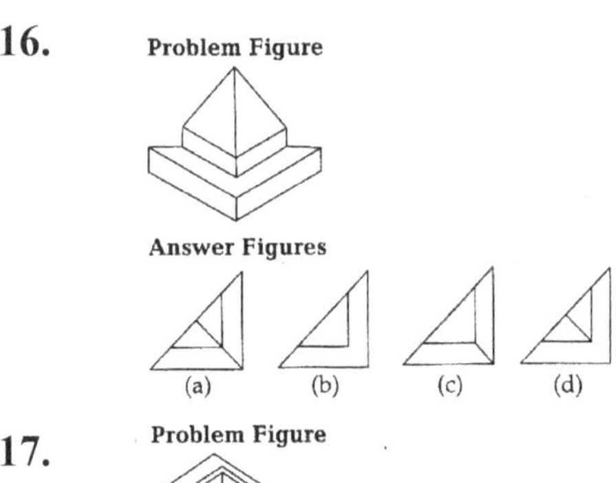

17.

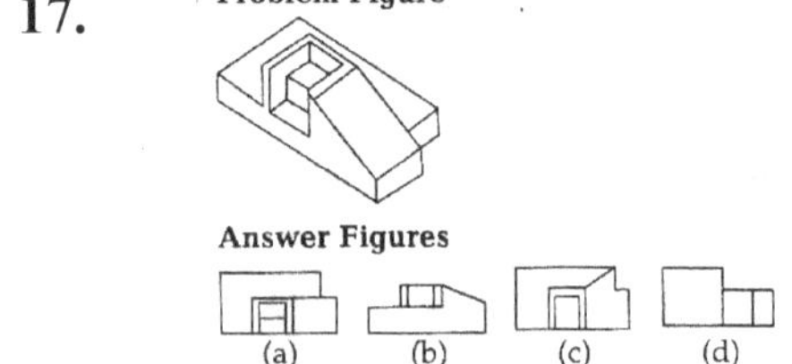

18.

19.

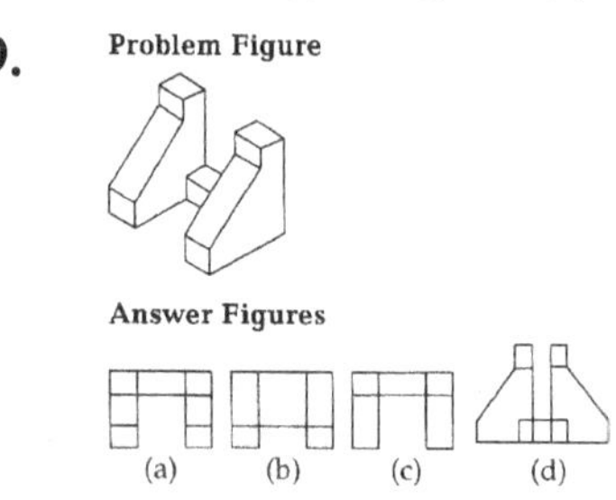

20. Lime cement plaster on external walls to prevent dampness due to rain uses
   a) Cement:Lime: Sand - 1:1:6
   b) Cement:Lime – 1:1
   c) Cement: Lime – 1:6
   d) Lime:Sand – 1:1

21. Cement concrete as D.P.C. uses cement, sand and stone ballast in ratio
   a) 1:2:4
   b) 1:2:1
   c) 2:2:1
   d) 1:1:1

22. Walls with dead air-space between them are
   a) Cavity walls   b) Gap walls
   c) Separation walls   d) Distant walls

23. Balustrade, nosing, handrail, soffit are related to
   a) Lifts   b) Skirting
   c) Staircases   d) Ramps

24. There were 40 girls in a class. One of them weighing 50 kg leaves the class. A new girl comes and increases the average weight of the class by ¼ kg. Find the weight of new girl.
   a) 40kg   b) 60kg   c) 30kg   d) none

25. There were 40 girls in a class. The average of the class is reduced by 1 year if 10 girls whose average age is 20 years leave the class and are replaced by 10 new girls. What is the average age of the new girls?
   a) 18 years   b) 16 years   c) 20 years   d) none

26. The average weight of class of 40 students is 25 kg. If the teachers weight be included, the average increases by 1.5 kg. Find the weight of teacher.
   a) 86.5 kg   b) 84.5 kg   c) 83.5 kg   d) none

NATA Practice Paper - 6

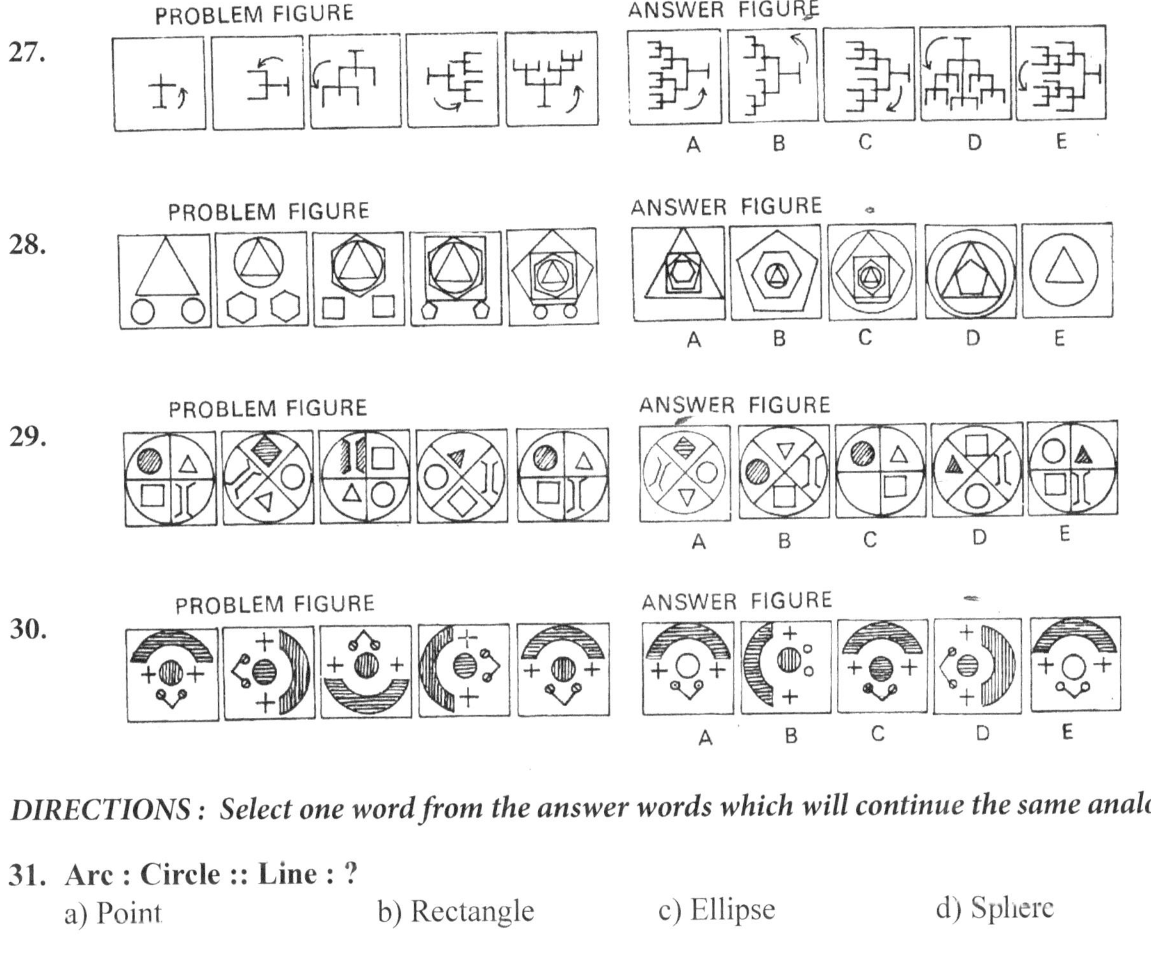

DIRECTIONS : Select one word from the answer words which will continue the same analogy.

31. Arc : Circle :: Line : ?
   a) Point   b) Rectangle   c) Ellipse   d) Sphere

32. Letter : Telegram :: Train : ?
   a) Aeroplane   b) Horse   c) Messenger   d) Telephone

33. Contamination : Food :: Infection : ?
   a) Germs   b) Diseases   c) Body   d) Microbes

34. Aluminium : Bauxite :: Iron : ?
   a) Pyrite   b) Magnesite   c) Pyrdusite   d) Haematite

35. England : London :: U.S.A : ?
   a) New York   b) Las Vegas   c) Los Angeles   d) None of these

NATA Practice Paper - 6

36. Identify this building:

1) Amer Fort
2) Agra Fort
3) Hawa Mahal
4) Red Fort

37. Identify this

1) NDMC Building, New Delhi
2) The Pyramids (Egypt)
3) India Habitat Centre
4) Hall of Nations, New Delhi

38. Identify the material
1) Draining Sheet
2) Corrugated Roof
3) Mangalore Tiles
4) Fibre Glass sheet

39. Identify:
1) Stone Wall
2) Brick wall
3) Mangalore Tiles
4) Ceramic Tiles

40. A cylinder has:-
a) 1 curve surface
b) 2 curve surfaces
c) 3 surfaces
d) both (a) and (c)

NATA Practice Paper - 7

DIRECTIONS : One set is called problem figures and the other is answer figures. Locate the figure from the answer figures which has in its pattern the problem figure embedded.

1. 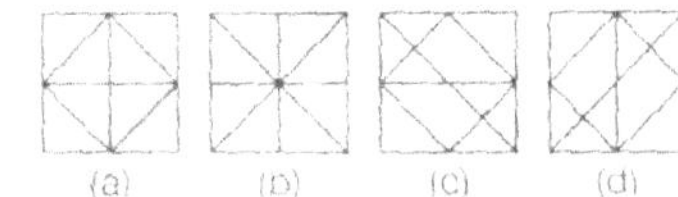

2. 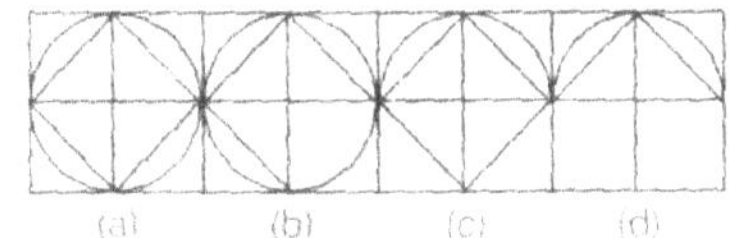

3. 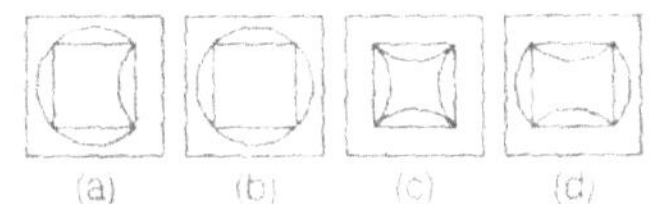

4. 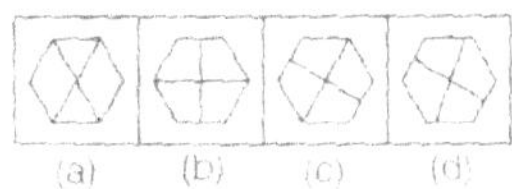

DIRECTIONS : One set is called problem figures and the other is answer figures. Find out the missing portion of the problem figure from the given answer figure.

5. 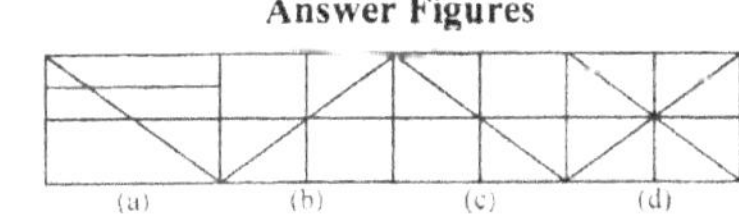

6. 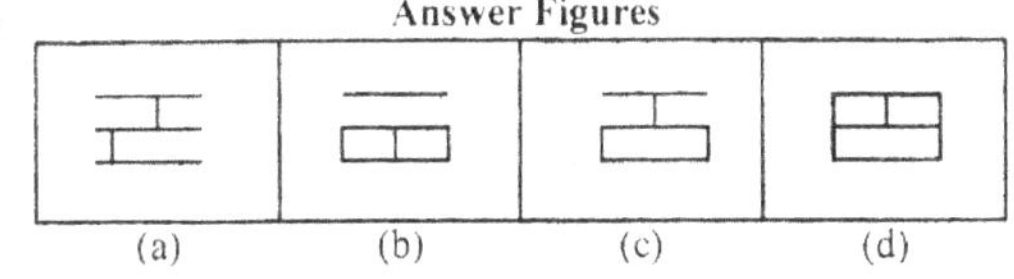

7. 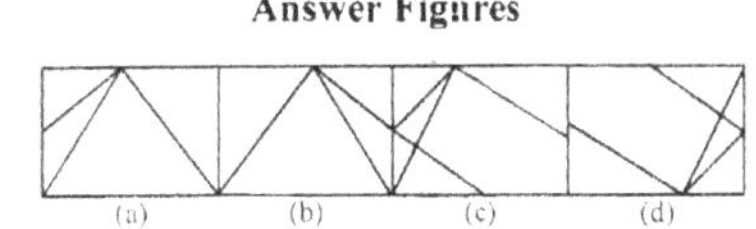

8. 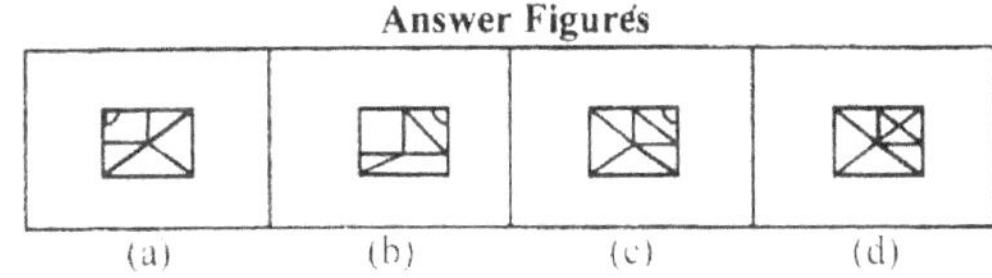

NATA Practice Paper - 7

> **Directions:** Find the total number of inclined surfaces of the object given below in the problem figure.

9. 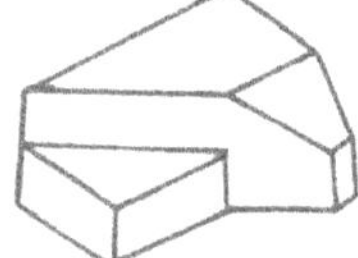
      (1) 1   (2) 4   (3) 2   (4) 3

10. 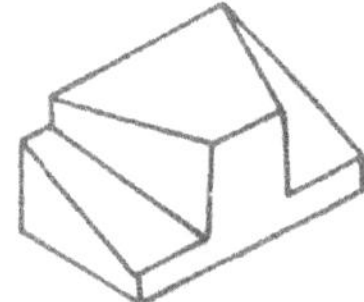
      (1) 2   (2) 9   (3) 7   (4) 3

11. 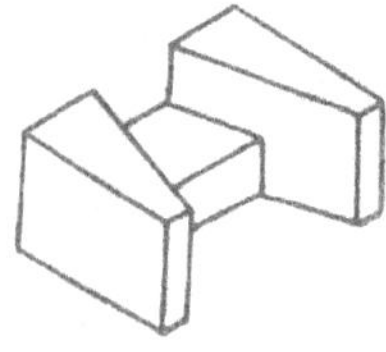
      (1) 1   (2) 0   (3) 3   (4) 5

12. Viceroy's Residence (Rashtrapati Bhawan) was designed by
 a) H. Baker
 b) E. Lutyens
 c) William Emerson
 d) Russell

13. Rashtrapati Bhawan has been designed in which style?
 a) Gothic   b) Baroque
 c) Classical   d) New Classical

14. Chandigarh was designed by
 a) Louis Kahn   b) Laurie Baker
 c) Le Corbusier   d) None of these

15. Chanakya Theatre was designed by :
 a) P.N. mathur   b) Ram Sharma
 c) Sharat Das   d) Ashok Goel

16. Parliament Annexe has been designed by
 a) Fariburz Sabha   b) F.W. Benjamin
 c) Laurie Baker   d) E. Lutyens

NATA Practice Paper - 7

Directions: Identify the correct top view of the given 3D figure.

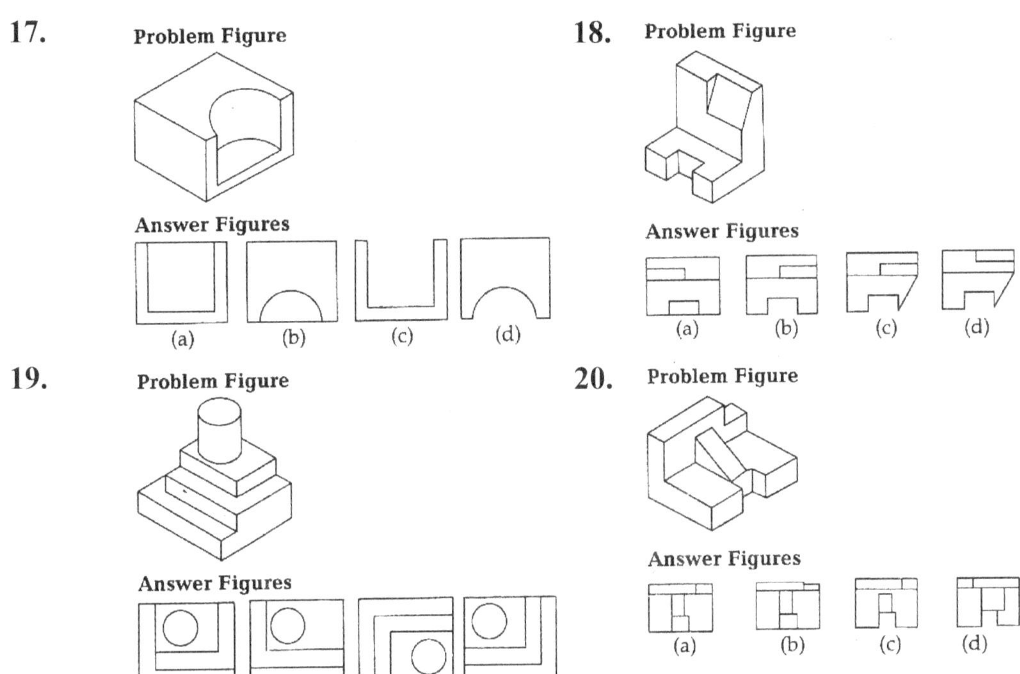

21. A certain work can be completed by 10 men and 8 women together in 20 days. The number of days 8 men and 10 women together will take to complete the same work is
a) 20
b) 64/5
c) 125/4
d) 15

22. A shopkeeper claims to sell all of his articles at a discount of 10% but marks his articles by increasing the cost price of each article by 20%. His gain on each article is
a) 6%
b) 8%
c) 10%
d) 12%

23. The ratio of the number of ladies to that of gents at a party was 3:2. When 20 more gents joined the party, the ratio was reversed. The number of ladies present at the party was]
a) 36
b) 32
c) 24
d) 16

24. Annual incomes of A and B are in the ratio 4:3 and their annual expenses are in the ratio 3:2. If each of them saves Rs. 600 at the end of the year, the annual income of A is
a) Rs. 4,800
b) Rs. 1,800
c) Rs 1,200
d) Rs 2,400

NATA Practice Paper - 7

25. Problem Figure

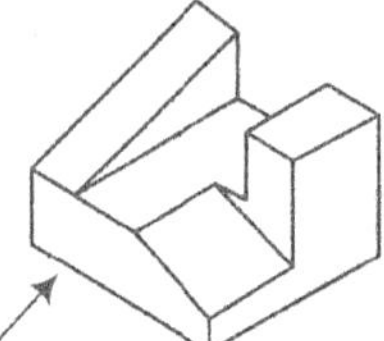

Answer Figures

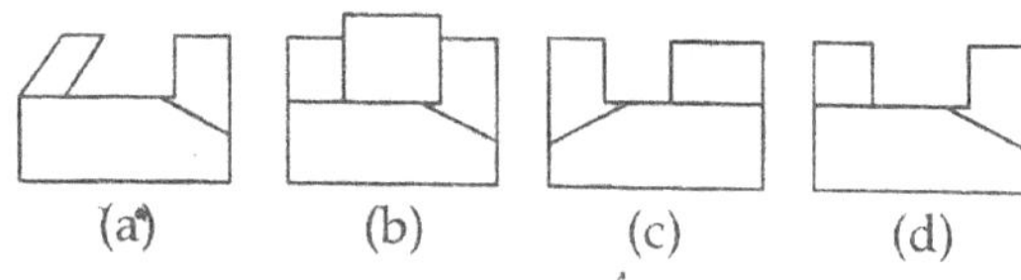

(a)   (b)   (c)   (d)

26. Problem Figure

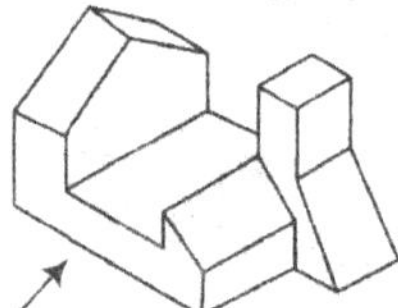

Answer Figures

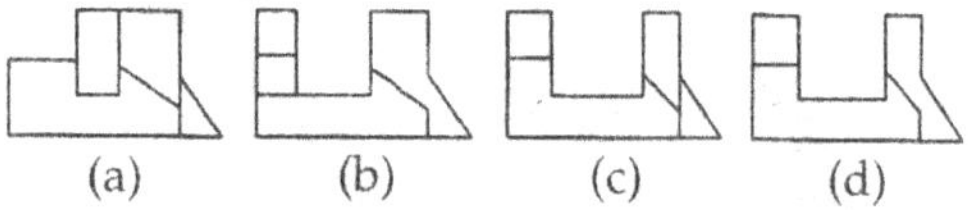

(a)   (b)   (c)   (d)

27. Problem Figure

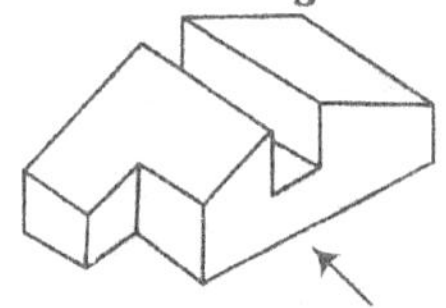

Answer Figures

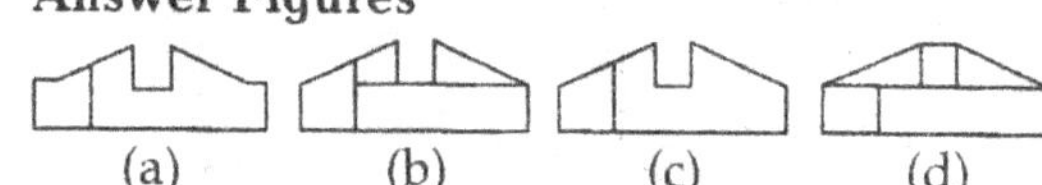

(a)   (b)   (c)   (d)

28. Problem Figure

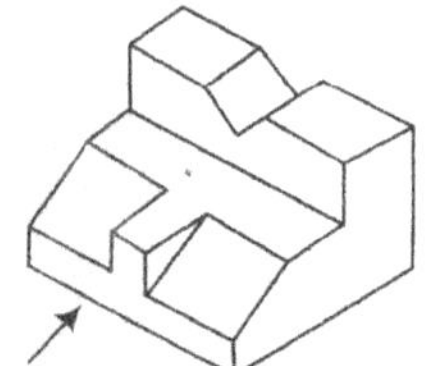

Answer Figures

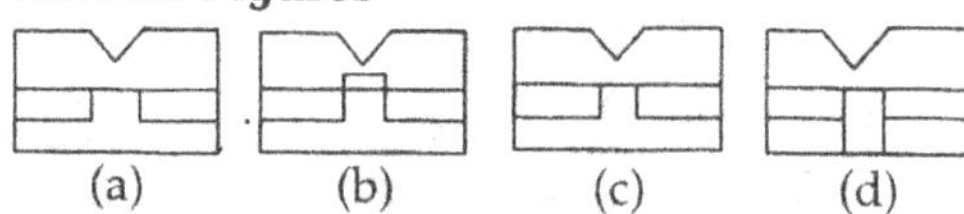

(a)   (b)   (c)   (d)

29. Identify the material:
1) Granite
2) Marble
3) Sand Plaster
4) Limestone

30. Identify the material:
1) Stone Slabs
2) Blockboard
3) Plywood
4) Glass

NATA Practice Paper - 7

31.	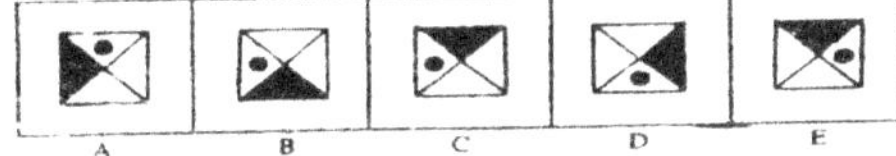	Identify the building : a) Talkatora Indoor Stadium b) Indira Gandhi Indoor Stadium c) Lotus Temple d) Matrimandir, Auroville
32.		Identify the building : a) Budhha Statue b) Statue Of Gomateshwara, c) Hanuman Murti, Delhi d) Shiv Statue

Directions: In each given problem, Out of the five figures (A), (B), (C), (D) and (E), four are similar in a certain way. However, one figure is not like the other four. Choose the figure which is different from the rest.

33. 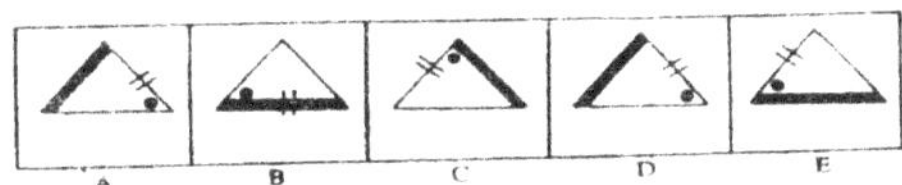

34. 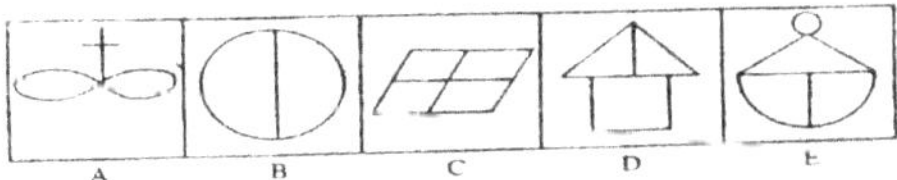

35. 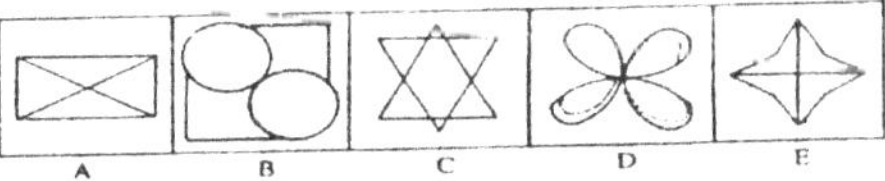

36. 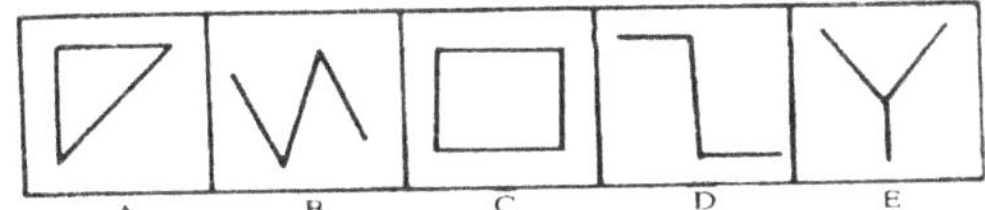

37.

Directions: Choose the word that is similar in meaning to the word given in capital letters.

38. REFUND

    A. deduct   B. receive   C. distribute   D. reimburse

39. CARELESS

    A. spotless   B. faceless   C. negligent   D. vigilant

40. ELOQUENT

    A. elusive   B. articulate   C. fluent   D. expressive

NATA Practice Paper - 8

DIRECTIONS : One set is called problem figures and the other is answer figures. Locate the figure from the answer figures which has in its pattern the problem figure embedded.

1. 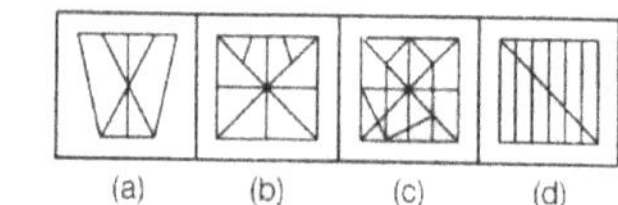

2. 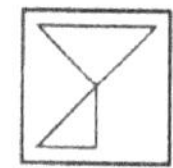 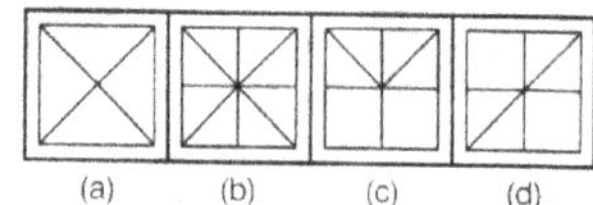

3.  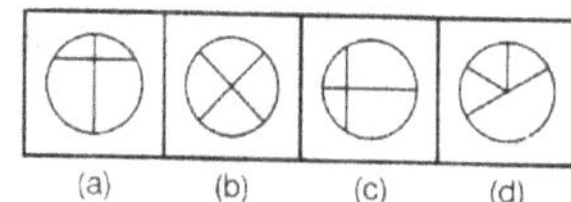

4.  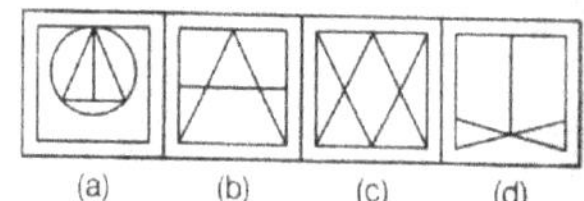

DIRECTIONS : One set is called problem figures and the other is answer figures. Find out the missing portion of the problem figure from the given answer figure.

5. 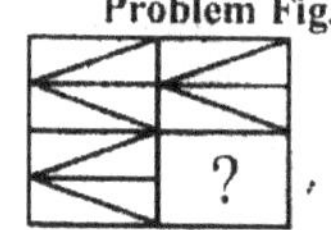 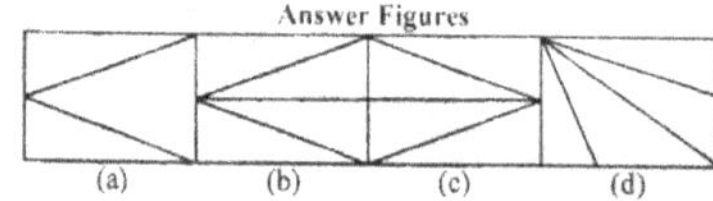

6.  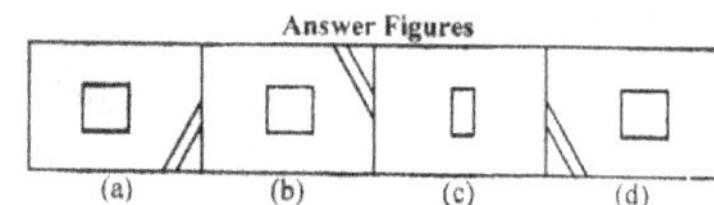

7. 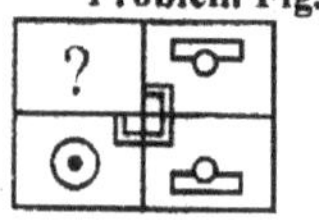 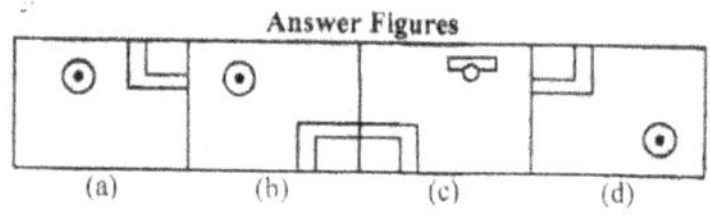

8. 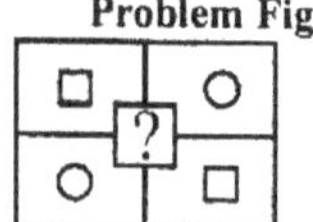 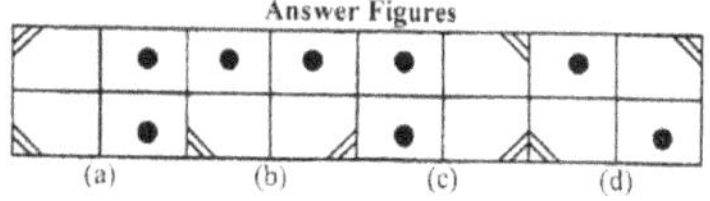

NATA Practice Paper - 8

> **Directions:** Find the total number of inclined surfaces of the object given below in the problem figure.

9. 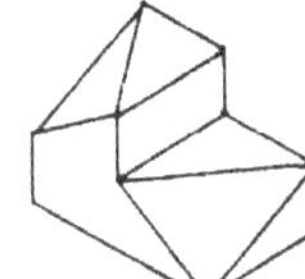   (1) 1   (2) 4   (3) 2   (4) 3

10. 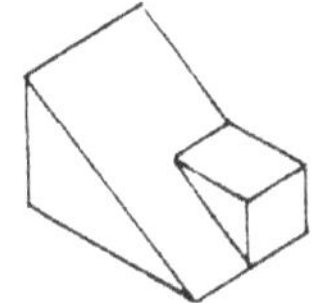   (1) 2   (2) 1   (3) 7   (4) 3

11. 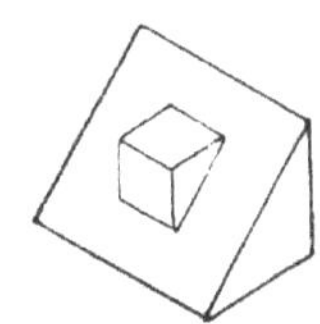   (1) 1   (2) 2   (3) 3   (4) 5

12. **JNU Complex has been designed by**
    a) C.P. Kukreja   b) ARCOP
    c) Sharad Jain   d) Uppal Ghosh

13. **India International Centre is associated with**
    a) Peter Eiesenman
    b) Charles Jeanneret
    c) Joseph Allen Stein
    d) None of these

14. **Laurie baker is associated with**
    a) Group Housing   b) Industrial design   c) Low cost housing   d) None of these

15. **Which of the following have been given 'Padma Shree' ?**
    a) M.M. Rana   b) Joseph Allen Stein   c) Both A & B   d) None of these

16. **LIC, Connaught Place has been designed by:**
    a) Charles Correa   b) Hafeez Contractor
    c) C.P. Kukreja   d) B.V. Doshi

NATA Practice Paper - 8

DIRECTIONS: The 3-D Problem figure shows an object. Identify the correct front view amongst the answer figures, looking in the direction of the arrow.

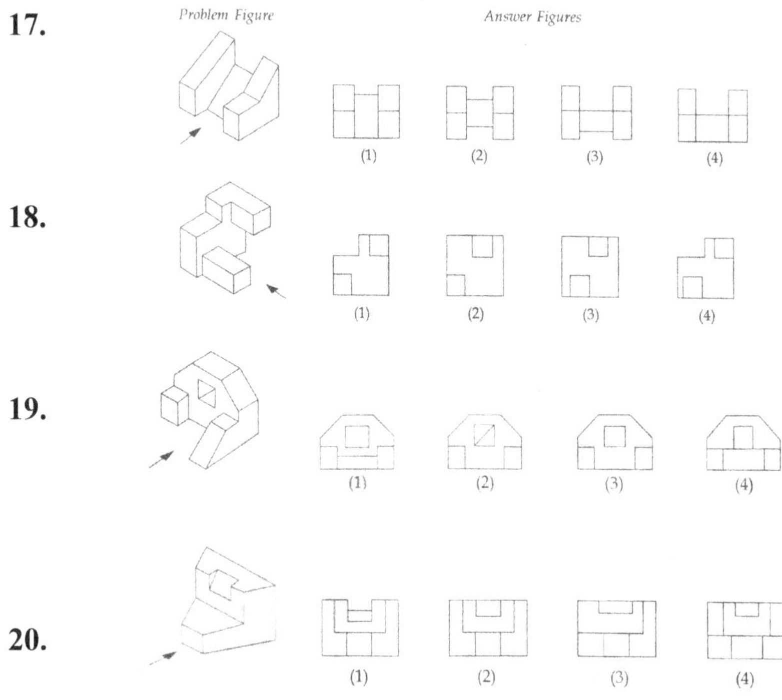

17.

18.

19.

20.

21. **A single discount, equivalent to successive discounts of 30%, 20% and 10% is**
    a) 50%   b) 49.60%   c) 50.40%   d) 51%

22. **A dealer offers a discount of 10% on the marked price of an article and still makes a profit of 20%. If its marked price is Rs. 800, then the price of the article is**
    a) Rs. 900
    b) Rs. 800
    c) Rs. 700
    d) Rs. 600

23. **If x: y = 2:3, then the value of $(3x+2y) \div (9x+5y)$ is equal to:-**
    a) 11/4
    b) 4/11
    c) 1/2
    d) 5/14

24. **Which of the following fractions lies between 2/3 and 3/5?**
    a) 2/5
    b) 1/3
    c) 1/15
    d) 31/50

NATA Practice Paper - 8

25. 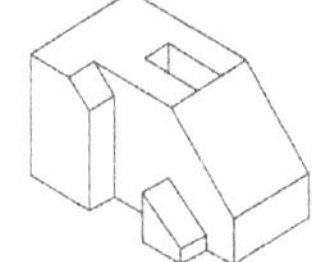 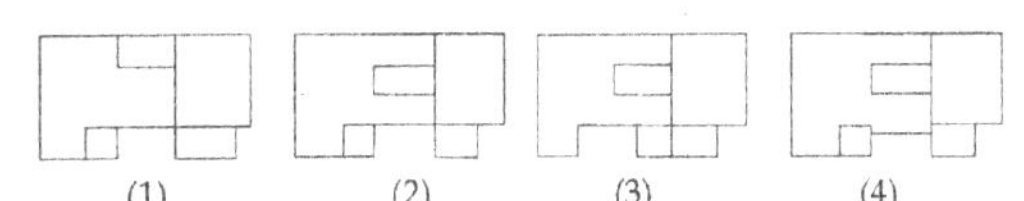

(1)   (2)   (3)   (4)

26. 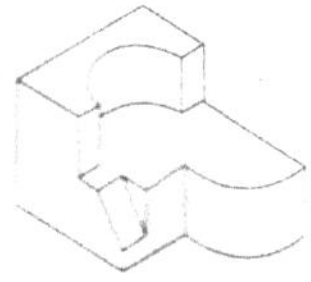 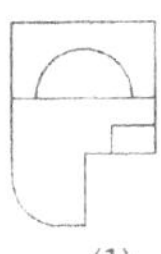 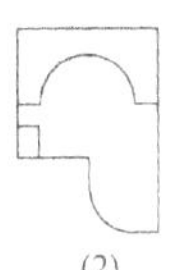 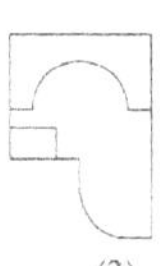 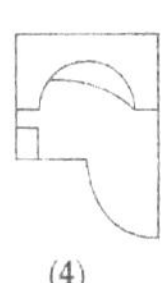

(1)   (2)   (3)   (4)

27. 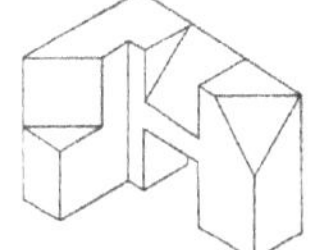 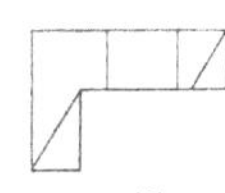 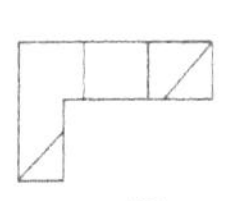 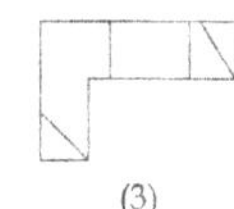 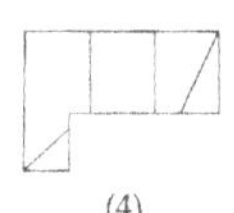

(1)   (2)   (3)   (4)

28. 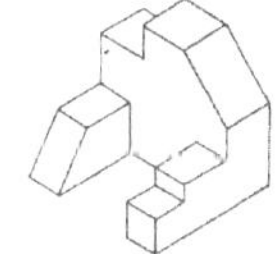 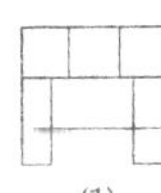 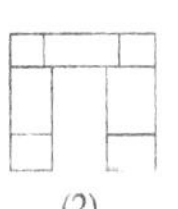 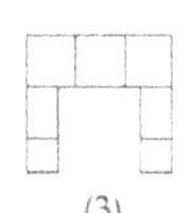 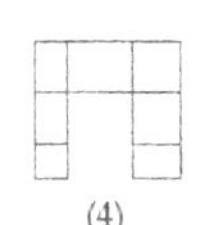

(1)   (2)   (3)   (4)

29. **Identify the material:**
1) Stone Wall
2) Brick wall
3) Mangalore Tiles
4) Ceramic Tiles

30. **Identify the material:**
1) Marble Slab
2) Granite Slab
3) Plywood
4) Glass

NATA Practice Paper - 8

31. Identify the building :
a) Fatehpur Sikri
b) Red Fort, Delhi
c) Agra Fort
d) Amer Fort

32. Identify the building :
a) Tower Bridge London
b) Gateway of India
c) Laxman Jhoola
d) Big Ben, London

Directions: In each given problem, Out of the five figures (A), (B), (C), (D) and (E), four are similar in a certain way. However, one figure is not like the other four. Choose the figure which is different from the rest.

33.

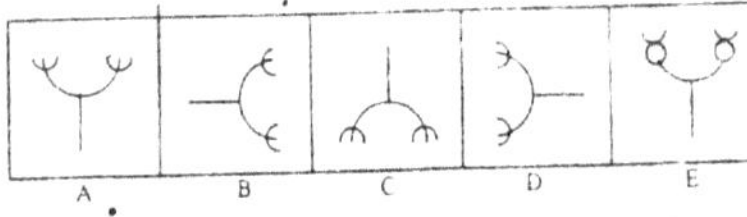

34.

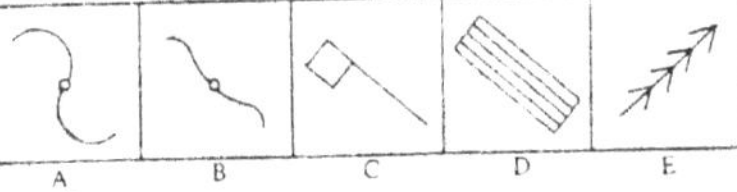

35.

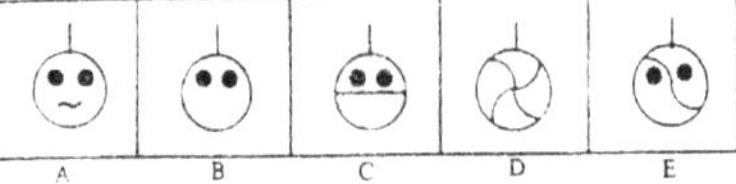

36.

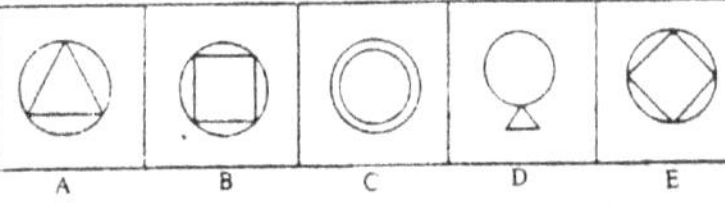

37.

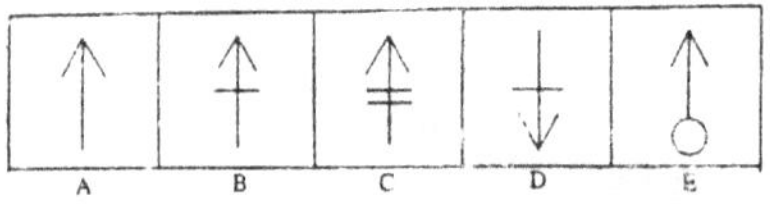

Directions: Choose the word that is similar in meaning to the word given in capital letters.

38. INEDIBLE
    A. unfit for human consumption   B. polluted   C. vitiated   D. eatable

39. DOCILE
    A. vague   B. gentle   C. stupid   D. stubborn

40. VIVID
    A. brilliant   B. fresh   C. explanatory   D. picturesque

NATA Practice Paper - 9

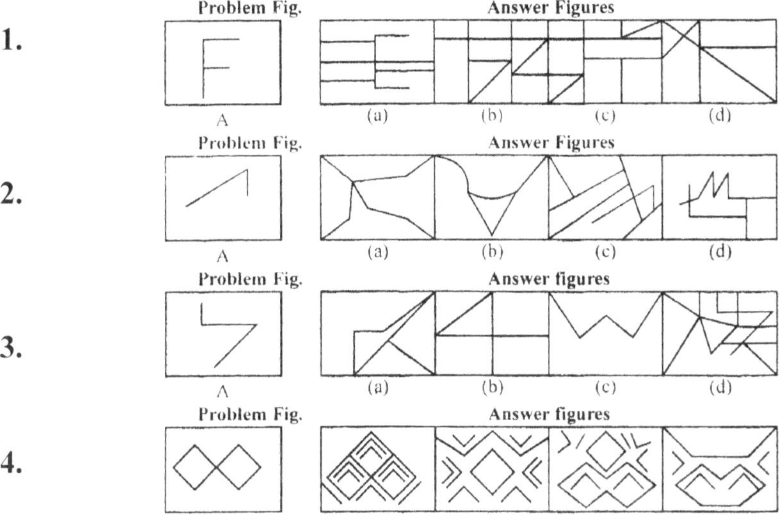

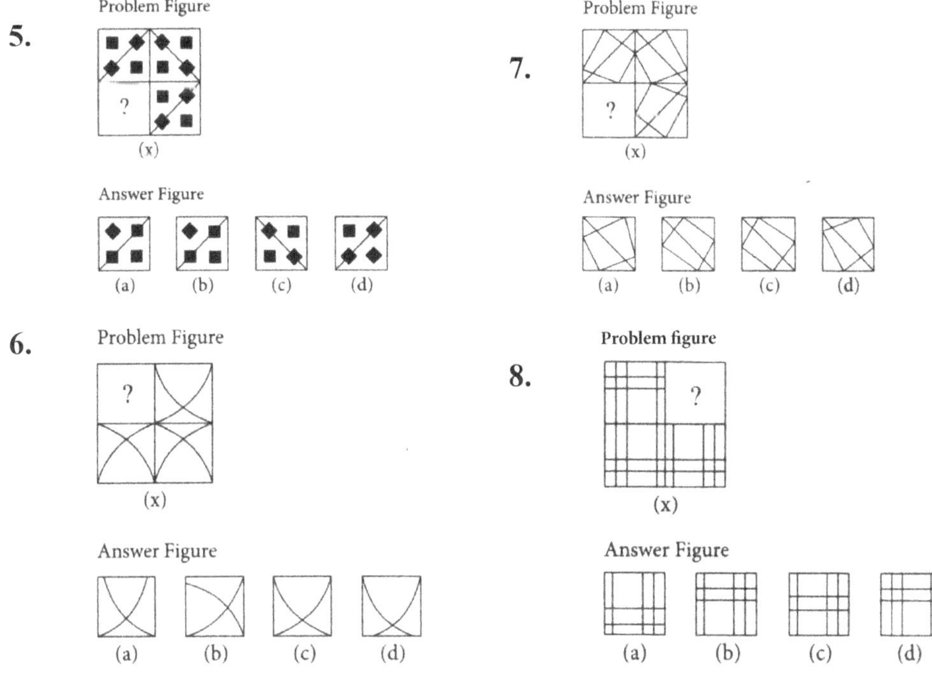

NATA Practice Paper - 9

9.  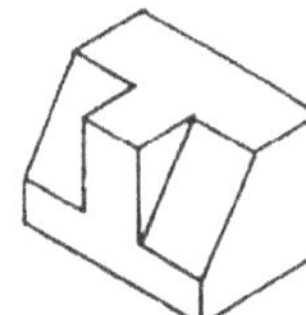   (1) 1   (2) 4   (3) 2   (4) 3

10. 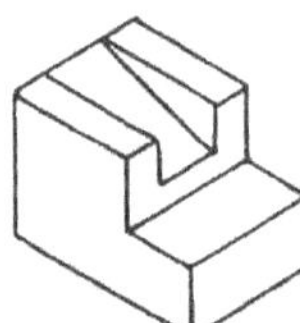   (1) 2   (2) 9   (3) 7   (4) 3

11. 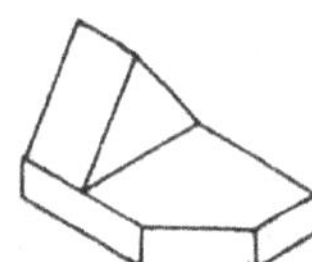   (1) 1   (2) 2   (3) 3   (4) 5

12. **Hussain – Doshi Gufa is situated in:**
    a) Bangalore   b) Ahmedabad   c) Kolkata   d) Jaisalmer

13. **Jantar Mantar was created by:**
    a) Jai Singh   b) Fidai Khan   c) Narsimh Dev   d) None of These

14. **Pinjore Gardens were designed by:**
    a) Fidai Khan   b) Habib Rehman   c) Jai Singh   d) None of the above

15. **"Falling Waters" has been done by**
    a) Frank Gehry   b) Frank Lloyd Wright
    c) Mies Van der Rohe   d) Eero Saarinen

16. **'Assembly Hall' Chandigarh has been designed by:**
    a) S.N. Prasad
    b) Le Corbusier
    c) F.L. Wright
    d) Ram Sharma

NATA Practice Paper - 9

Directions: Identify the correct top view of the given 3D figure.

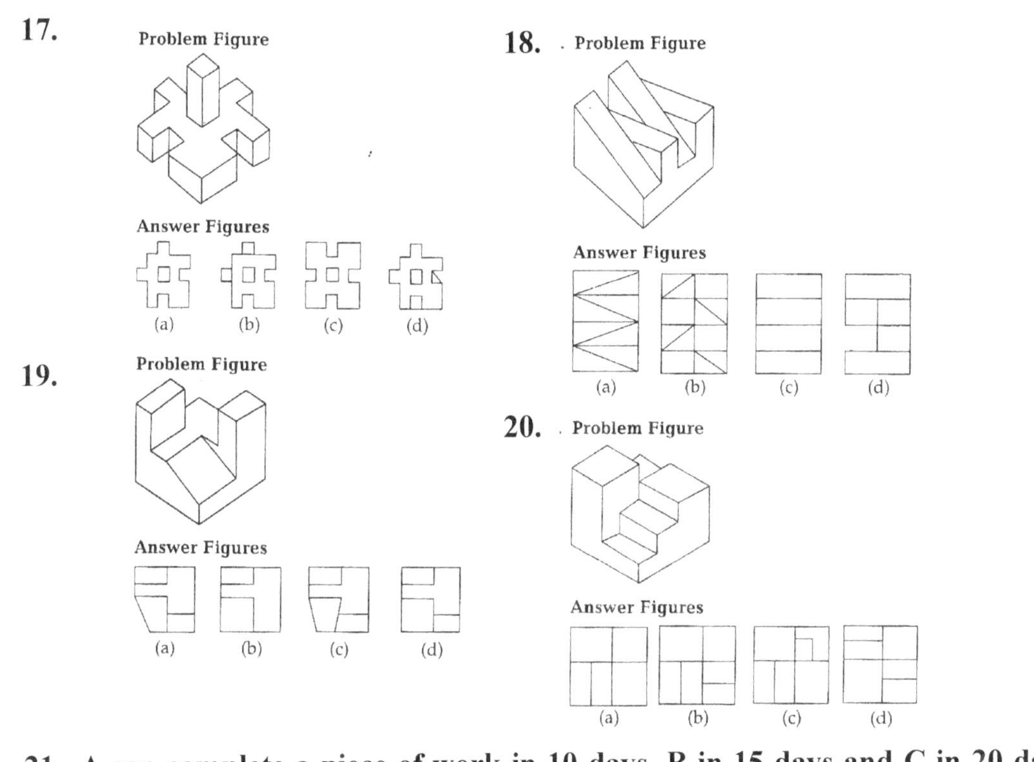

17. Problem Figure

Answer Figures

(a) (b) (c) (d)

18. Problem Figure

Answer Figures

(a) (b) (c) (d)

19. Problem Figure

Answer Figures

(a) (b) (c) (d)

20. Problem Figure

Answer Figures

(a) (b) (c) (d)

21. A can complete a piece of work in 10 days, B in 15 days and C in 20 days. A and C worked together for 2 days and then A was replaced by B. In how many days, altogether, was the work completed?

a) 12 b) 10 c) 6 d) 8

22. A,B and C can complete a work in 10,12 and 15 days respectively. They started the work together. But A left the work before 5 days of its completion. B also left the work 2 days after A left. In how many days was the work completed?

a) 4 b) 5 c) 7 d) 8

23. Two pipes A and B can fill a water tank in 20 and 24 minutes respectively and a third pipe C can empty at the rate of 3 gallons per minute. If A, B and C opened together fill the tank in 15 minutes, the capacity (in gallons) of the tank is

a) 180 b) 150 c) 120 d) 60

24. If 10 men or 20 boys can make 260 mats in 20 days, then how many mats will be made by 8 men and 4 boys in 20 days?

a) 260 b) 240 c) 280 d) 520

NATA Practice Paper - 9

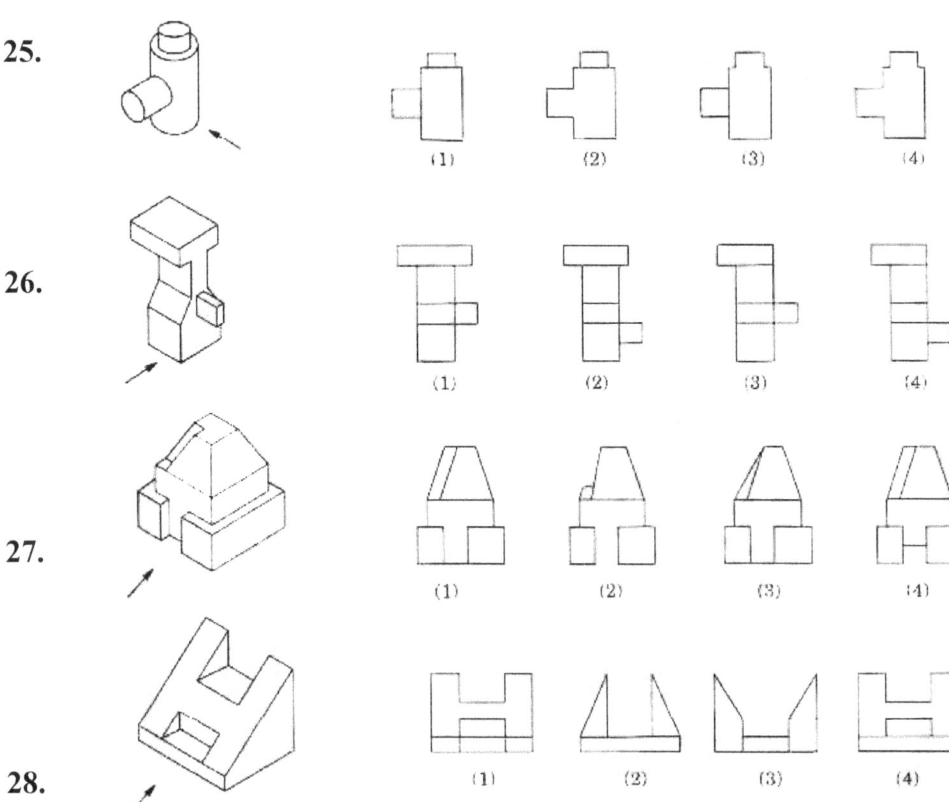

25. (1) (2) (3) (4)

26. (1) (2) (3) (4)

27. (1) (2) (3) (4)

28. (1) (2) (3) (4)

29.

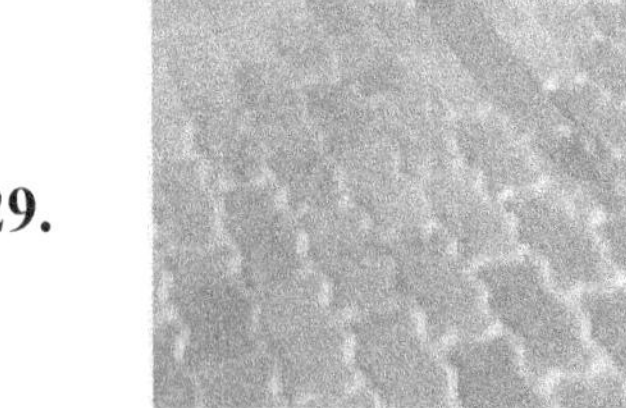

These tiles are better used for
a) Bathroom
b) Lounge
c) Pavement
d) Road

30.

Identify the material
a) Limestone
b) Stone aggregate
c) Brick Wall
d) Slate

NATA Practice Paper - 9

31. Identify the building :
a) Ashoka Pillar
b) Kirti Stambh
c) Qutub Minar
d) Vijay Stambh

32. Identify the building :
a) Birla Mandir
b) Badrinath Temple
c) ISKON Temple
d) Kedarnath Mandir

DIRECTIONS: Choose the word which is most OPPOSITE in meaning as the word printed

33. CIVILISED
    a) palpable   b) civic   c) incongruent d) barbarian

34. WEALTHY
    a) wicked   b) famous   c) ill   d) poor

35. TRANSPARENT
    a) translucent   b) vague   c) blind   d) opaque

36. URBAN
    a) rustic   b) rural   c) civil   d) domestic

37. ANXIOUS
    a) crafty   b) metier   c) carefree   d) slapdash

DIRECTIONS: Find the odd figure out in the problem figures given below:

38
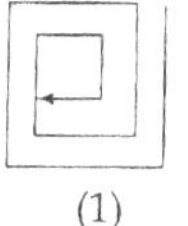 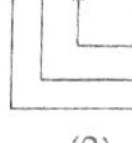 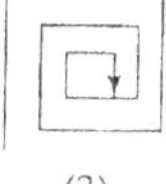 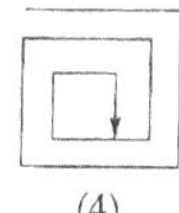

(1)   (2)   (3)   (4)

39.
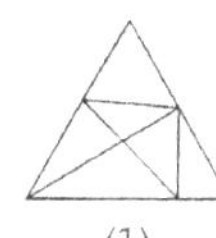 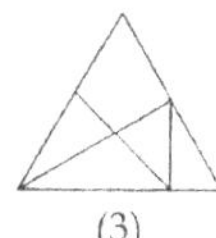 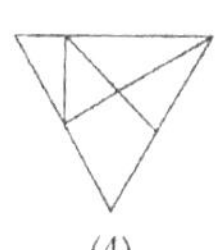

(1)   (2)   (3)   (4)

40.
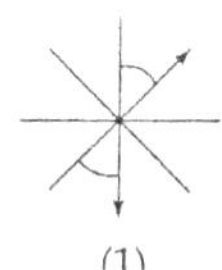 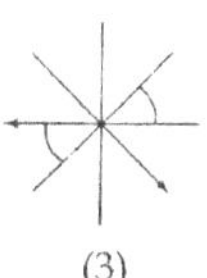 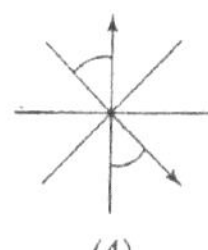

(1)   (2)   (3)   (4)

NATA Practice Paper - 10

Directions: In each given problem, Out of the five figures (A), (B), (C), (D) and (E), four are similar in a certain way. However, one figure is not like the other four. Choose the figure which is different from the rest.

1.
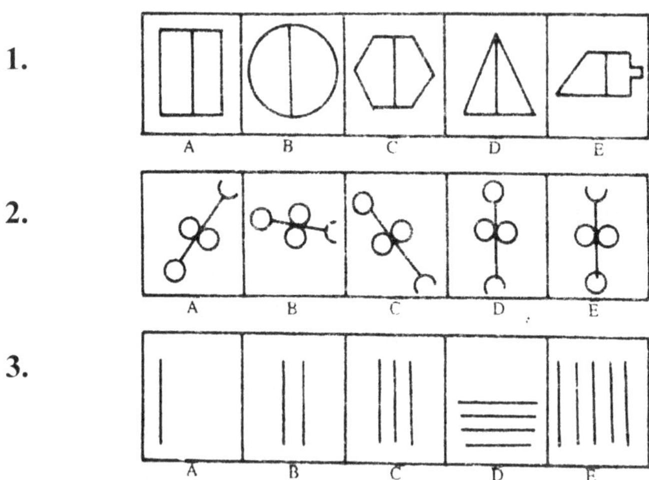

2.

3.

DIRECTIONS: *The problem figure shows the **top** view of an object. Identify the correct front view amongst the answer figures.*

4.
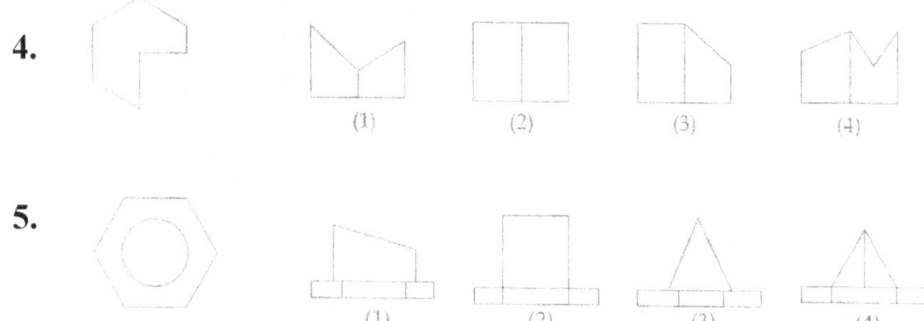

5.

DIRECTIONS: *The problem figure shows the **front** view of an object. Identify the correct 3D figure amongst the answer figures.*

6.
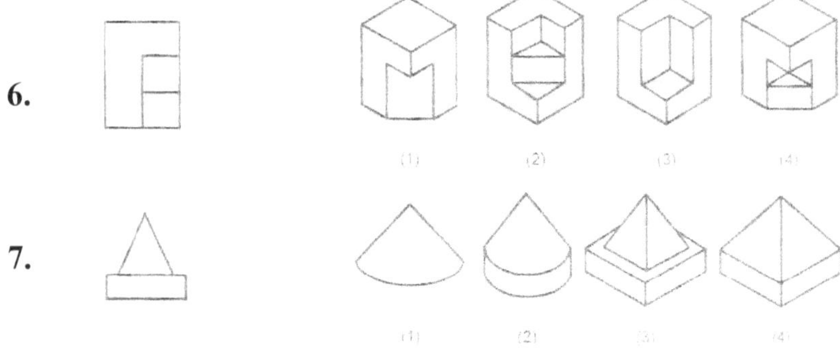

7.

NATA Practice Paper - 10

8. 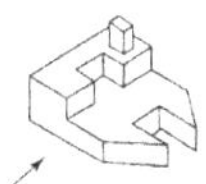 (1) 1 (2) 0 (3) 2 (4) 3

9. 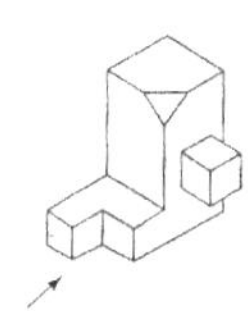 (1) 1 (2) 2 (3) 3 (4) 4

10. 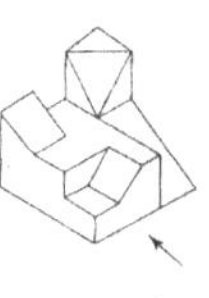 (1) 3 (2) 1 (3) 2 (4) 4

11. 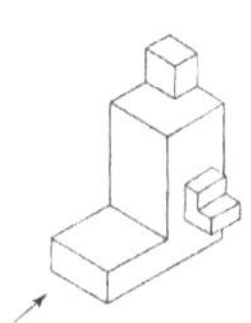 (1) 3 (2) 0 (3) 1 (4) 2

DIRECTIONS: The question figures form a series. You have to find which one of the answer figure would be the next one in the given series.

12. 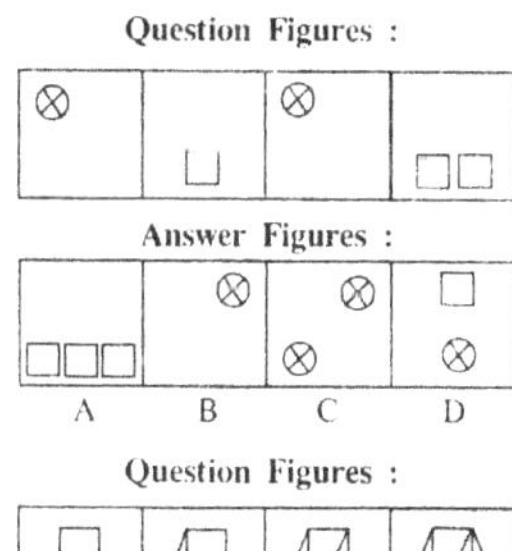

13. 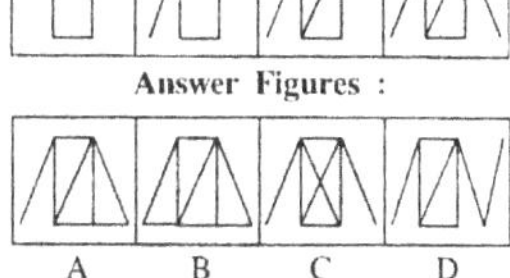

14. 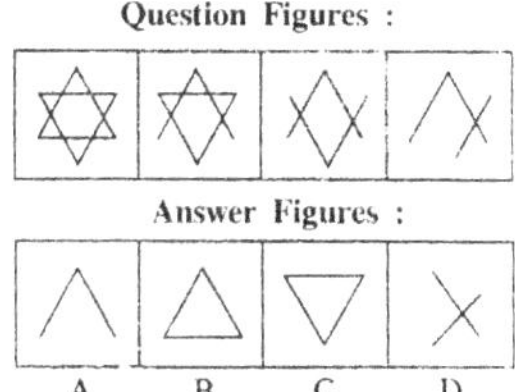

NATA Practice Paper - 10

Directions: Identify the correct top view of the given 3D figure.

15.

16

17.

18.

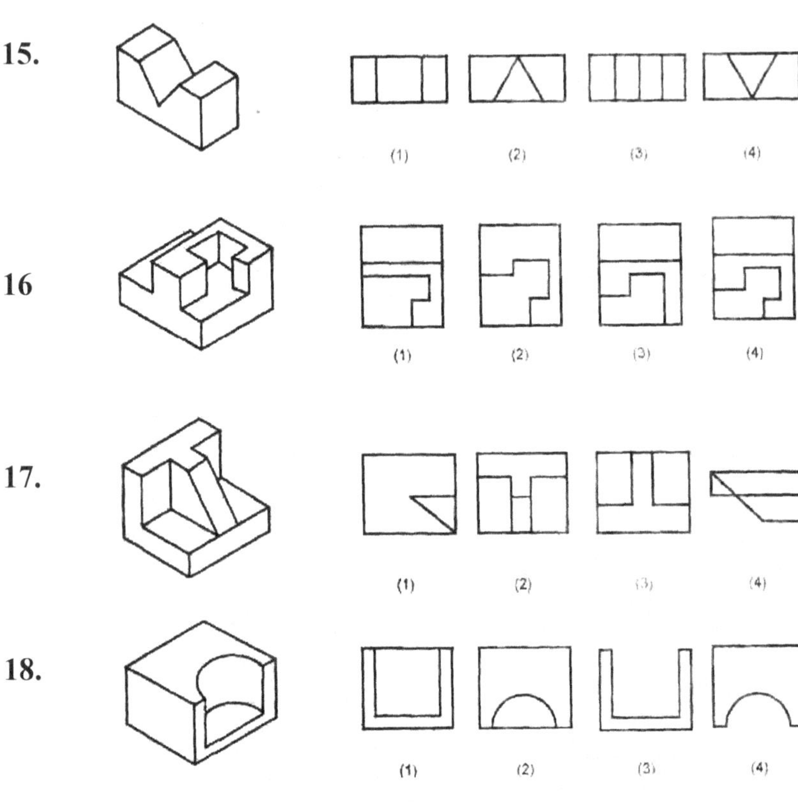

Directions :Choose the most appropriate option to fill in the blank.

19. The .... transformation of the former Soviet Union or Russia as it was popularly known, remains one of the biggest stories of the decade.
   A. smooth   B. singular   C. tumultuous   D. prophetic

20. Paper money is merely a representation of wealth; therefore unlike gold or any other precious metal, it has no .... value.
   A. financial   B. fiscal   C. inveterate   D. intrinsic

21. We must .... the tickets for the movie in advance.
   A. draw   B. buy   C. remove   D. take

22. The stenographer is very efficient. He is........ to his firm.
   A. a credit   B. a blessing   C. an asset   D. a boon

23. The police .... the mob.
   A. scattered   B. disbanded   C. drove   D. dispersed

NATA Practice Paper - 10

24. The difference between a number and its three-fifth is 50. What is the number?

a) 75   b) 100

c) 125   d) None of these

25. $837.62 + 8.591 + 34.4 = ?$

a) 870.611   b) 880.511

c) 880.611   d) 926.97

26. If a and b are both odd numbers, which of the following is an even number?

a) a+b   b) a+b+1

c) ab   d) ab+2

27. By how much does 48/7 exceed 6/48?

a) $6\ ^{41}/_{56}$ b) $6\ ^3/_4$ c) $7\ ^3/_4$ d) $7\ ^5/_6$

28. Mahesh obtained 67,82, 76, 65 and 85 marks (out of 100) in English, Mathematics, Physics, Chemistry and Biology respectively. What are his average marks?

a) 65   b) 69   c) 72   d) None of these

DIRECTIONS : One set is called problem figures and the other is answer figures. Find out the missing portion of the problem figure from the given answer figure.

---

29. 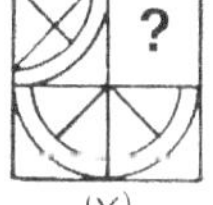   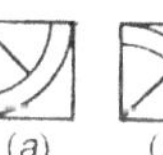   

30. 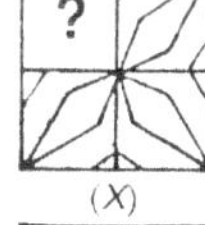 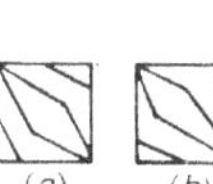   

31. 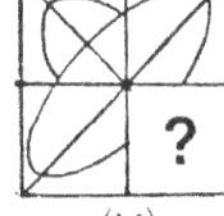 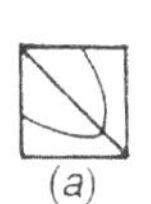   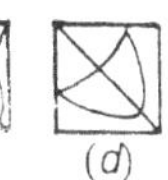

32. 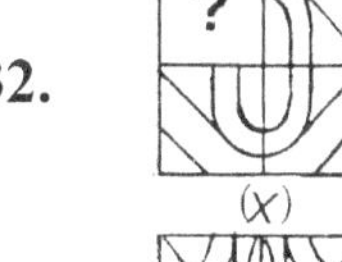  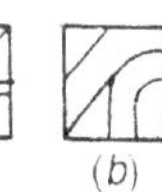 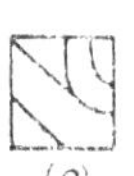 

33. 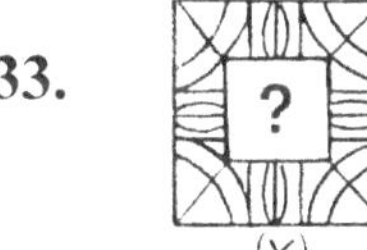    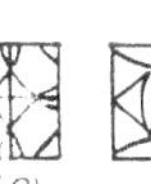 

NATA Practice Paper - 10

34. Identify this building:

1) Lotus Temple
2) Birla Mandir, Delhi
3) ISKON Temple
4) Akshardham Temple, Delhi

35. Identify this building:

1) Grey Taj Mahal
2) Bibi Ka Makbara
3) Gol Gumbaz, Bijapur
4) Humayun's Tomb, Delhi

36. Identify:
a) Brick Masonry
b) Slate Roof
c) Stone Masonry
d) Ceramic Tiles

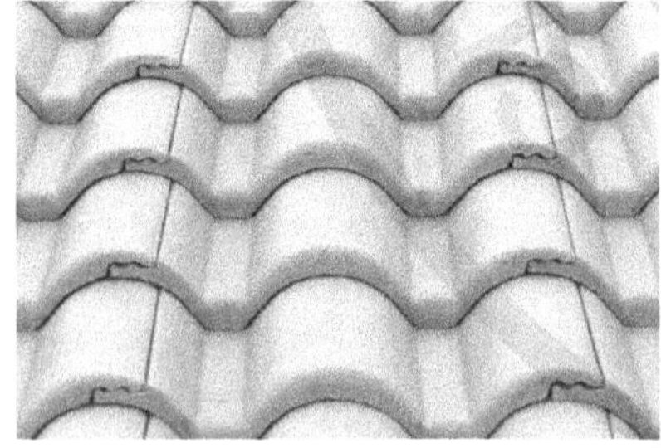

37. Identify the material:
a) Mangalore Tiles
b) Asbestos Roofing
c) Fibreglass roofing
d) Corrugated Sheet

38. A square pyramid has the following:-
    a) 5 triangular surfaces   b) 3 triangular surfaces
    c) 5 triangular surfaces and 5 vertex   d) 4 triangular surfaces and 5 vertex

39. A hexagonal pyramid has:-
    a) 11 surfaces   b) 6 surfaces   c) 8 surfaces   d) 7 surfaces

40. A pentagonal pyramid has:-
    a) 7 surfaces   b) 4 surfaces
    c) 6 surfaces   d) 5 surfaces

NATA Practice Paper - 11

Directions: In each given problem, Out of the five figures (A), (B), (C), (D) and (E), four are similar in a certain way. However, one figure is not like the other four. Choose the figure which is different from the rest.

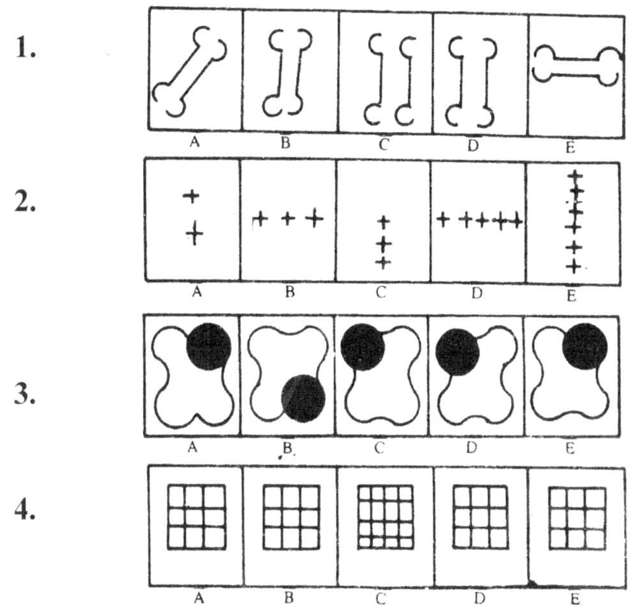

DIRECTIONS: The 3-D Problem figure shows an object. Identify the correct front view amongst the answer figures, looking in the direction of the arrow.

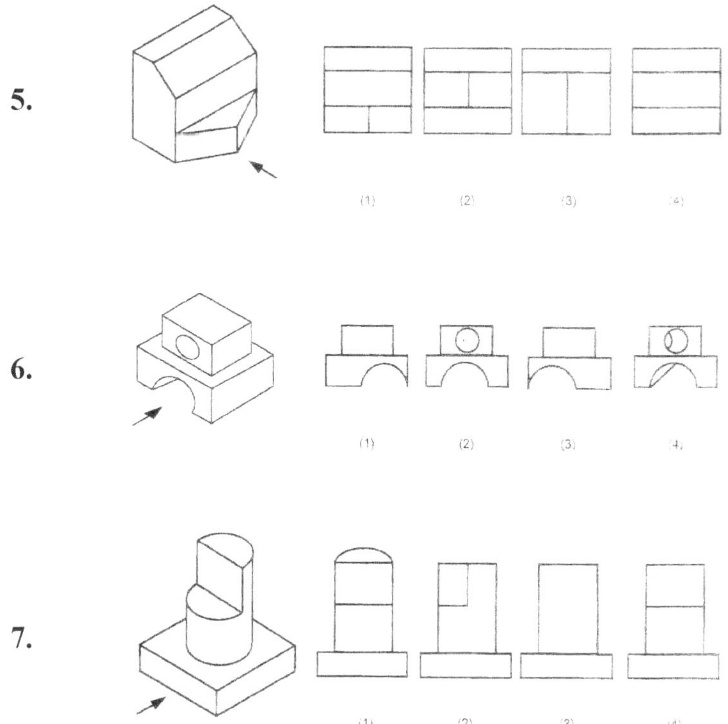

NATA Practice Paper - 11

8.  (1) 1 (2) 3 (3) 2 (4) 0

9. 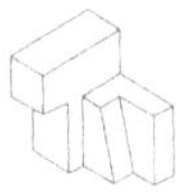 (1) 2 (2) 4 (3) 1 (4) 4

10. 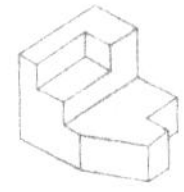 (1) 1 (2) 3 (3) 2 (4) 0

11. 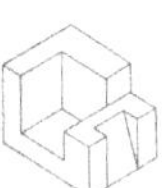 (1) 1 (2) 3 (3) 0 (4) 4

DIRECTIONS: The question figures form a series. You have to find which one of the answer figure would be the next one in the given series.

12.
Question Figures :

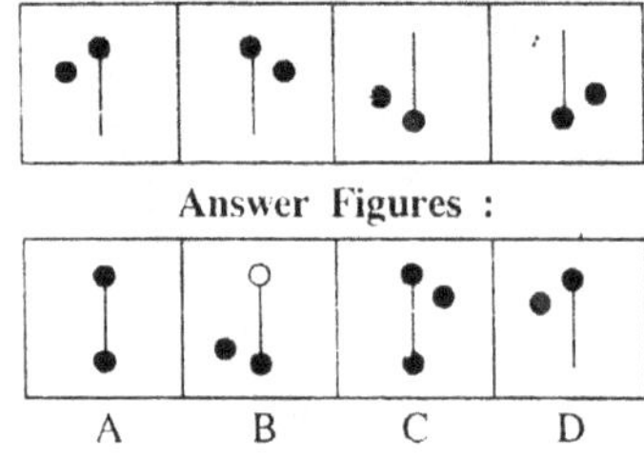

Answer Figures :

A   B   C   D

13.
Question Figures :

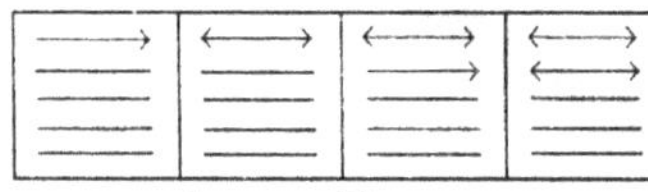

Answer Figures :

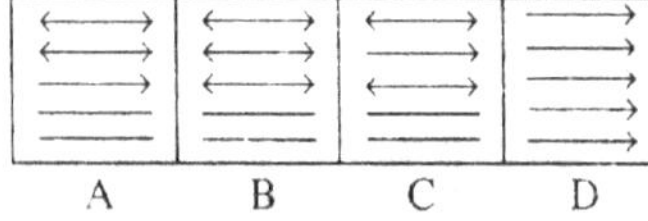

A   B   C   D

14.
Question Figures :

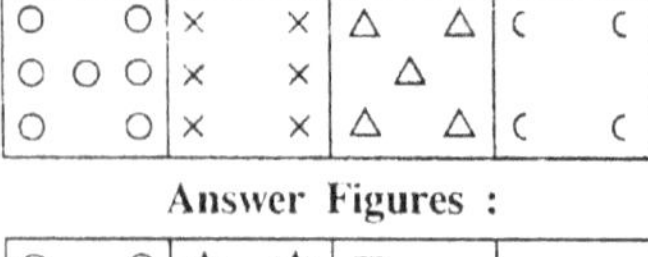

Answer Figures :

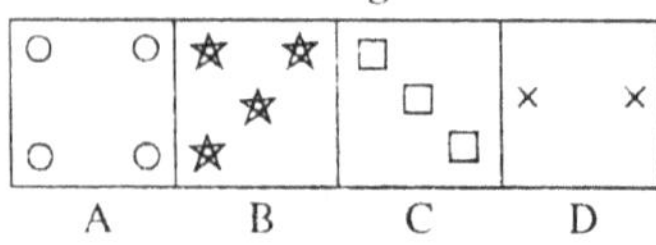

A   B   C   D

NATA Practice Paper - 11

> **Directions: Identify the correct top view of the given 3D figure.**

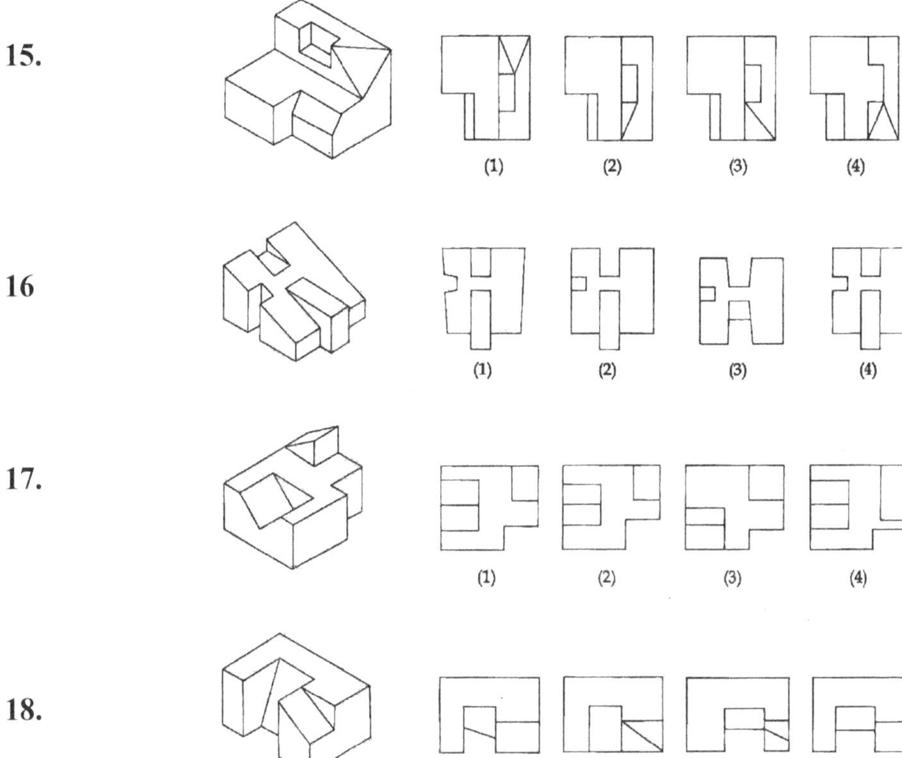

15.

16

17.

18.

Directions : Choose the most appropriate option to fill in the blank.

19. I cannot .... to know much about it.
    A. imagine   B. conceive   C. pretend   D. contemplate

20. Satish was .... with a natural talent for music.
    A. given   B. found   C. endowed   D. entrusted

21. If you drink too much, it will .... your judgement.
    A. impede   B. impair   C. impose   D. impel

22. I did .... I could which wasn't much.
    A. that   B. what   C. how much   D. which

23. Put your signature .... blue ink.
    A. in   B. through   C. by   D. with

24. Varun ranks sixteenth from the top and forty-ninth from the bottom in a class. How many students are there in the class?

    a) 64   b) 65   c) 66   d) Cannot be determined

25. There are five different houses, A to E, in a row. A is to the right of B and E is to the left of C and right of A. B is to the right of D. Which of the houses is in the middle?

    a) A   b) B   c) D   d) E

26. Ramesh is twice as old as Anil. Three years ago, he was three times as old as Anil. How old is Ramesh?

    a) 6 years   b) 7 years   c) 8 years   d) None of these

27. Ranvir was counting down from 32. Shashi was counting upwards starting from 1 and he was calling out only the odd numbers. What common number will they call out the same time if they are calling out at the same speed?

    a) 19   b) 21   c) 22   d) None of these

28. Going 50m to the South of her house, Kapil turns left and goes another 20m. Then, turning to the North, he goes 30m and then starts walking to his house. In which direction is he walking now?

    a) North-west   b) North   c) South-east   d) East

DIRECTIONS : One set is called problem figures and the other is answer figures. Locate the figure from the answer figures which will continue the same series as given in the Problem figure.

Problem Figures   Answer Figures

29.

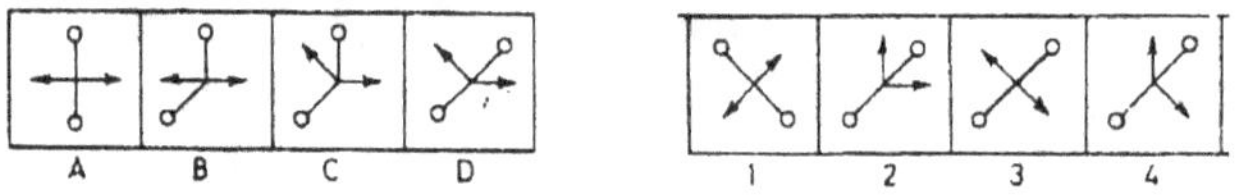

30.

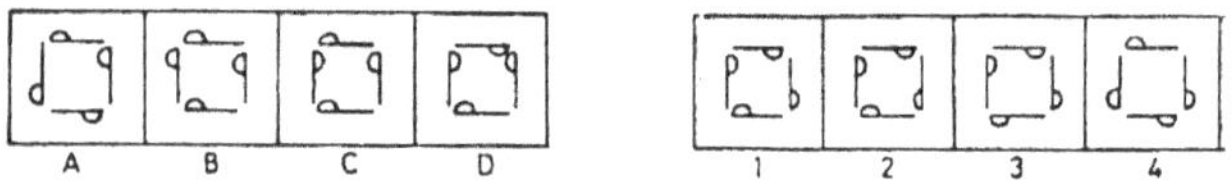

31.

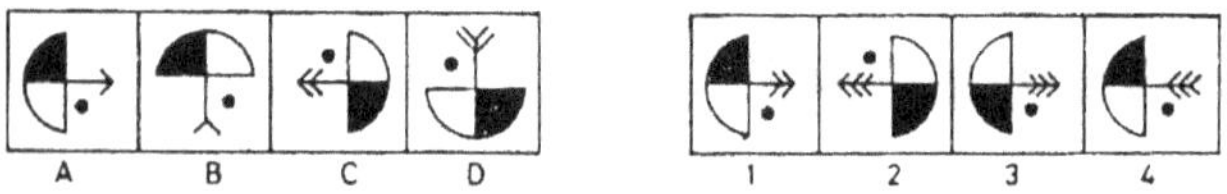

32.

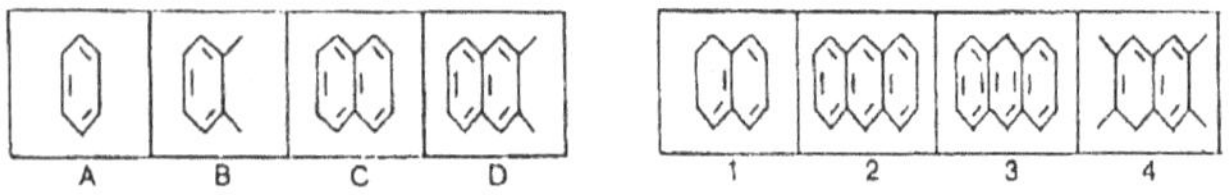

33.

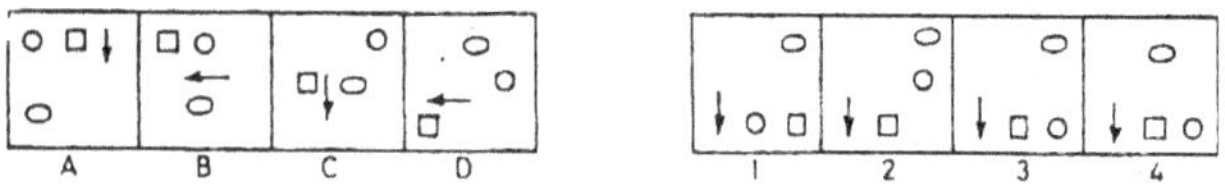

34.

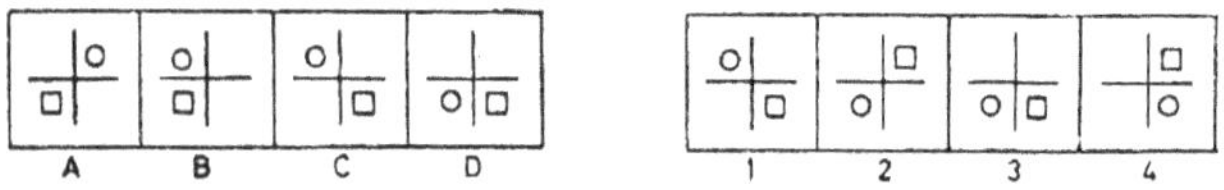

NATA Practice Paper - 11

35. Identify this building:

1) Lotus Temple
2) Birla Mandir, Delhi
3) Lingaraja Temple
4) Sun Temple, Konark

36. Identify this building:

1) Pyramids
2) Sphinx
3) Stonehenge, UK
4) Char Minar

37. Identify:
a) Marble Floor
b) Slate Roof
c) Granite Floor
d) Ceramic Tiles

38. Identify the material:
a) Particle Board
b) Plywood
c) Blockboard
d) Mineral Fibre Board

39. A cube has the following:-
a) 5 surfaces   b) 6 surfaces   c) 6 surfaces and 8 vertex   d) both (b) & (c)

40. A octagonal pyramid has:-
a) 9 surfaces   b) 6 surfaces   c) 8 surfaces   d) 7 surfaces

NATA Practice Paper - 12

Directions: In each given problem, Out of the five figures (a), (b), (c), (d) and (e), four are similar in a certain way. However, one figure is not like the other four. Choose the figure which is different from the rest.

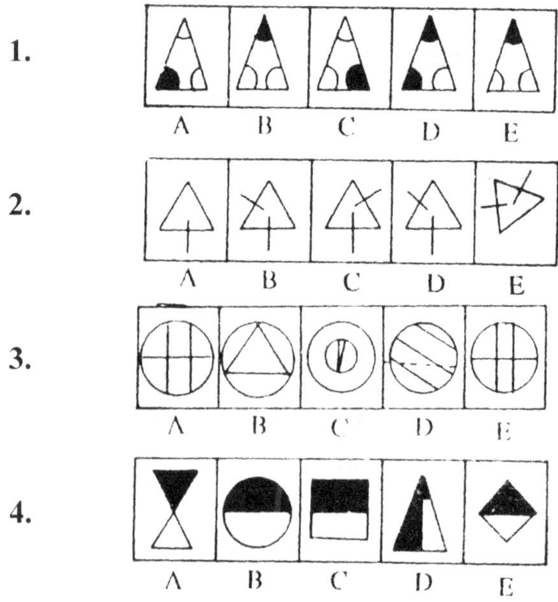

1. A   B   C   D   E

2. A   B   C   D   E

3. A   B   C   D   E

4. A   B   C   D   E

DIRECTIONS: The 3-D Problem figure shows an object. Identify the correct front view amongst the answer figures, looking in the direction of the arrow.

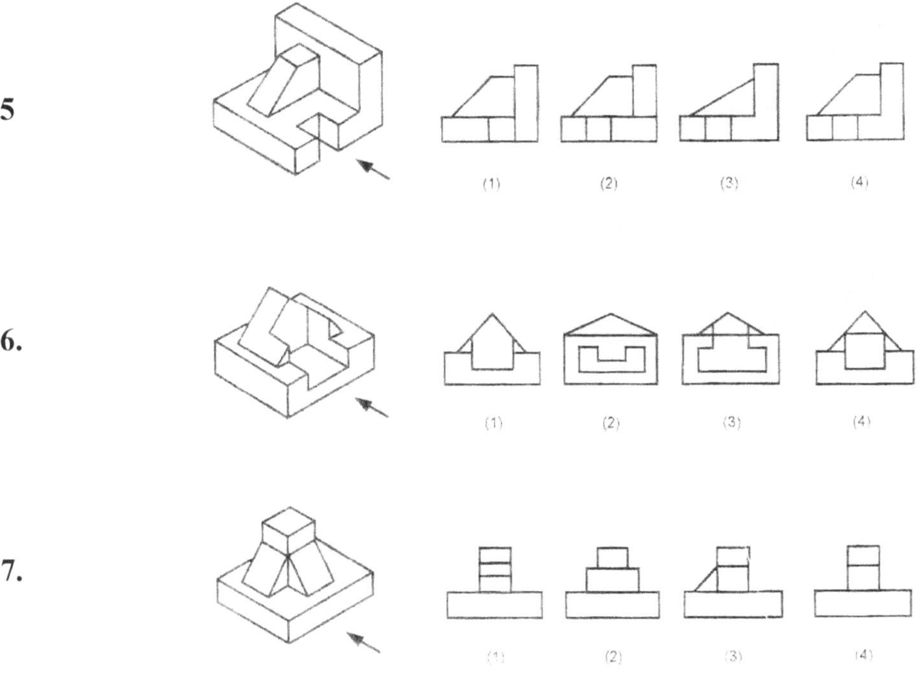

5

6.

7.

NATA Practice Paper - 12

Directions: Find the total number of inclined surfaces of the object given below in the problem figure.

---

8. 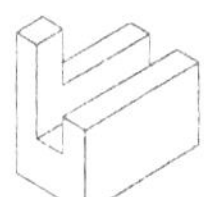   (1) 1   (2) 3   (3) 2   (4) 0

9. 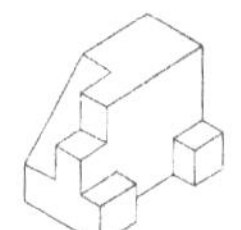   (1) 2   (2) 4   (3) 0   (4) 4

10. 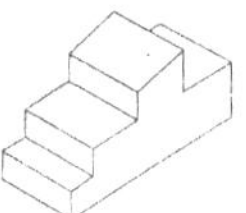   (1) 1   (2) 3   (3) 2   (4) 0

11. 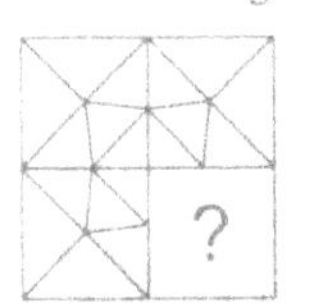   (1) 1   (2) 3   (3) 0   (4) 4

DIRECTIONS: The question figures form a series. You have to find which one of the answer figure would be the next one in the given series.

12. 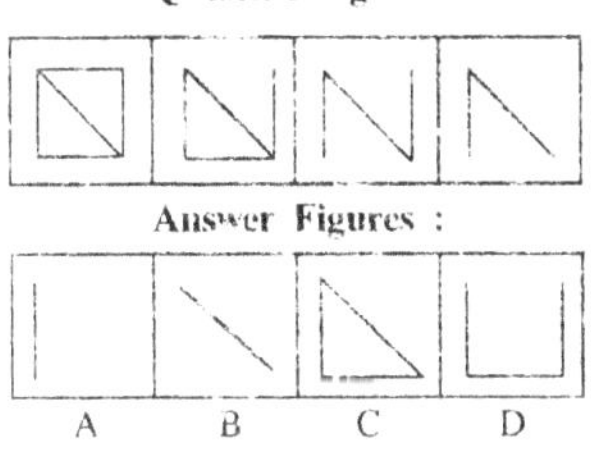

DIRECTIONS: Choose the correct options from the answer figures that will complete the pattern given in the Question Figure

13. Problem Figures

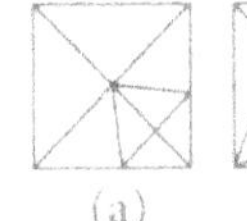

Answer Figures

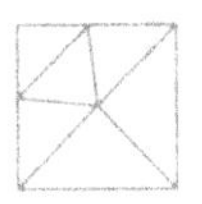

14. Problem Figure

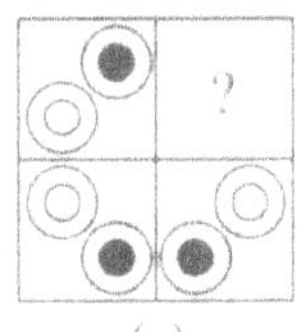

(x)

Answer Figure

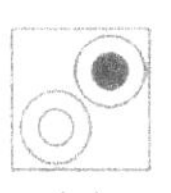 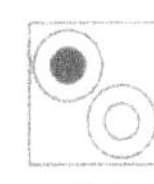 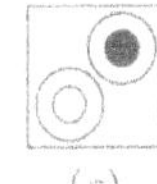 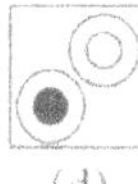

(a)   (b)   (c)   (d)

NATA Practice Paper - 12

15. 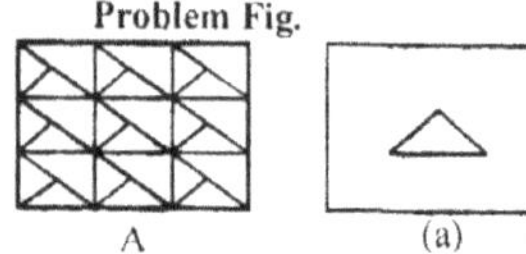

16. 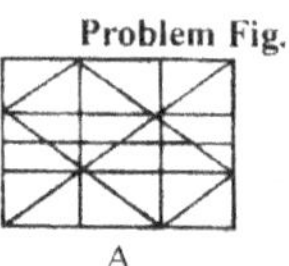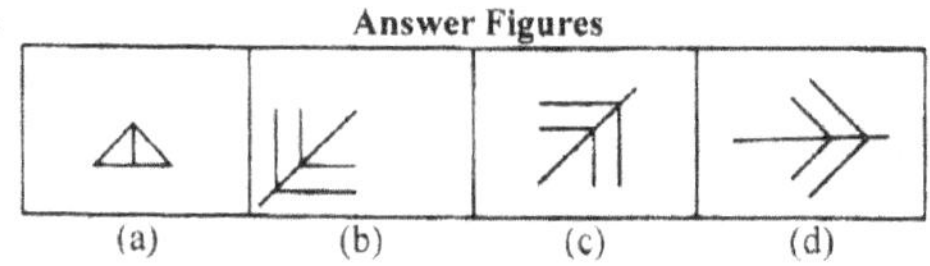

17. 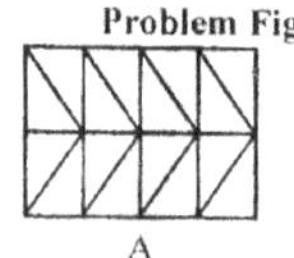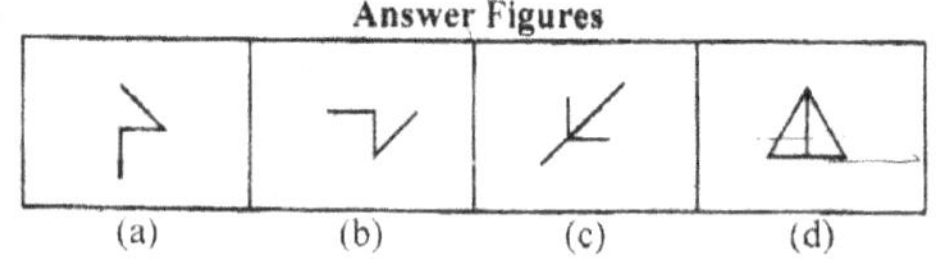

18. 'A' is multiple of 3 and less than 10. It is an odd number and more than 5 the number is:
   1. 6
   2. 9
   3. none
   4. incomplete data

19. Ravi is twice as old as Vinay. Ravi is now 12 years older than Vinay. What are the ages of Ravi and Vinay now?

   a) 24, 12   b) 12,6   c) 24,48   d) 12,24

20. $(x+1)(x-1)$ is equal to 3 find the value of 'x'
   a) -2,+2   b) +4,-4   c) 4   d) 2

21. Find the value of $(3a+3b)\times(3a+3b)$
   a) $9a^2+9b^2+18ab$ b) $6a^2+6b^2$ c) $9a^2-9b^2+18ab$ d) $6a^2+6b^2+12ab$

22. 'a' is less than zero, a+b is also < 0 then
   A) b is less than zero   B) b < a   C) a < b   D) none

23. A writes 50 pages in 10 hours. A and B both can write 70 pages in 10 hours together. In how many hours B can write 26 pages?
   a) 13   b) 15   c) 26   d) 14

NATA Practice Paper - 12

DIRECTIONS: Choose the word which is most nearly the SAME in meaning as the word printed

24. ADMONISH
   a) punish   b) curse   c) dismiss   d) reprimand

25. WRETCHED
   a) poor   b) foolish   c) insane   d) strained

26. ARCHAIC
   a) earlier   b) outdated   c) complex   d) ancient

27. NIMBLE
   a) unrhythmic   b) lively   c) quickening d) clear

How many squares are there in the following diagram ?

28.

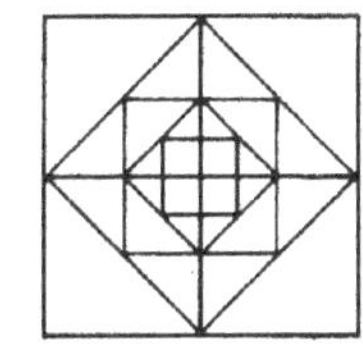

(a) 16   (b) 17   (c) 14   (d) 18

Count the rectangles in the below given figure ?

29.

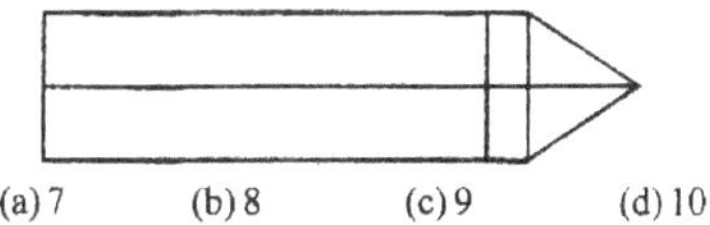

(a) 7   (b) 8   (c) 9   (d) 10

How many triangles does the following diagram have ?

30.

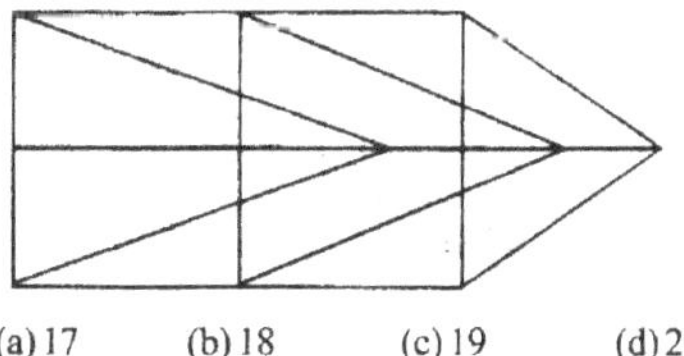

(a) 17   (b) 18   (c) 19   (d) 20

Count the number of triangles and squares in the following figure.

31.

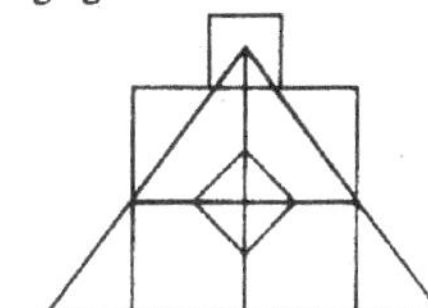

(a)   15 triangles 6 squares
(b)   18 triangles 7 squares
(c)   12 triangles 8 squares
(d)   16 triangles 8 squares

NATA Practice Paper - 12

32. Identify this building:

1) Ellora Temple
2) Birla Mandir, Delhi
3) Lingaraja Temple, Bhubhaneshwar
4) Sun Temple, Konark

33. Identify this building:

1) Pyramids
2) Stupa of Sanchi
3) Stonehenge, UK
4) Gol Gumbaz, Bijapur

34. A square pyramid has:-
a) 4 surfaces
b) 6 surfaces
c) 5 surfaces
d) 7 surfaces

35. Horizontal sun shades are required to protect windows on which facade of a building?
    1) East   2) West   3) North   4) South

36. Palace of winds (Hawa Mahal) is located in :
    1) Rajasthan   2) Jammu and Kashmir   3) Andhra Pradesh   4) Madhya Pradesh

37. Which one is not a sound absorbing material?
    1) Thermocol   2) Glass wool   3) Ground glass   4) Jute bags

38. Which one of the following is a horizontal member in a building that carries load?
    1) Column   2) Vault   3) Beam   4) Arch

39. Qutab Minar is largely cladded with
    1) Red sand stone   2) Marble   3) Brick   4) Granite

40. The summer sun in northern hemisphere rises from
    1) South east   2) North east   3) East   4) North

ANSWERS

Paper-1

1	2	3	4	5	6	7	8	9	10
(a)	(c)	(b)	(4)	(1)	(1)	(1)	(1)	(4)	(4)
11	12	13	14	15	16	17	18	19	20
(3)	C	B	B	D	(3)	(1)	(1)	(1)	(b)
21	22	23	24	25	26	27	28	29	30
(d)	(b)	(c)	(a)	(b)	(d)	(c)	(c)	(a)	(b)
31	32	33	34	35	36	37	38	39	40
(c)	(a)	(b)	(c)	(b)	(1)	(2)	(a)	(d)	(d)

Paper-2

1	2	3	4	5	6	7	8	9	10
(b)	(d)	(e)	(4)	(3)	(2)	(2)	(1)	(1)	(2)
11	12	13	14	15	16	17	18	19	20
(1)	D	B	B	A	(2)	(1)	(3)	(4)	(d)
21	22	23	24	25	26	27	28	29	30
(c)	(a)	(a)	(d)	(c)	(c)	(b)	(a)	(b)	(a)
31	32	33	34	35	36	37	38	39	40
(c)	(a)	(b)	(a)	(a)	(3)	(1)	(d)	(d)	(d)

Paper-3

1	2	3	4	5	6	7	8	9	10
(d)	(d)	(a)	(3)	(1)	(3)	(1)	(1)	(3)	(1)
11	12	13	14	15	16	17	18	19	20
(2)	C	D	C	D	(3)	(4)	(2)	(3)	(d)
21	22	23	24	25	26	27	28	29	30
(b)	(b)	(b)	(c)	(b)	(b)	(b)	(b)	(d)	(b)
31	32	33	34	35	36	37	38	39	40
(a)	(d)	(b)	(a)	(d)	(2)	(2)	(d)	(d)	(d)

Paper-4

1	2	3	4	5	6	7	8	9	10
(c)	(b)	(d)	(4)	(4)	(3)	(2)	(4)	(2)	(2)
11	12	13	14	15	16	17	18	19	20
(4)	(2)	(2)	(4)	(4)	(b)	(c)	(c)	(b)	(b)
21	22	23	24	25	26	27	28	29	30
(b)	(a)	(d)	(b)	(b)	(c)	(a)	(b)	(a)	(b)
31	32	33	34	35	36	37	38	39	40
(a)	(d)	(b)	(b)	(b)	(3)	(2)	(d)	(d)	(b)

Paper-5

1	2	3	4	5	6	7	8	9	10
(a)	(b)	(c)	(1)	(1)	(3)	(1)	(1)	(2)	(2)
11	12	13	14	15	16	17	18	19	20
(2)	(d)	(a)	(c)	(b)	(b)	(a)	(b)	(c)	(b)
21	22	23	24	25	26	27	28	29	30
(c)	(d)	(b)	(c)	(b)	(c)	B	A	C	A
31	32	33	34	35	36	37	38	39	40
(b)	(a)	(c)	(c)	(c)	(3)	(2)	(d)	(b)	(c)

Paper-6

1	2	3	4	5	6	7	8	9	10
(b)	(c)	(e)	(2)	(4)	(2)	(2)	(1)	(3)	(1)
11	12	13	14	15	16	17	18	19	20
(2)	(b)	(a)	(b)	(c)	(d)	(a)	(d)	(c)	(a)
21	22	23	24	25	26	27	28	29	30
(a)	(a)	(c)	(b)	(b)	(a)	B	C	A	D
31	32	33	34	35	36	37	38	39	40
(b)	(a)	(c)	(d)	(d)	(3)	(4)	(2)	(1)	(d)

Paper-7

1	2	3	4	5	6	7	8	9	10
(b)	(a)	(a)	(a)	(c)	(a)	(c)	(c)	(1)	(1)
11	12	13	14	15	16	17	18	19	20
(2)	(b)	(d)	(c)	(a)	(b)	(b)	(b)	(a)	(c)
21	22	23	24	25	26	27	28	29	30
(c)	(b)	(c)	(d)	(d)	(d)	(c)	(c)	(1)	(3)
31	32	33	34	35	36	37	38	39	40
(d)	(b)	C	E	C	B	C	D	C	C

Paper-8

1	2	3	4	5	6	7	8	9	10
(a)	(b)	(d)	(b)	(b)	(c)	(b)	(d)	(3)	(2)
11	12	13	14	15	16	17	18	19	20
(1)	(a)	(c)	(c)	(d)	(a)	(4)	(4)	(3)	(2)
21	22	23	24	25	26	27	28	29	30
(b)	(d)	(b)	(d)	(2)	(2)	(2)	(3)	(2)	(1)
31	32	33	34	35	36	37	38	39	40
(c)	(a)	E	E	D	D	E	A	B	A

Paper-9

1	2	3	4	5	6	7	8	9	10
(b)	(c)	(d)	(a)	(c)	(a)	(d)	(b)	(3)	(2)
11	12	13	14	15	16	17	18	19	20
(2)	(b)	(a)	(a)	(b)	(b)	(a)	(c)	(d)	(a)
21	22	23	24	25	26	27	28	29	30
(d)	(c)	(c)	(a)	(1)	(3)	(1)	(4)	(c)	(b)
31	32	33	34	35	36	37	38	39	40
(b)	(b)	(d)	(d)	(d)	(b)	(c)	(3)	(1)	(3)

Paper 10

1	2	3	4	5	6	7	8	9	10
E	E	D	(2)	(2)	(4)	(3)	(2)	(1)	(1)
11	12	13	14	15	16	17	18	19	20
(2)	B	D	A	(3)	(4)	(2)	(2)	(B)	(D)
21	22	23	24	25	26	27	28	29	30
B	C	D	(c)	(c)	(a)	(a)	(d)	(c)	(a)
31	32	33	34	35	36	37	38	39	40
(d)	(b)	(c)	(2)	(3)	(c)	(a)	(d)	(d)	(C)

Paper-11

1	2	3	4	5	6	7	8	9	10
C	C	C	C	(1)	(2)	(4)	(4)	(3)	(4)
11	12	13	14	15	16	17	18	19	20
(1)	D	A	C	(3)	(4)	(1)	(4)	C	C
21	22	23	24	25	26	27	28	29	30
B	C	A	(a)	(a)	(d)	(d)	(a)	(3)	(1)
31	32	33	34	35	36	37	38	39	40
(3)	(2)	(3)	(2)	(4)	(3)	(d)	(c)	(d)	(a)

Paper-12

1	2	3	4	5	6	7	8	9	10
D	A	C	D	(4)	(1)	(3)	(1)	(3)	(1)
11	12	13	14	15	16	17	18	19	20
(1)	B	(c)	(b)	(a)	(a)	(a)	(2)	(a)	(a)
21	22	23	24	25	26	27	28	29	30
(a)	D	(a)	(d)	(a)	(d)	(b)	(b)	(c)	(c)
31	32	33	34	35	36	37	38	39	40
(b)	(3)	(2)	(c)	(4)	(1)	(3)	(3)	(1)	(2)

IMPORTANT NATA INFORMATION

English Vocabulary

Serial No.	Word	Synonym/Meaning
1	Taciturn	Silent, quiet
2	Urbane	Suave
3	Disparate	Unlike
4	Nadir	Lowest point
5	Belligerent	Aggressive
6	Recalcitrant	Unruly
7	Jingoistic	Nationalistic
8	Incandescent	Bright
9	Elan	Style
10	Oar	Broad wooden blade to propel boats
11	Cantankerous	Ill-natured
12	Opprobrium	Disgrace
13	Ostentatious	Showy, (Antonym - Modest)
14	Obsolete	Out-dated, old fashioned
15	Airy	Open, roomy
16	Ponder	Consider
17	Resplendent	Shining brilliantly
18	Stentorian	Extremely loud
19	Suave	Polished
20	Fulmination	Flash, explosion with noise and violence
21	Satiate	Satisfy
22	Erudite	Learned
23	Wont	Custom
24	Cogent	Well convincing
25	Illumination	Brightness
26	Gluttony	Greediness
27	Sojourn	Holiday Break
28	Pretence	To pretend
29	Admonitory	Caution
30	Panoramic	Picturesque
31	Espousal	Adoption
32	Terrific	Excellent
33	Dream	Series of images, events & feelings that happen in your mind when you are asleep
34	Hidden	Concealed
35	Guesstimate	An attempt to calculate something that is based more on guessing than information
36	Reconciliation	Reunion, Recheck
37	Efficacy	Effectiveness
38	Retraction	The art of pulling back
39	Delicate	Fragile
40	Arms	Weapons especially used by the army
41	Arsenal	A collection of weapons such as guns and explosives
42	Credentials	Qualifications
43	Vivacious	Lively
44	Durable	Sturdy, long lasting
45	Pleasant	Something pleasing

IMPORTANT NATA INFORMATION
English Vocabulary

46	Aspirant	Hopeful
47	Petrified	Scared
48	Encapsulation	To brief up, to sum up
49	Irrational	Illogical
50	Incandescence	Light emission
51	Esperanto	A language
52	Notorious	Well known for being bad
53	Disquisition	A long complicated speech or report
54	Glib	Clever
55	Serendipity	Luck
56	Tenacious	Firm
57	Veteran	Experienced
58	Unanimous	Supported by all
59	Pungent	Strong smell
60	Congenital	Inborn
61	Congenial	Pleasant, friendly
62	Desultory	Unplanned
63	Jurisprudence	Scientific study of law
64	Querulous	Argumentative, Habitually complaining
65	Athwart	Not agreeing with, At an oblique angle
66	Cogency	Force
67	Constellation	Group
68	Sculptor	A person who makes statue
69	Greet	Welcome
70	Propeller	A type of fan that transmits power by converting rational motion into thrust
71	Verse	Poetry (Antonym - Prose)
72	Chronic	Difficult to cure
73	Virtue	Good worth (Antonym- Vice)
74	Capricious	Impulsive
75	Circuitous	Indirect (Antonym-Direct)
76	Admonish	Caution
77	Reticence	Reserve
78	Assertive	Forceful
79	Desirous	Eager
80	Thoroughly	In detail
81	Resistance	Inclination to resist
82	Resilient	able to revert to normal size
83	Suspect	Suspicious
84	Erratic	Lacking a definite plan (Antonym-Organized)
85	Predilection	Fondness (Antonym-dislike)
86	Equanimity	Calmness
87	Prodigal	Wasteful
88	Renounce	Give up something
89	Elucidate	To make clear (Antonym-confuse)
90	In toto	All together (Antonym-partially)

FAMOUS BUILDINGS (INDIA)

- Parliament House/Sansad Bhawan, Delhi
- Rashtrapati Bhawan, Delhi
- India Gate, Delhi
- Humayun's Tomb, Delhi
- Safdarjung Tomb, Delhi
- Qutub Minar, Delhi
- National Gallery of Modern Art, Delhi
- DLF Building- Connaught place & Gurgaon
- Gopaldas Bhawan, CP, Delhi
- NDMC Building, Delhi
- Statesman House, CP, Delhi
- British Council Library, Delhi
- MCD Civic Centre, Delhi
- India Habitat Centre, Delhi
- Jama Masjid, Delhi
- Red Fort, Delhi
- Iron Pillar, Qutub Minar Complex
- Firoz Shah Kotla,Delhi
- Purana Qila- Delhi, Jaipur
- Akshardham Temple-Delhi, Ahmedabad,
- Jantar Mantar- Delhi, Jaipur
- Fatehpur Sikri, Agra
- IIT-Delhi, Mumbai
- IIM Ahmedabad
- Houseboat-Srinagar & Kerela
- Vidhan Sabha Bhawan-Bhopal and Bangalore
- Port Trust, Kolkata
- Dakhineshwar temple, Kolkata
- Belur Math, Kolkata
- Writers Building, Kolkata
- The Victoria Memorial, Kolkata
- Buland Darwaza, Fatehpur Sikri
- Panchmahal, Fatehpur sikri
- Hawa Mahal, Jaipur
- Amer fort, Jaipur
- Victory tower, Chittorgarh
- Pushkar Ghat, Pushkar
- Udaipur Palace, Rajasthan
- Umaid Bhawan Palace, Jodhpur
- Sun Temple at Konark, Orissa
- Sun Temple at Modhera, Gujarat,
- Jain Temples at Rajgir, Bihar
- Dilwara Jain Temples, Mount Abu, Rajasthan
- Jain temples in Gujarat. Meenakshi Temple, Madurai
- Gopurams-South Indian temples
- Stone rathas- Bhubaneshwar
- Rock temples/stone rathas/Temple rathas at Mahabalipuram, Tamilnadu
- Vithal Rath(stone ratha temple), Hampi, Karnataka
- Kailasanatha temple,Ellora (cave 16)
- Khajurao temples, Madhya Pradesh
- Birla temples
- Vivekananda Rock Temple, Kanyakumari
- Jagannath Temple, Puri
- Brihadeshwara Temples, Thanjavur
- Rajabari tower, Mumbai
- The Gateway of India, Mumbai
- Victoria Terminus, Mumbai
- Ajanta Ellora Caves, Mumbai
- Shanivarwada, Pune
- Bibi Ka Makbara-Aurangabad
- Basilica of Bom Jesus, Goa
- Gateway of Sanchi Stupa(Madhya Pradesh)
- Bodhgaya, Bihar
- Palace at Padmanabhapuram, Tamilnadu
- Charminar, Hyderabad
- High Court, Chandigarh
- The Secretariat, Chandigarh
- Gandhi Bhawan, Chandigarh
- Legislative Assembly, Chandigarh

FAMOUS BUILDINGS (WORLD)

- Stonehenge, Great Britain, UK
- Bigben, London
- Buddhist Stupa at Borbodur, Indonesia
- Brasilia, Brazil
- Nepal pagoda
- Palace Entrance, Nepal
- Swayambhunath Stupa, Kathmandu, Nepal
- Petronas Twin Towers, Malaysia
- White House, Washington
- Hanging Gardens of Babylon
- Pyramids of Giza at Egypt
- Pyramids at Mexico
- Berlin Buildings, Germany
- Beijing Stadium, China
- Tinanmen Square, China
- Burj-Al-Arab, Dubai
- Burj Khalifa, Dubai
- Hagia Sophia, Constantinople/Istanbul
- Colosseum Rome
- Pantheon, Rome
- Machu Picchu
- Parthenon, Greece
- Red Square, Moscow
- Louvre Museum, Paris
- Chapel Notredame, Paris
- Chapel Ronchamp, France
- UN Headquarters, Newyork
- Diet (Japanese parliament)
- Sydney opera house, Sydney, Australia

PROMINENT FOREIGN ARCHITECTS

S. No.	ARCHITECT	MAJOR WORKS
1.	Cesar Pelli	• World Financial Center, New York City • Petronas Towers, Kuala Lumpur, Malaysia (1998)
2.	Sir Christopher Wren	• Saint Paul's Cathedral, London • Monument to the Great Fire of London (with Robert Hooke)
3.	Daniel Libeskind	Freedom Tower at Ground Zero, New York
4.	Eugene	Statue of Liberty
5.	F.W. Stevens	Victoria Terminus
6.	Frank Lloyd Wright	• Falling Waters, USA • Guggenheim Museum, USA .
7.	Gustav Eiffel	Eiffel Tower
8.	I.M. PIE	• Louvre Pyramid • Bank of China Tower, Hong Kong He won the prestigious Pritzker Prize (Highest Prize in Architecture)
9.	Jorn Utzon	Sydney Opera House
10.	James Hoban	White House, Washington DC
11.	Kevin Eamonn Roche	• IBM Pavilion World's Fair, New York • Union Carbide Corporation • World Head Quarters
12.	Mies Van Der Rohe	Barcelona Pavilion Seagram Building, New York (with Philip Johnson)
13.	Moshe Safdie	Habitat Housing, Montreal
14.	Minora Yamasaki	World Trade Centre, New York
15.	Norman Foster	• Hong Kong and Shanghai Bank, Hong Kong • Hearst Tower, New York • Wembley Stadium, London • New German Parliament, Berlin, Germany • Terminal T3, Beijing, China Sir Norman Foster won Pritzker Architecture Prize
16.	Philip Johnson	• Glass House, New Canaan, CT • Seagram Building (with Mies van der Rohe), New York
17.	Richard Rogers	• Charles de Gaulle Airport, Paris • Lloyds Building, London
18.	Skidmore, Owings and Merrill	• Sears Tower, Chicago • Burj Khalifa, Dubai (Tallest Building) • John Hancock Tower, Chicago
19.	Walter Gropius	• The Bauhaus Building, Dessau, Germany • University of Baghdad, Iraq

PROMINENT INDIAN ARCHITECTS

S.No.	ARCHITECT	MAJOR WORKS
1.	Achyut P. Kanvinde (1916)	• IIT, Kanpur • National Science Centre, Delhi • National Institute of Immunology (NII), Pune • ISKON Temple, Delhi
2.	B.V. Doshi (1927)	• Centre of Environmental Planning and Technology, Ahmedabad • Husain-Doshi Gufa Art Gallery, Ahmedabad • Indian Institute of Management, Bangalore • National Institute of Fashion Technology, New Delhi • Sangath, Ahmedabad • Bhabha Atomic Research Centre, Kota, Rajasthan
3.	Charles Correa (1930)	• Tata Centre for Performing Arts, Mumbai • Bharat Bhawan, Arts Complex, Bhopal • Vidhan Bhawan/Sabha, Bhopal • LIC Building, Connaught Place • British Council Library, Connaught Place • Tara Apartment Alaknanda, New Delhi • Crafts Museum, Delhi • Jawahar Kala Kendra, Jaipur • Indira Gandhi International Airport, Delhi • Memorial of Mahatma Gandhi, Sabarmati Ashram, Ahmedabad
4.	CP Kukreja (1938)	• Jawaharlal Nehru University (JNU), Delhi • Amba Deep Tower/Connaught Place, New Delhi • Signature Tower Gurgaon • Ansal Bhawan, New Delhi • Hudco Lodhi Road, New Delhi • Sir Ganga Ram Hospital • Apollo Hospital, New Delhi • IIM, Lucknow • Delhi-Gymkhana Club, New Delhi
5,	Edwin Lutyens (British)	Planning of New Delhi (also known as Lutyens' Delhi) Main Features- (landscaped round-abouts; VIP Bunglows; Rashtrapati Bhawan; Colonial style Architecture)
6.	Fariburz Saabha	Bahai Temple (Lotus Temple), New Delhi
7.	F.W. Benjamin	Parliament Annexe, New Delhi
8.	Herbert Baker (English Architect)	He designed Prominent buildings in New Delhi along with Lutyens North and South Block, New Delhi Parliament House Secretariat, New Delhi
9.	Habib Rehman (1916)	• Mandi house, New Delhi • R.K. Puram housing (Y shaped structure), New Delhi • Rabindra Bhavan, New Delhi

10.	Hafeez Contractor (1950)	• Hiranandani Gardens • Mumbai Airport redesign • Infosys - Bangalore, Mangalore, Mysore, Trivandrum • Rajneesh Osho Ashram, Pune • NICMAR, Pune • DLF Centre, Connaught Place, New Delhi (in association with Architect Ranjit Sabikhi) • Beverly Park Apartments, Gurgaon
11.	Joseph Allen Stein(1912- 2001) (American architect)	• India International Center, Lodhi Estate, New Delhi • India Habitat Centre, Lodhi Estate, New Delhi • Ford Foundation HQ, Lodhi Estate, New Delhi • UNICEF HQ Lodhi Estate, New Delhi • World Wide Fund for Nature, Lodhi Estate, New Delhi • Indian Institute of Management, Kozhikhode- campus, Kerala • Triveni Kala Arts Center, New Delhi • Kashmir Conference Center, Srinagar • Tata Iron and Steel Township, Orissa • Relandscaping of Lodhi Gardens, along with Garrett Eckbo
12.	K.T. Ravindran	Rajiv Gandhi Memorial, Sriperumbudur
13.	Kuldip Singh (1934)	NDMC Building, New Delhi
14.	Le Corbusier (Charles Edduard Jeanneret) Swiss Architect	• Villa La Roche/Villa Jeanneret, Paris • Villa Savoye / France United Habitation, France, History of the Prefabricated Home • Chapelle Notre Dame du Haut, Ronchamp, France • Mill Owners Association Building, Ahmedabad, India • Villa Sarabhai and Villa Schodan, Ahmedabad, India • Museum at Ahmedabad, India • Buildings in Chandigarh, India (1952-1959) -Palace of Justice / High Court, Chandigarh -Museum and Gallery of Art, Chandigarh -Secretariat Building, Chandigarh -Governor's Palace, Chandigarh -Palace of Assembly / Assembly Hall, Chandigarh -Government College of Arts (GCA), Chandigarh -Chandigarh College of Architecture(CCA), Chandigarh
15.	Laurie Baker (1917-2007)	• Centre for Development Studies ,Trivandrum • Literacy Village, Lucknow • Low Cost Housing, Auroville • International Leprosy Mission • Latur Earthquake Proof Housing Project
16.	Louis Kahn	• Indian Institute of Management, Ahmedabad, India (1962) • National Assembly Building (Jatiyo Sangshad Bhaban), Dhaka, Bangladesh (1962)

17.	M.M.Rana	Buddha Jayanti Gardens
18.	P.N. Mathur	Chanakya Theatre, New Delhi
19.	Pierre Jeanneret (Swiss architect)	• Housing, Chandigarh • Punjab Technical University, Chandigarh • Gandhi Bhawan, Chandigarh
		Pierre Jeanneret was a Swiss architect who collaborated with his more famous cousin Le Crbusier on the plan and architecture for the planned city of Chandigarh in India.
20.	Raj Rewal	• ASIAN Games Village/ New Delhi • Sheikh Sarai Housing; New Delhi • Hall of Nations, Pragati Maidan, New Delhi • Scope Complex Lodhi Road, New Delhi • Bhikaji Cama Place, New Delhi • Engineers. India House, New Delhi • State Trading Corporation; New Delhi • Indian National Science Academy, New Delhi, India • National Institute of Immunology, New Delhi, India • Parliament Library Building, New Delhi, India
21.	Ravindra Bhan	Shakti Sthala
22.	Sharat Das	Indira Gandhi Indoor Stadium, New Delhi
23.	Shiv Nath Prasad(1922)	Shri Ram Centre, New Delhi
24.	Satish Grover 1940	Talkatora Swimming Pool, New Delhi

PROMINENT HISTORICAL ARCHITECTS

l.	Shahjahan	Chashma Shahi, Kashmir
2.	Pallavas	Mahabalipuram Temples
3.	Ashoka	Sanchi Stupa
4.	Narsingh Dev	Sun Temple, Konark
5.	Jai Singh	Jantar Mantar, Delhi & Jantar Mantar, Jaipur
6.	Ustad Isa	Taj Mahal, Agra
7.	Mirak Mirza Ghiyas	Humayun Tomb, Delhi
8.	Khalil and Sadulla Khan	Jama Masjid, Delhi
9.	Fidai Khan	Pinjore Gardens, Chandigarh
10.	Rana Kumbha	Victory Tower, Chittorgarh

National Aptitude Test in Architecture

YX4MR3BW-APC15-20110048

AP: ABC College of Architecture

Name of Candidate	ABC	Candidate ID	2011593432
Appointment ID	APE0-20110048	**Date of generation**	Friday, June XX, 2014 11:01:02 AM
Total Marks	100	**Time Allowed**	2 Hours 10 Minutes

1	Imagine that your size has been reduced to 6 cms and you are on your study table standing on the keyboard of your computer. Draw a pencil sketch of what you would see from there along with the view of the computer etc.	50
2	In the given space design and draw a pattern using circles and triangles for a saree palloo (Anchal). Colour with any 3 colours of your choice.	25
3	Arrange four pieces of luggage in an intesrsting composition. The light is falling on the composition from left hand side. Draw the composition in pencil with shades and shadows.	25

This is an actual

sample page

of

NATA

Question Paper

× Q1

Please Do NOT write anything above this line. This Sheet is to be used to solve Question No 1 ONLY.

This is an actual

sample page

of

NATA

Answer Sheet

Q2

Please Do NOT write anything above this line. This sheet is to be used to solve Question No 2 ONLY.

Please Do NOT write anything above this line. This sheet is to be used to solve Question No 3 ONLY.

Q3

IMPORTANT NATA QUESTIONS

1. Draw a pencil sketch of the dilapidated ruins of an old fort in the given space.

2. One morning you went to visit a small temple on the hilltop with your friends. You still have to climb a little to reach the temple when you see the temple on the top with a few people standing/sitting near it looking down at your group. Make a pencil sketch as you will see it from below.

3. Your size has been reduced to 2 inch and you are on your study table, standing on the keyboard of your computer. Draw, what you would see from there along with the view of the computer etc.

4. You are standing in the door-way of a bus as it passes by a local street market on a Sunday. Draw, what you would see from your position in the bus.

5. You are standing in the passage way between the book shelves in your college library. Draw from your memory of what you see around in the library.

6. Design a logo for Water polo Game to be used by national water polo players' association, using Rectangles, Triangles and circles. Colour the logo using three colours of your choice.

7. Draw in the given space a mural to be used in an upmarket bicycle shop using various parts of bicycle. Colour the mural with THREE colours of your choice.

8. Make a two dimensional composition using profiles of pet animals of various sizes, shapes and colours. (You must overlap profiles) Colour your composition using not more than FOUR colours

9. Using line profiles of leaves and flowers create an interesting composition to serve as a signage for a showroom selling Herbal Products. Colour the same using not more than three colours of your choice. Note: Internal details in shapes are not expected. Use not more than 3 basic profiles. Repetition of single profile in different sizes and orientation is allowed.

10. Draw a composition using form of a Peepal leaf (Use the form maximum 4 times) and colour it using warm colour scheme

11. Draw an interesting three dimensional stable composition by using four tubes (like tubelights) four bricks, two wooden planks. Show the effect of light & shadow of the composition.

12. Draw a three dimensional, stable composition (still life) with 3 bricks & 2 stones of similar size in the space provided. Also show the effect of light & shadow on it

13. Arrange number of cubes of different sizes to create a sense of opening & steps. Show shades & shadows on the composition.

14. Draw a three dimensional, stable composition (still life) with 2 earthen pots & 3 glass bottles in the space provided. Also show the effect of light & shadow on it.

ORIGINAL
DRAWING QUESTIONS

1. Imagine that your size has been reduced to 6 cms and you are on your study table standing on the keyboard of your computer. Draw a pencil sketch of what you would see from there along with the view of the computer etc.
2. In the given space design and draw a pattern using circles and triangles for a saree palloo (Anchal). Colour with any 3 colours of your choice.
3. Arrange four pieces of luggage in an interesting composition. The light is falling on the composition from left hand side. Draw the composition in pencil with shades and shadows.
4. Imagine yourself to be a trapeze artist performing in a circus. Draw a pencil sketch of what you see around and below from the trapeze swing high up in the circus tent as you are performing the act in one of the shows.
5. In the given rectangle, using basic shapes like squares, triangles & circles create a design to depict motion. Render the same in a pleasing colour scheme of your choice.
6. In the given space draw a still life arrangement made of two square boxes, one rectangular box & one pyramid. It should make an interesting, abstract, stable three dimensional composition. Also show the effect of light & shade on the objects. Draw your drawing sufficiently large to fill the given blank space.
7. There is a festive procession in your town where people are dancing in the procession in front of floats mounted on trucks. You are riding on one of the trucks. There is huge crowd to greet and cheer on both sides of the road and in the buildings facing the road. Draw a pencil sketch of what you will see from your position on top of the truck.
8. Create a composition using form of a Peepal leaf (Use the form maximum 4 times) and colour it using warm colour scheme.
9. Make a 3D composition using 3 cubes & 2 rectangular boxes in the space provided. Also show the effect of light & shadow on it.
10. Imagine that your size has been reduced to 6 cms and you are standing on an open newspaper lying in your room. Draw a pencil sketch of what you would see of the newspaper along with some view of the room.
11. In the given space, make a two dimensional composition using profiles of cooking vessels of various sizes, shapes and colours. (You must overlap profiles) Colour your composition using not more than FOUR colours.
12. Arrange 7 cylinders of different heights & diameters on the ground in any pattern. Show shades & shadows on the composition.
13. A mother is giving a toy to her baby lying in his cradle. Draw pencil sketch of what the baby would see from his cradle.
14. Depict, draw and colour a fruit basket as a two dimensional composition with at least three to four variety of fruits, in multiple numbers.
15. 3 to 4 Books of sizes 20 cm x 10 cm and 300 to 500 pages each are kept vertically at a distance 8cmfrom each other on a book rack. The light source on the left at angle of 45 degrees. Draw out the 3D composition showing the shadow pattern.

Set-1

1. On rainy day you are standing at a window of your third floor house. Some children are playing football in the open place below. Draw a pencil sketch of the scene as you would see it from the window.

2. Make a visually appealing two dimensional composition using the basic geometric shape of a mango. You may use the shape any number of times and overlap it. Colour the composition in shades of two colours in a medium of your choice.

3. You are given three glass pyramids and two wooden cubes. Make an interesting three dimensional composition which can be placed in the corner of the sit-out of your house as an artifact. A creeper growing near the sit out has to be used to adorn the composition. Show the effect of shades and shadows on your sketch.

Set-2

1. You are a cricket umpire for an inter-club match. At this moment you are leg umpire and fielding team has broken the stumps and appealed for run out. The batsman has dived to the crease with bat extended to touch base. Draw a pencil sketch of what you see from your position.

2. Design and draw in the given space a square graphic composition to be used on Tee Shirts to be given to Members of a TREKKING EXPEDITION. Colour the design using maximum four colours.

3. Make a three dimensional composition using seven empty matchboxes. Draw the same and show shade and shadows on the composition.

Set-3

1. Imagine that you are standing in the door-way of a bus as it passes by a local street market on a Sunday. Draw a pencil sketch of what you would see from your position in the bus.

2. Using basic primary shapes design a bed sheet for children's bedroom. Draw and colour your design in the given space. Each shape should be used maximum two times and not more than four colours should be used.

3. You are provided with a small clock, a talcum powder tin, a can of a soft drink and a roll of paper. Make an interesting three dimensional composition. Draw the composition in pencil and show the effect of shades and shadows.

Set-4

1. An inter school quiz competition being held in the assembly hall in one of the new modern school in town. There are three teams each with two participants- one teacher and one student and the quiz master conducting the proceedings is standing in the middle with audience on rest of the three sides. Imagine you are one of the participants in the quiz along with your teacher. Draw a pencil sketch of what you will see from your position.

2. Design and draw in the given space a square graphic composition to be used on Tee Shirts for Save Trees Campaign. Colour the design using maximum four colours. The words (Save Trees) should NOT be used within the square graphic.

3. In the given space draw a still life arrangement made of two square boxes, one rectangular box & one pyramid. It should make a interesting, abstract, stable three dimensional composition. Also show the effect of light & shade on the objects. Draw your drawing sufficiently large to fill the given blank space.

Set-5

1. Imagine yourself to be an Umpire for a Badminton match, sitting on a high chair. A doubles match is going on with the badminton hall packed with spectators. Draw a sketch as to how you, as an umpire, would see the court, the players and the hall.

2. God has decided to create a company promoting the sky. Design a logo for this company. Colour it in any medium using not more than three colours of your choice.

3. A clay pot, A bamboo basket & a brass cooking pot are kept on the dining table. You have to keep appropriate materials in all the 3 objects & compose them. Draw a pencil sketch of the 3D composition on the table top with the shade and shadow effects showing the materials of the objects.

Set-6

1. Imagine you are moving around with a shopping trolley in a grocery store. Draw a memory sketch in pencil of what you see around you.

2. Design and draw in the given space a square graphic composition to be used on Tee Shirts for EDUCATION FOR EVERYONE Campaign. Colour the design using maximum four colours.The words (Education for everyone) should NOT be used within the square graphic as it will be printed separately on the Tee shirt.

3. A metal lunch box, a glass water bottle, two spoons and a cap are kept on a table as preparation for a trip. Arrange these objects to form a three dimensional composition and draw it showing shades and shadows.

Set-7

1. You are on the school playground to watch a n inter-school football match. You are seating on the ground just behind the goal post and net of the opposition team. Your school team is awarded a free kick against the opposition team just outside the D and your friend is on the spot to take the kick. Other team mates and players have taken their positions. Draw a pencil sketch of what you see from you seat.

2. Compose and draw in given space a flooring pattern for center of the entrance lobby of a resort hotel on beach using 4 circles of varying size, 2 squares and 1 triangle. You can use maximum three colours.

3. Two tooth brushes and a toothpaste are kept in a glass on a table. A shaving brush is lying near it. Draw a three dimensional sketch of these objects showing shades and shadows.

Set-8

1. Imagine yourself to be a 5 year old naughty boy/ girl always upto some mischief. Today for some mischief that you have played, your mother is furious and she puts you on top of a 2 meters (6.5 feet) tall cupboard in your living room. You are unable to get down from this cupboard on your own and have no choice but to sit quietly there. Draw a pencil sketch showing how you will see your living room sitting on top of cupboard.

2. Using straight lines and angular lines create a composition in the given space which will indicate 'confusion' and colour it with 3 primary colours.

3. Arrange number of cubes of different sizes to create a sense of opening (Door, Arch, etc.) & steps leading to the opening. Show shades & shadows on the objects. Draw a sufficiently large sketch in the given space.

Set-9

1. Imagine yourself to be a 12 years old boy/ girl visiting a Mela (fair) in your town. In the mela you are sitting in a merry-go-round with friends. You can see around you number of food stalls, games including giant wheel, toy train and other attractions in the Mela. Draw a pencil sketch of the scene as visible from your seat in the merry go round.

2. Using at least four shapes of the moon in various phases make an interesting composition by overlapping / repeating these shapes. Colour the composition in shades of any one colour.

3. Four cubes and 5 circular wooden logs in different sizes are available with you. Make use of these 3 Dimensional objects to create a stable interesting sculpture. Draw the same and show the effect of shade and shadow on the composition.

Set-10

1. Imagine you are sitting on a bench at a small town railway station. While a train stops at the platform with people trying to get out of the train. There is a soft drink stall to your right and the train indicator in your frame of view, Draw the scene in pencil as you would see with at least 5 people in your sketch doing different activities.

2. Create a composition using form of a Peepal leaf (Use the form maximum 4 times) and colour it using warm colour scheme.

3. Arrange 7 cylinders of different heights & diameters on the ground in any pattern. Show shades &shadows on the composition.

Set-11

1. Children from your neighbourhood are flying kites. You are reduced to small size to ride a Kite and you are riding one of the kites. Draw a pencil sketch of what you see below riding on the kite.

2. In the given space design and draw a pattern using circles and triangles for a saree palloo (Anchal). Colour with any 3 colours of your choice.

3. Make an interesting balanced composition of two chilies, two tomatoes and two slices of bread on a square plate. Draw the composition in three dimensions showing shades and shadows.

Set-12

1. Imagine you are sitting on a chair in barber shop or a boutique. Barber or make up artist is cutting your hair. Draw what you see in the Mirror, which is in front of you.

2. Design and draw in the given space a square graphic composition to be used on Tee Shirts for SAVE OUR PLANET Campaign. Colour the design using maximum four colours. The words (Save Our Planet) should NOT be used within the square graphic as it will be printed separately on the Tee shirt.

3. Two tooth brushes and a toothpaste are kept in a glass on a table. A shaving brush is lying near it. Draw a three dimensional sketch of these objects showing shades and shadows.

Set-13

1. You are standing in your balcony and looking at a cricket match in y our building compound or colony or a small ground. You can also see your friends in their balconies on the other side cheering the players. Draw the entire scene in pencil including your friends in their balconies.

2. Imagine you are studying in a School of Architecture. Your School decides to manufacture a designed student Architect's bag to be put on sale for student Architects in India. Design a suitable and attractive logo for the student Architect's bag. Colour your logo using primary colours only.

3. Use six candles, one square box and three prisms to create a stable three dimensional form. Also draw the shadows cast on your 3D composition by lighting one of the candles.

Set-14

1. An inter school quiz competition being held in the assembly hall in one of the new modern school in town. There are three teams each with two participants- one teacher and one student and the quiz master conducting the proceedings is standing in the middle with audience on rest of the three sides. Imagine you are one of the participants in the quiz along with your teacher. Draw a pencil sketch of what you will see from your position.

2. In the given space, design and draw a pattern for a stained glass window using only lines. Colour in 5 colours. Stained glass windows have panels of coloured glass arranged as per design.

3. Imagine that you are given 4 cubical concrete blocks, 6 wooden logs and a thin piece of cloth for making a sculptural composition. Make a three dimensional sketch to show your composition. Show the effect of shades & shadows.

Set-15

1. You have gone with your sister to select a jewellery item to a jewellery shop. The shop is not much crowded and you can see the counters and display. Draw a pencil sketch of what you see around in the shop.

2. Using 8 equilateral triangles of various sizes create an interesting two dimensional composition in the given rectangle and colour it in three colours of your choice.

3. Create a stable sculpture using four cubes interlocking into each other. Some cubes may be opaque and some may be transparent. Draw a pencil sketch of the composition and imagining light falling from one of the corners, also show shades and shadows.

Set-16

1. There is a workshop organised on painting by renowned painter in an art gallery. He is explaining process of painting right from beginning. Crowd of 10 to 15 young children is watching the process. You are standing at the back of the crowd. Make a pencil sketch of the activity as YOU see it from your position.

2. Create a composition using form of a Peepal leaf (Use the form maximum 4 times) and colour it using warm colour scheme.

3. Draw a three dimensional composition using various size cylinders (Minimum 4) to represent a tall building. Draw using pencil only and show shades and shadows on the composition.

Set-17

1. Imagine you visiting a public garden. In the garden they have a sculpture made of 8 cubes at the centre & you are standing at the corner of a cube. Draw a pencil sketch of what you can see from the corner.

2. Using curved and straight lines, design and draw in the given space, a two dimensional composition to indicate "Peace". Colour the composition in a colour scheme of your choice.

3. Arrange number of cubes of different sizes to create a sense of opening & steps. Show shades & shadows on the composition.

Set-18

1. You are on the school playground to watch an inter-school football match. You are sitting on the ground just behind the goal post and net of the opposition team. Your school team is awarded a free kick against the opposition team just outside the D and your friend is on the spot to take the kick. Other team mates and players have taken their positions. Draw a pencil sketch of what you see from you seat.

2. Design and draw in the given space a square graphic composition to be used on Tee Shirts for SAVE WATER Campaign. Colour the design using maximum four colours. The words (Save Water) should NOT be used within the square graphic.

3. Four pieces out of eight pieces of a round birthday cake are remaining on a plate with the knife in the plate and two extinguished candles near the plate. Draw a three dimensional composition of these objects showing shades and shadows.

Set-19

1. In the summer season, one morning you went to visit a small temple on the hilltop with your friends. You still have to climb a little to reach the temple when you see the temple on the top with a few people standing/ sitting near it looking down at your group. Make a pencil sketch of the scene as you will see it from below.

2. In the given space, create a geometrical composition by using three primary shapes circle/ triangle and square. The composition is to be created by using each shape not more than 4 times. Colour the composition using secondary colours

3. Four cubes and 5 circular wooden logs in different sizes are available with you. Make use of these 3 Dimensional objects to create a stable interesting sculpture. Draw the same and show the effect of shade and shadow on the composition.

Set-20

1. Imagine yourself to be a 12 years old boy/ girl visiting a Mela (fair) in your town. In the Mela you are sitting in a merry-go-round with friends. You can see around you a number of food stalls, games including giant wheel, toy train and other attractions in the Mela. Draw a pencil sketch of the scene as visible from your seat in the merry go round.

2. A car manufacturing company wants to design its logo to be used on the front and rear bonnet of the car. The same logo will also be used in advertisements in colour. You can use primary shapes like square, rectangle, circle, etc. and also few letters (alphabets) to compose the logo. Draw the logo in the given space and colour the composition using 2 colours.

3. Make a 3D composition using 3 cubes & 2 rectangular boxes in the space provided. Also show the effect of light & shadow on it.

Set-21

1. You are standing in a que at a cinema hall to get the ticket for the feature film that is popular (hit) today. You can view others standing in a que till the booking window, people standing around (not in the Que) looking at hoardings / banners and those entering the hall beyond. Draw a pencil sketch of what you see from your position.

2. Design and draw in the given space a square graphic composition to be used on Tee Shirts for Save Trees Campaign. Colour the design using maximum four colours. The words (Save Trees) should NOT be used within the square graphic.

3. Using the objects - 3 notebooks, one orange and two walking sticks create a stable form and draw its view from interesting angle. Then show the effect of light thrown at your form from the left direction and draw the shadow cast by it on the ground.

Sketching

Introduction: Art is an integral part of architecture. As a matter of fact architecture is combination of art and technology. Through painting, sketches and drawings, one gets an opportunity to express one's feelings, experiences and ideas. You may say art as a subject provides an opportunity to us for satisfying our creative thirst.

The main aim of sketching is to draw and graphically represent any scene, human, animal or landscape correctly. The final outcome of sketch is often governed by the creative ability and perception of the artist. But no doubt the sketch must have some degree of realism. The subject drawing or sketch should be recognizable. For example, a sketched boat ought to look like a boat and not a house or ship.

Observation and Recording: We must spend some time to observe various things carefully which we want to sketch. Observation must be sharp and accurate. Memory drawing is a subject for architecture entrance exams. If you want to depict any scene of a mela or railway station or road side "dhaba" you have to recall your past experiences of visiting those places. The sketch drawn by you should be accurate as well as aesthetically pleasing and beautiful. Composition and sense of proportion are also very important.

We must know how to balance tone and value and how to create a focal point or center of interest in the sketch. A good composition has the ability to unite the artist and viewer emotionally. One should learn how to draw various objects like furniture, clothes, human figures, landscape, animals, houses, vehicles, utensils, flowers, etc. Start by trying to draw simple figures like, cone, cylinder, prism, pyramid, sphere, cube, cuboid and then go for utensils, flowers, plants and trees. For sketches of vehicles you should observe the cars, buses, bikes, etc. from various angles. It needs little extra effort to draw human figures. Gradually, step by step, with practice you will learn to draw, correct human figures.

Still Life Sketching: Pencils are the most important tools of an artist as they are used for sketching as well as shading. The study of still objects is known as still life and sketching of still objects is known still life drawing. In the beginning, draw figures of objects by keeping them in front of you. You can use glass,

katori, earthen pots, books, fruits, etc. for this purpose. Observe the light and shade and try to draw shadows according to light source. Each object has a unique form and that defines its appearance and shadow.

Though objects have lot of details if we see it from near but these details are hardly visible if seen from a distance. Therefore do not try to fill in minute details unnecessarily. As a matter of fact it is a race against time to complete the memory drawing in the allotted time. While making coloured posters, again, we advise not to fill in minute details. Try to make maximum use of contrast to enhance the beauty of the drawing.

Students' Sketches

These sketches have been prepared by the students preparing for NATA Exams. There may be various errors in these sketches because they are not drawn by any professional artist and the students have been asked to prepare 3 sketches in 2 hours time.

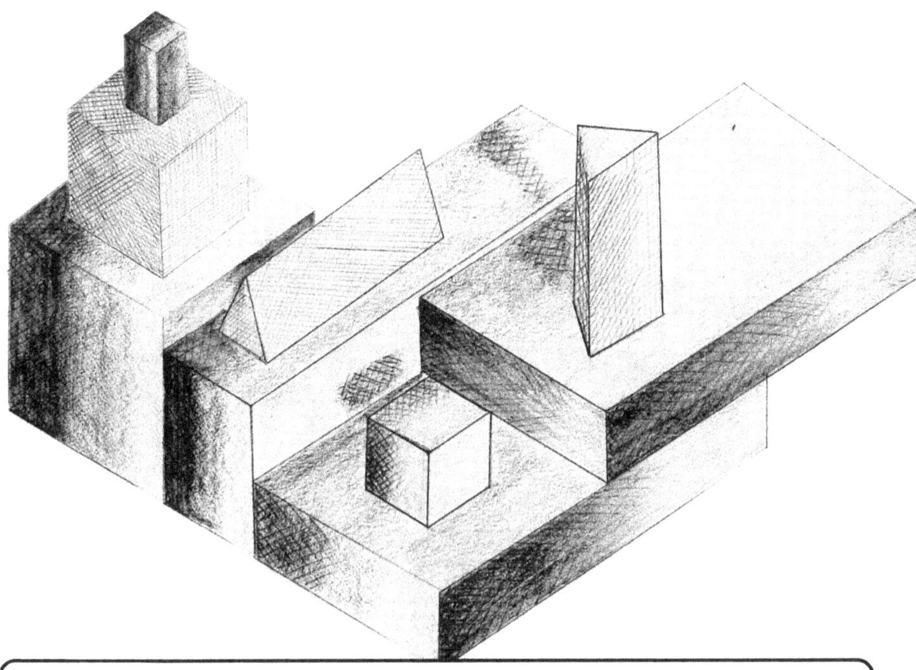

Make an interesting three dimensional composition using cubes, cuboids and prisms, showing the effect of light and shadow on the composition.

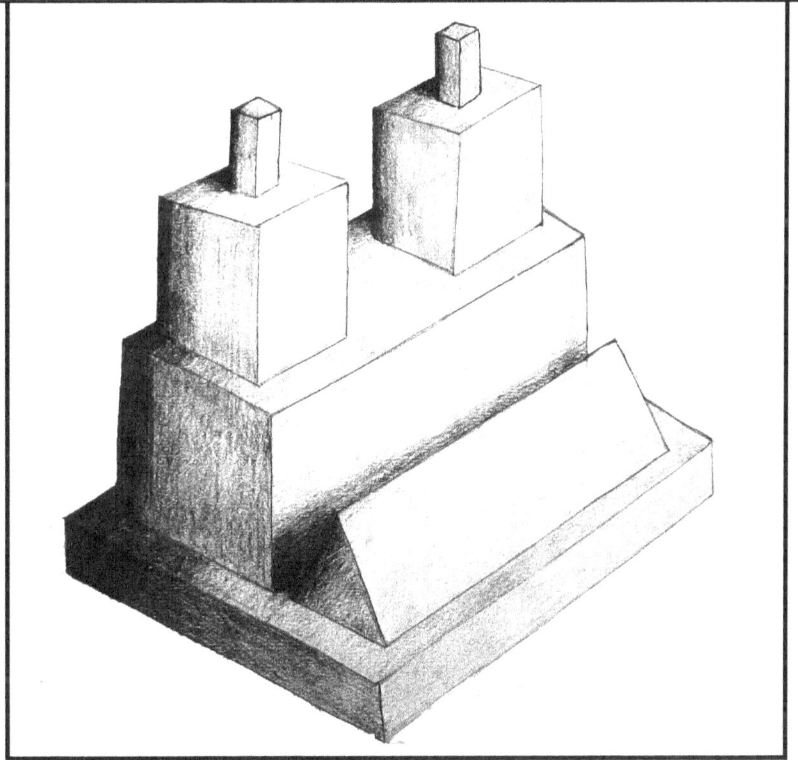

Compose a visually appealing composition with squares and circles using minimum of three and not more than six each and colour the same composition with primary colours.

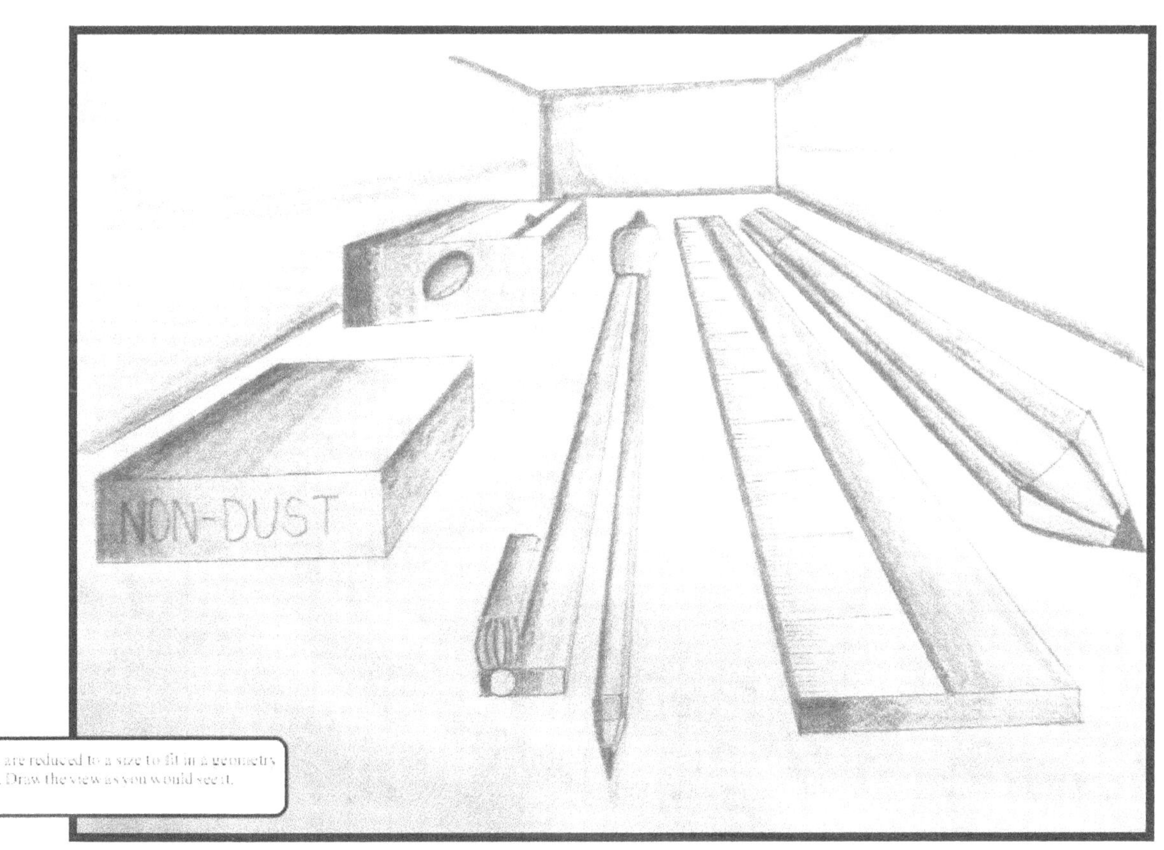

You are reduced to a size to fit in a geometry box. Draw the view as you would see it.

Make a three dimensional composition using six automobile tyres. Draw the same and show shade and shadows on the composition.

You are standing in a que at a cinema hall to get the ticket for the feature film that is popular (hit) today. You can view others standing in a que till the booking window, people standing around (not in the Que) looking at hoardings / banners and those entering the hall beyond. Draw a pencil sketch of what you see from your position.

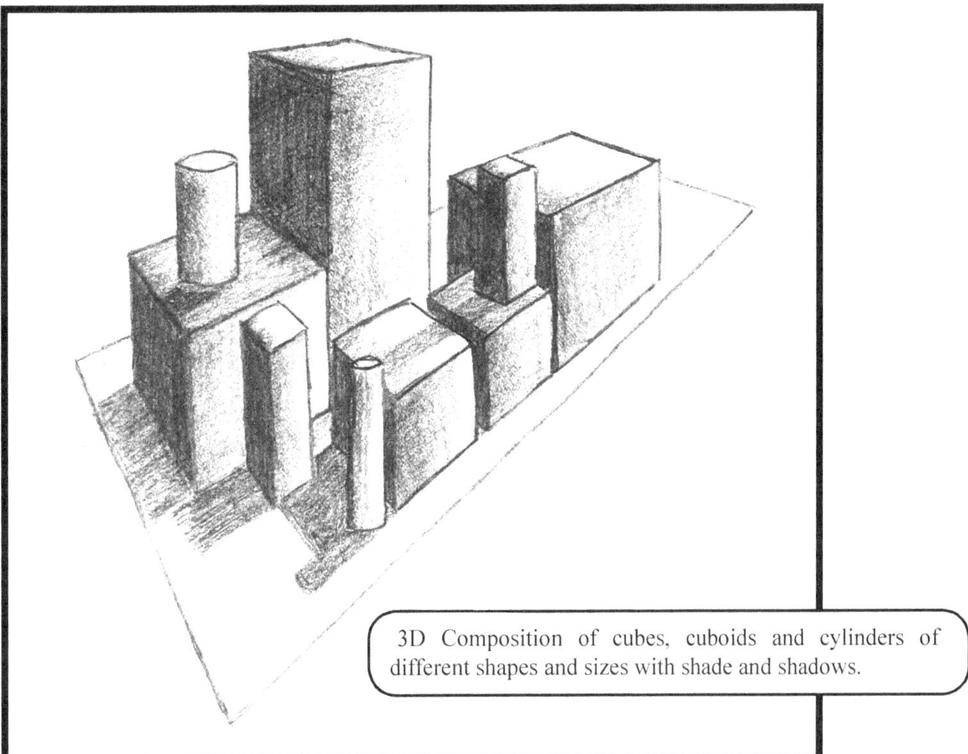

3D Composition of cubes, cuboids and cylinders of different shapes and sizes with shade and shadows.

Make an interesting three dimensional composition using three cubes and two cones, showing the effect of light and shadow on the composition.

In the given space arrange 5 earthen pots of any shape and size to make interesting looking stable composition. Draw the composition from an interesting angle and show shades and shadow on the composition.

In the given space arrange 5 earthen pots of any shape and size to make interesting looking stable composition. Draw the composition from an interesting angle and show shades and shadow on the composition.

Art Gallery

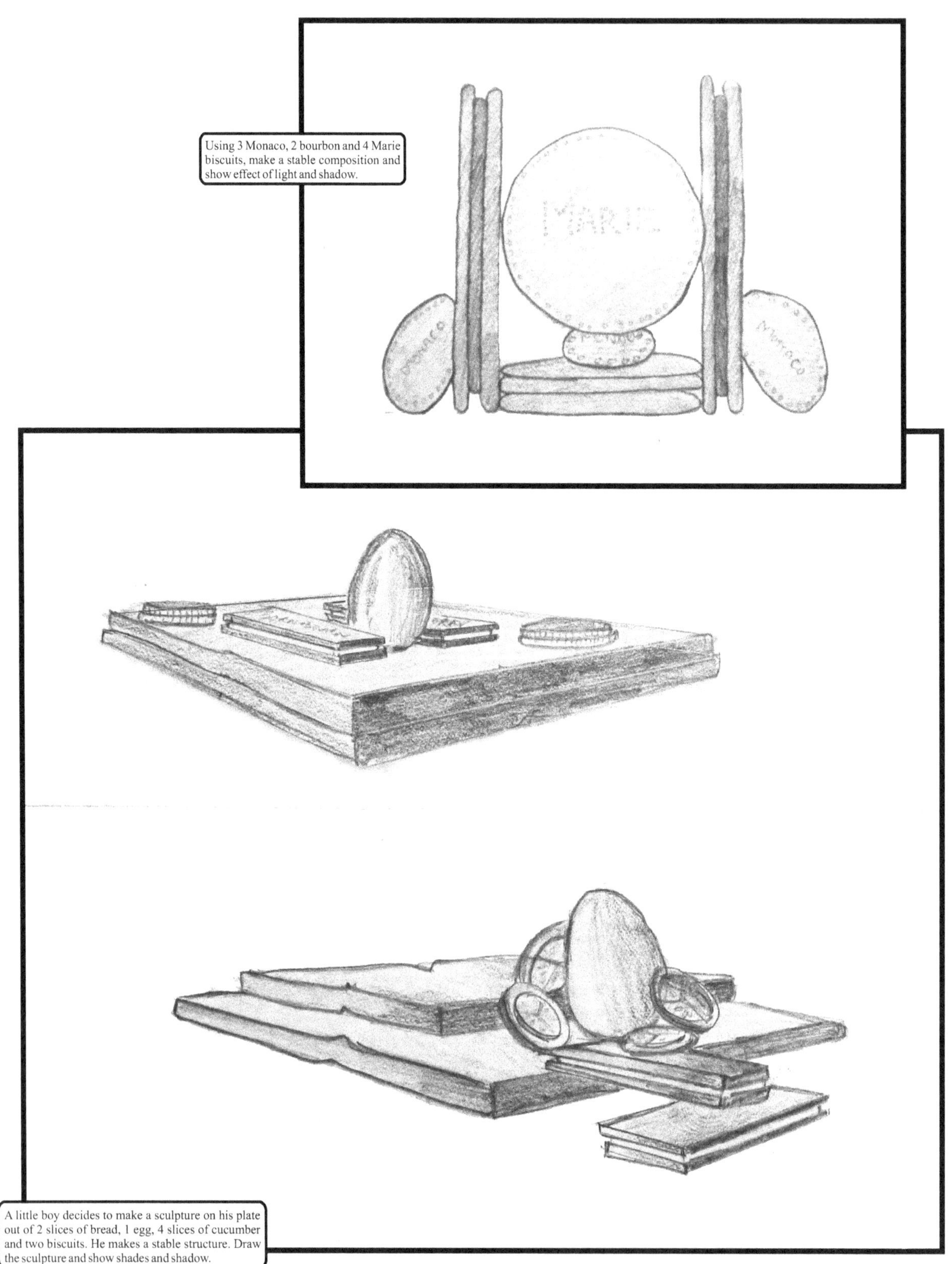

Using 3 Monaco, 2 bourbon and 4 Marie biscuits, make a stable composition and show effect of light and shadow.

A little boy decides to make a sculpture on his plate out of 2 slices of bread, 1 egg, 4 slices of cucumber and two biscuits. He makes a stable structure. Draw the sculpture and show shades and shadow.

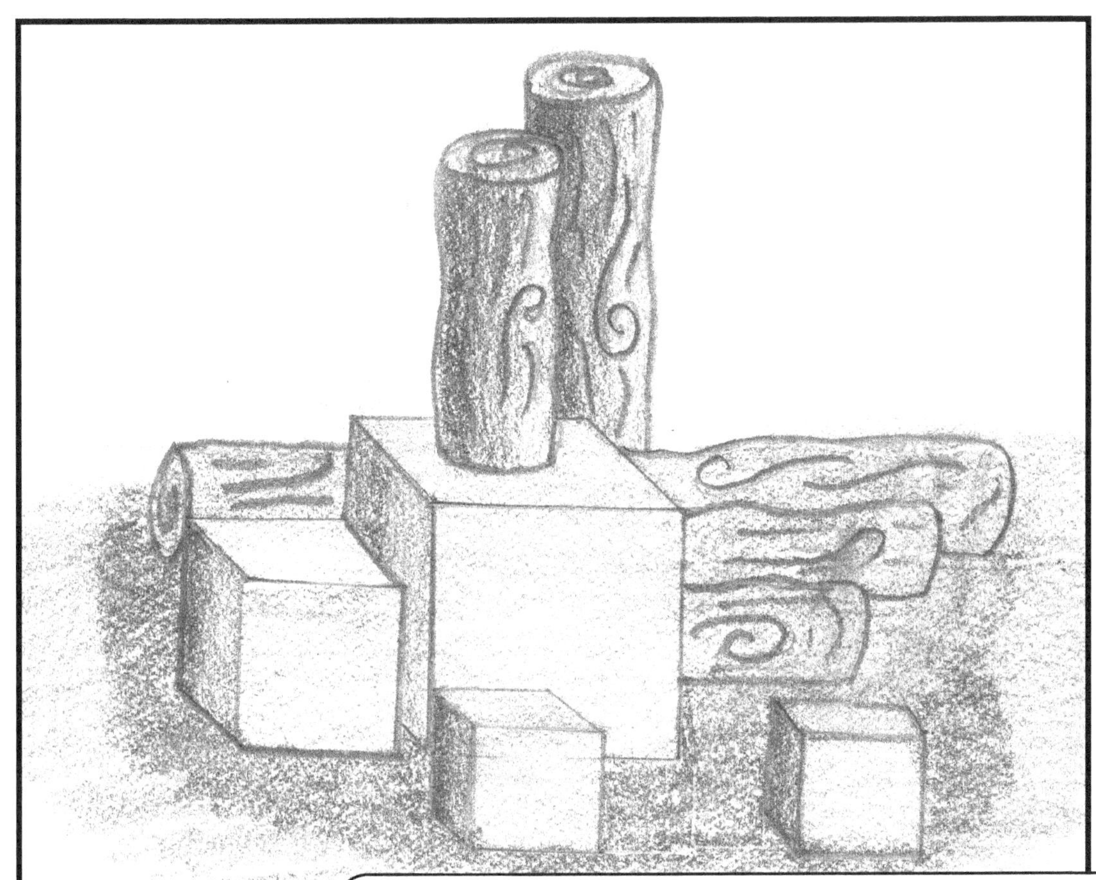

Four cubes and 5 circular wooden logs in different sizes are available with you. Make use of these 3 dimensional objects to create a stable interesting sculpture. Draw the same and show the effecet of shade and shadow on the composition.

Bedroom

You have gone with your sister to select a jewellery item to a jewellery shop. The shop is not much crowded and you can see the counters and display. Draw a pencil sketch of what you see around in the shop.

Imagine you have reduced to 5 cm size and sitting in a kitchen rack (cupboard). There are cups, plates, bottles kept in the rack. Sketch what you see.

Drawing Room
One - Point Perspective

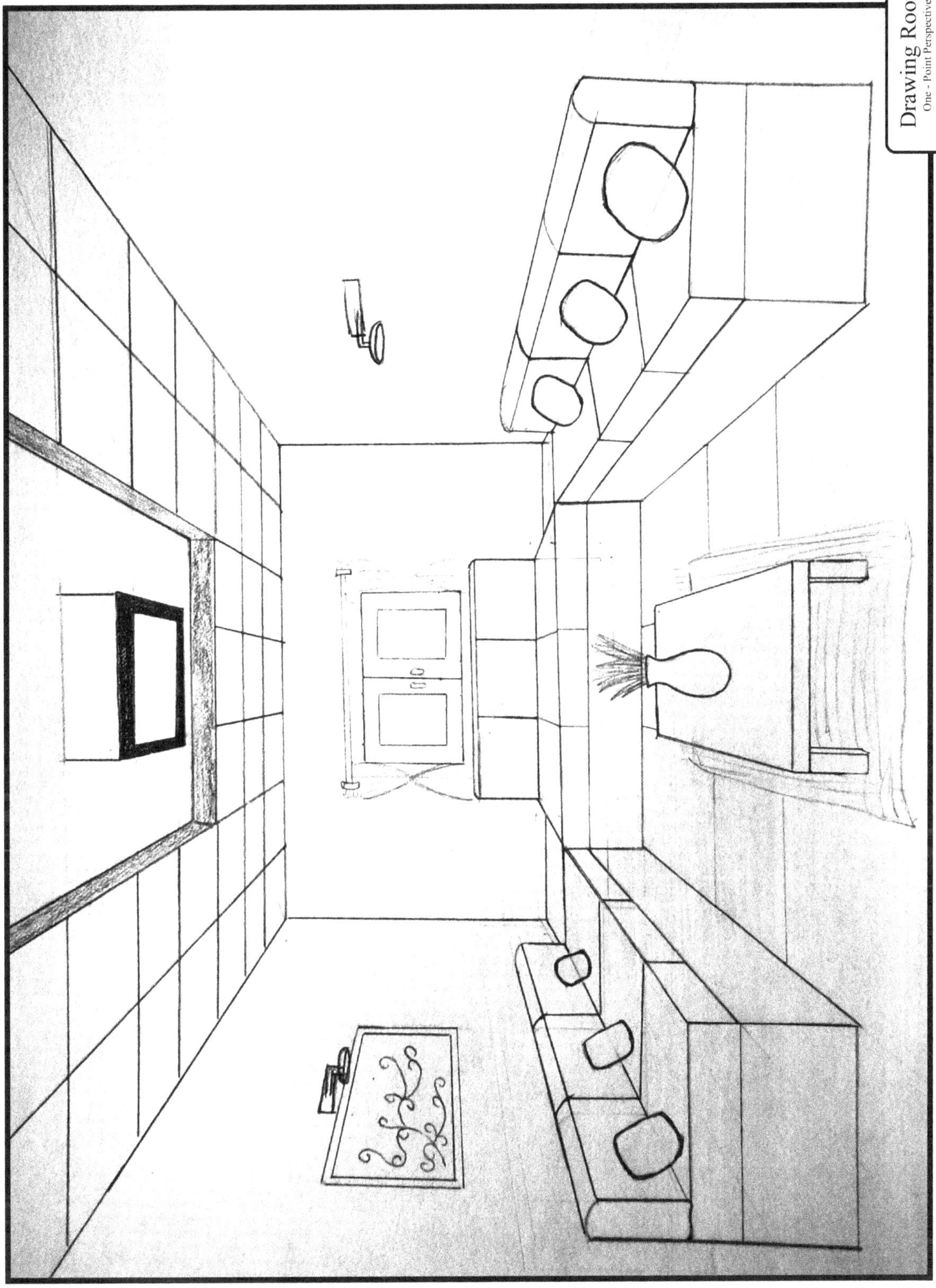

STUDENT'S SKETCHES

A zebra, an elephant and a giraffe have come from zoo into your street. Draw a pencil sketch of what you see around in the street.

Imagine you are a fish and you are in aquarium with your fish friends and a family of four is watching you and a girl of that family is pointing her finger towards you. Sketch the scene you see.

Imagine you are moving around with a shopping trolley in a grocery store. Draw a memory sketch in pencil of what you see around you.

Imagine you are sitting on a chair in barber shop or a boutique. Barber or make up artist is cutting your hair. Draw what you see in the Mirror, which is in front of you.

Make a three dimensional composition using five bottles. Draw the same and show shade and shadows on the composition.

A metal lunch box, a glass water bottle, two spoons and a cap are kept on a table. Arrange these objects to form a three dimensional composition and draw it showing shades and shadows.

Drawing Room
Two Point perspective

Make an interesting balanced composition of two chillies, two tomatoes and two slices of bread on a square plate. Draw the composition in three dimensions showing shades and shadows.

On the flag hosting day at your school you are with your school in the assembly ground attended by all your teachers, school principal and school staff. The scene should be complete and drawn in pencil as you see it from where you are standing, highlighting the main subject of the day in the given space

A dance competition is being held in the assembly hall of your school. You are standing in the last row. Draw a pencil sketch of what you will see from your position.

Imagine you are a bird flying above a temple. Draw the sketch of the scene viewed from above.

Imagine you are a bird. You are flying over the remnants of a historical site. Make a pencil of sketch of what you see.

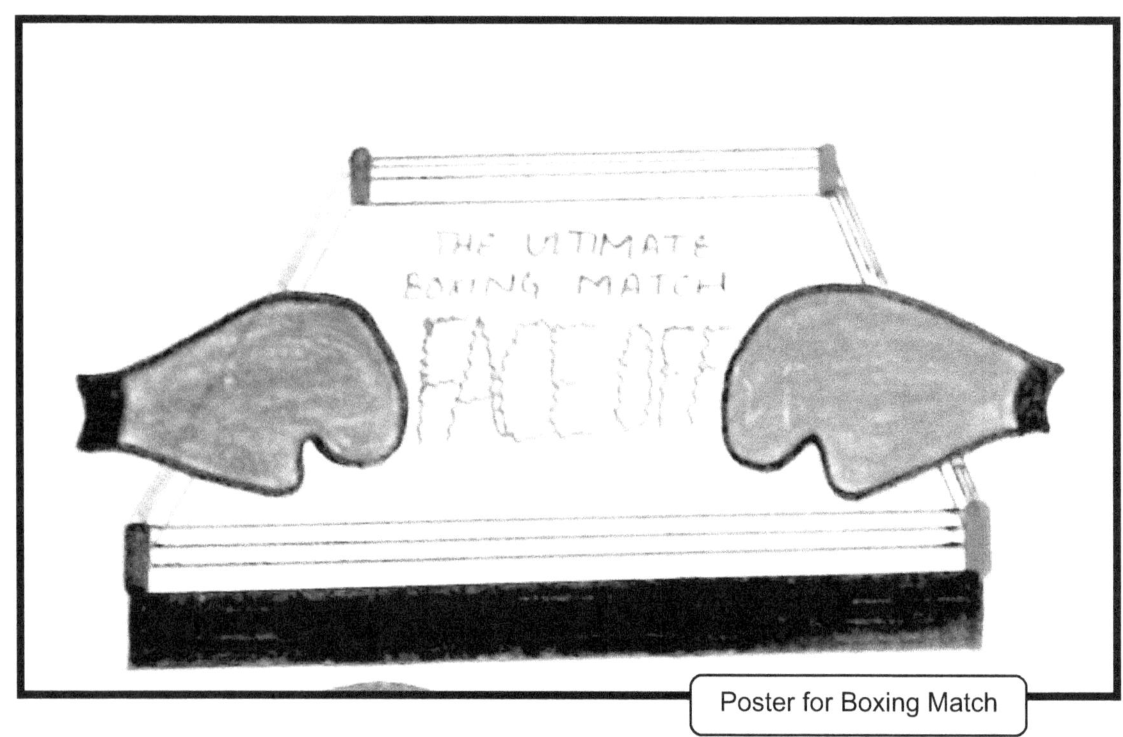

Poster for Boxing Match

Imagine you have reduced to 5 cm size and sitting in a kitchen rack (cupboard). There are cups, plates, bottles kept in the rack. Sketch what you see.

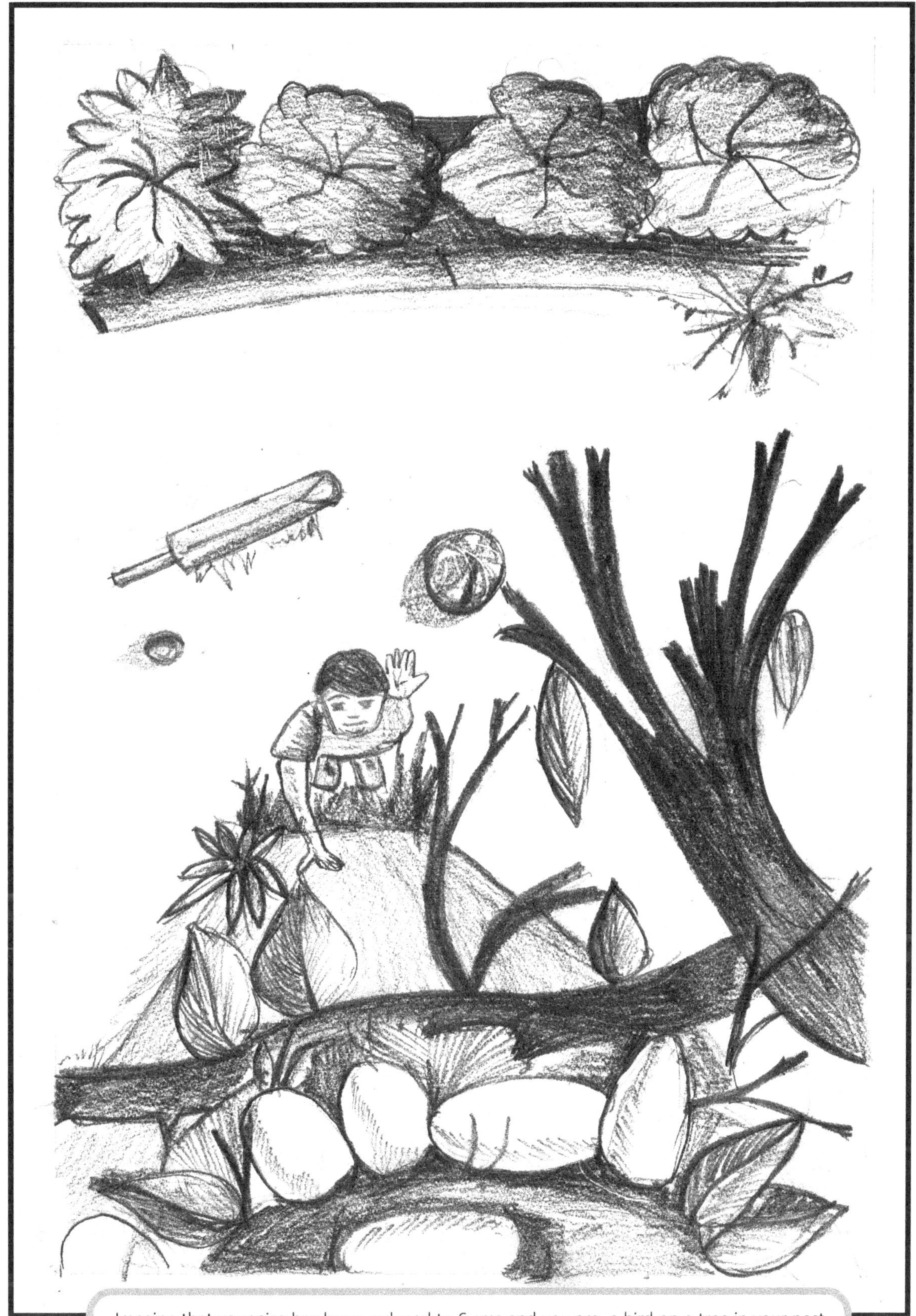

Imagine that your size has been reduced to 6 cms and you are a bird on a tree in your nest. A boy is approaching you. Draw a pencil sketch of what you would see from there, along with the nest and the eggs.

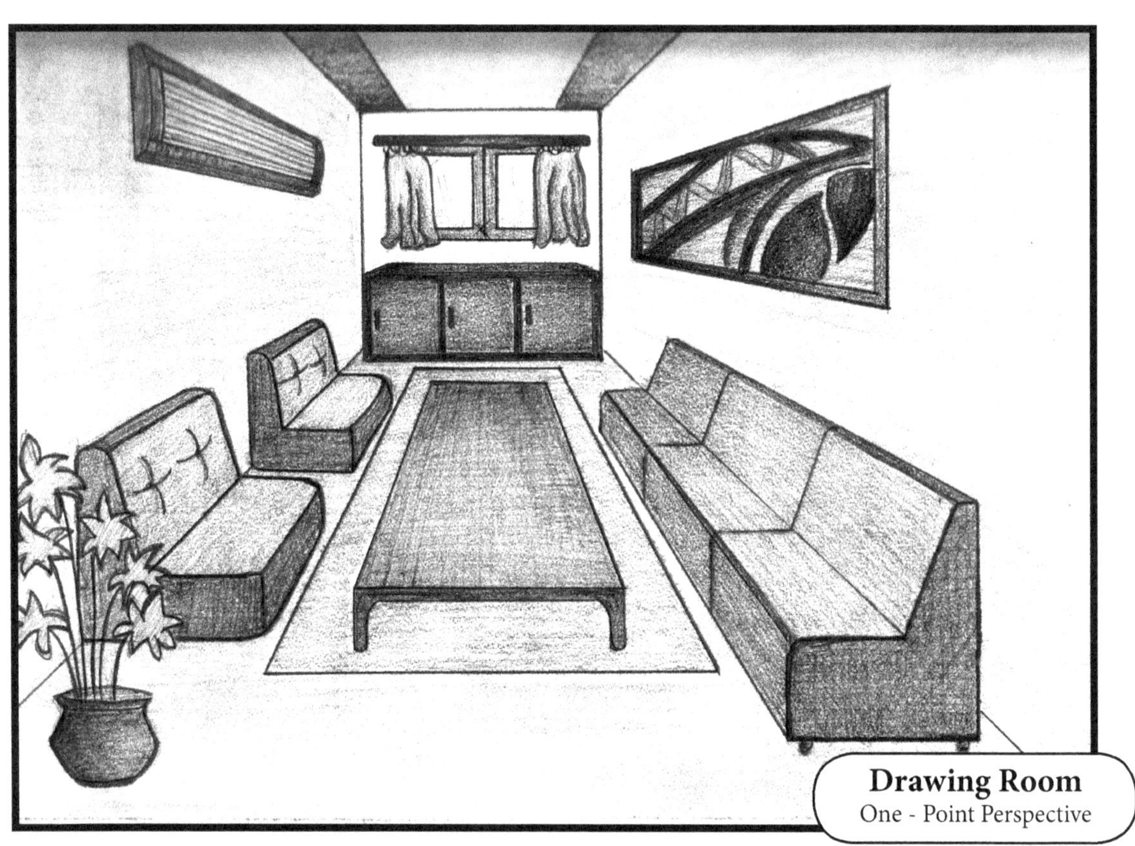

Drawing Room
One - Point Perspective

Kitchen
One - Point Perspective

Make a 3D composition using three prisms , one cube and six candles. Show shade and shadow.

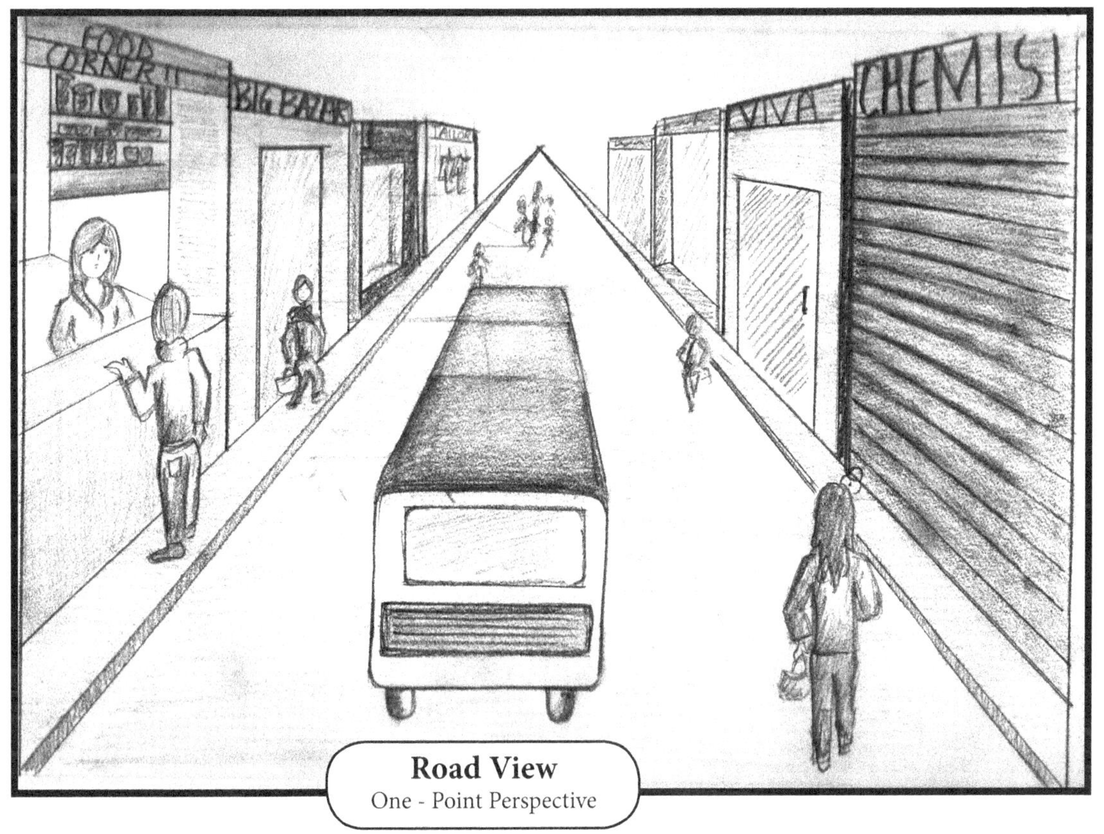

Road View
One - Point Perspective

Design a logo for water polo.

In the given space arrange three luggage pieces [suitcase, trunk, sleeping bag, etc.] make an interesting, abstract, stable, three dimensional composition like a still life. Also show the efect of light & shade on the objects. Your composition should be su ciently large to ill the draw ing space.

Two tooth brushes and a toothpaste are kept in a glass on a table. A shaving brush is lying near it. Draw a three dimensional sketch of these objects showing shades and shadows.

You are provided with a small clock, a talcum powder tin, a can of a sot drink and a roll of paper. Make an interesting three dimensional composition. Draw the composition in pencil and show the efect of shades and shadows.

Bird's Eye view
Old Fort Below

One morning, you went to visit a small temple on the hilltop with your friends. Make a pencil sketch of the scene as you will see it from below.

Imagine that you are inside a ticket counter of a cinema hall issuing tickets, and sketch the view of the people lined in the queue as seen from inside the counter by you.

Imagine that your size has been reduced to 6 cms and you are standing on an open newspaper lying in your room. Draw a pencil sketch of what you would see of the newspaper along with some view of the room.

A zebra, an elephant and a giraffe have come from zoo into your street. Draw a pencil sketch of what you see around in the street.

Imagine you are standing in front of a coconut tree and a rose shrub in a garden. However, the coconut tree is shrunk to the size of the rose shrub and the rose shrub has enlarged to the size of the coconut tree. Draw the scene in pencil as you would see.

Design and draw in the given space a square graphic composition to be used for Bharat Jodo Campaign. Colour the design using maximum four colours.

Design and draw in the given space a square graphic composition to be used on Tee Shirts for Save Trees Campaign. Colour the design using maximum four colours.
The words (Save Trees) should NOT be used within the square graphic.

Art Gallery

Imagine you have reduced to 5 cm size and sitting in a kitchen rack (cupboard). There are cups, plates, bottles kept in the rack. Sketch what you see.

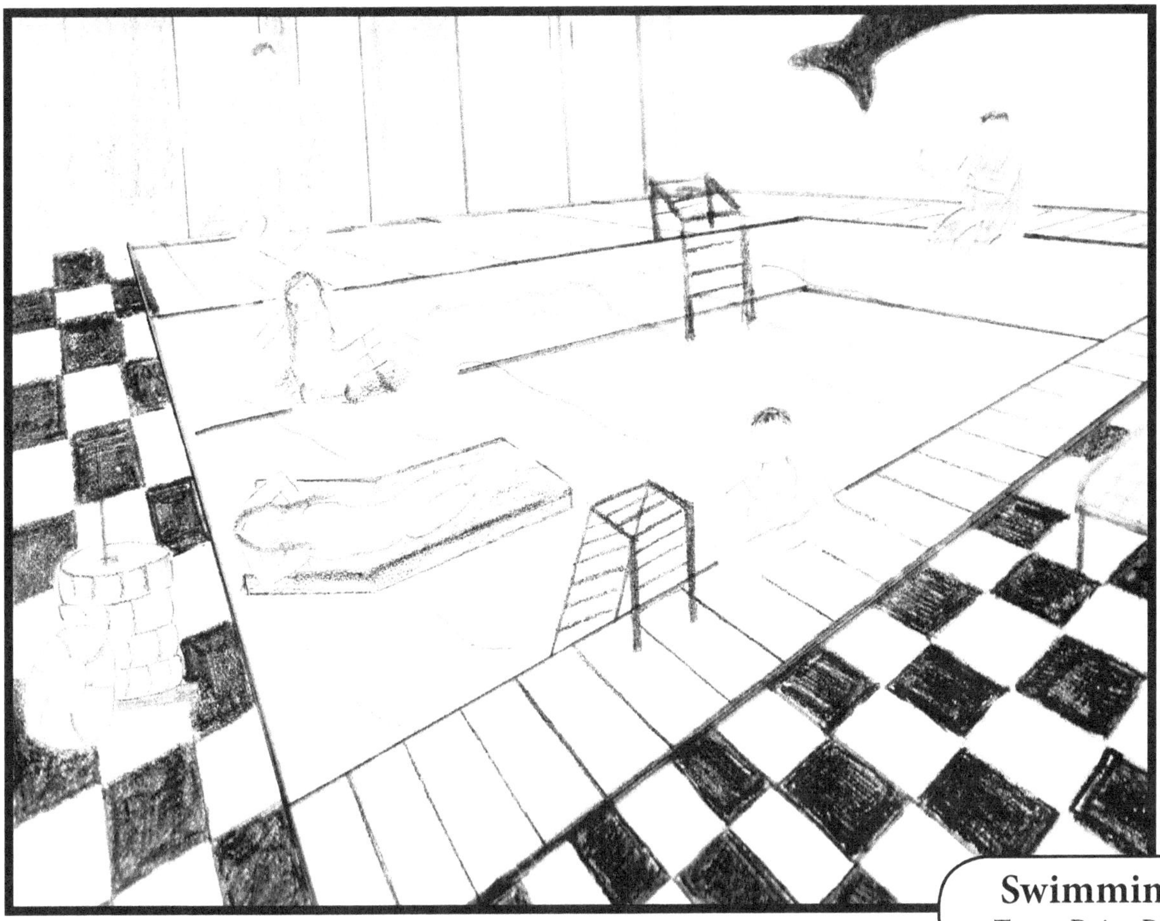

Swimming Pool
Two - Point Perspective

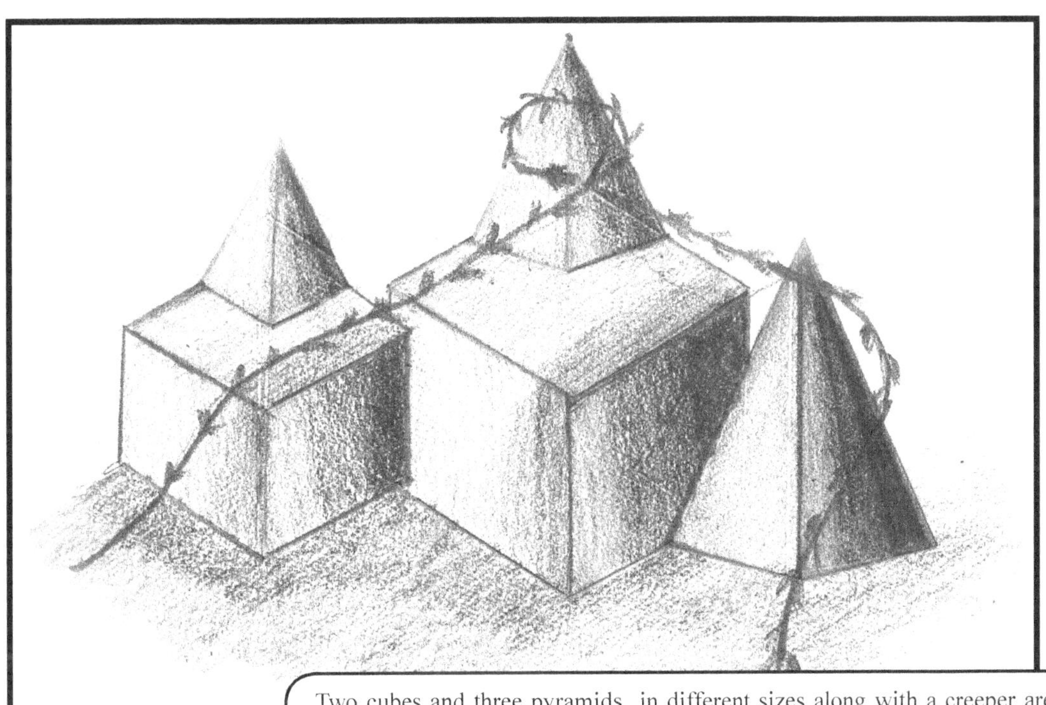

Two cubes and three pyramids in different sizes along with a creeper are available with you. Make use of these 3 dimensional objects to create a stable interesting sculpture. Draw the same and show the effecet of shade and shadow on the composition.

Bedroom
Two - Point Perspective

Bedroom
Two - Point Perspective

Bus-Terminal
One - Point Perspective

Bus-Stop
One - Point Perspective

Temple view from below

Cinema Ticket Window
View from inside

Doctor's Reception
Two-Point Perspective

Railway Station
One-Point Perspective

Fruit Basket

Fruit Basket

Design and draw in the given space a square graphic composition to be used on Book Cover for GEOMETRY FOR EVERYONE. Colour the design using maximum four colours.

Imagine you are a fish and you are in aquarium with your fish friends and a family of four is watching you and a girl of that family is pointing her finger towards you. Sketch the scene you see.

Imagine you are sitting on a chair in barber shop or a boutique. Barber or make up artist is cutting your hair. Draw what you see in the Mirror, which is in front of you.

An inter school quiz competition being held in the assembly hall in one of the new modern school in town. here are three teams each with two participants- one teacher and one student and the quiz master conducting the proceedings is standing in the middle with audience on rest of the three sides. Imagine you are one of the participants in the quiz along with your teacher. Draw a pencil sketch.

Using the objects - 3 notebooks, one orange and two walking sticks create stable from and draw its view from an interesting angle. Then show the effect of light thrown at your form form the left direction and draw the shadow cast by it on the ground.

Roadside View
One-Point Perspective

Imagine you are visiting a public garden. In the garden children are playing. There are swings, see-saw, trees and plants, and an old man reading newspaper

On rainy day you are standing at a window of your third loor house. Some children are playing football in the open place below. Draw a pencil sketch of the scene as you would see it from the window.

View inside a bus
One-Point Perspective

Design and draw in the given space a square graphic composition to be used on Tee Shirts to be given to Members of a TREKKING EXPEDITION. Colour the design using maximum four colours.

Design and draw in the given space a square graphic composition to be used on Tee Shirts for blood donation Campaign. Colour the design using maximum four colours.
The words (blood donation) should NOT be used within the square graphic.

Children Playing On Road

Four pieces out of eight pieces of a round birthday cake are remaining on a plate with the knife in the plate and two extinguished candles near the plate. Draw the view showing shades and shadows.

Village Market

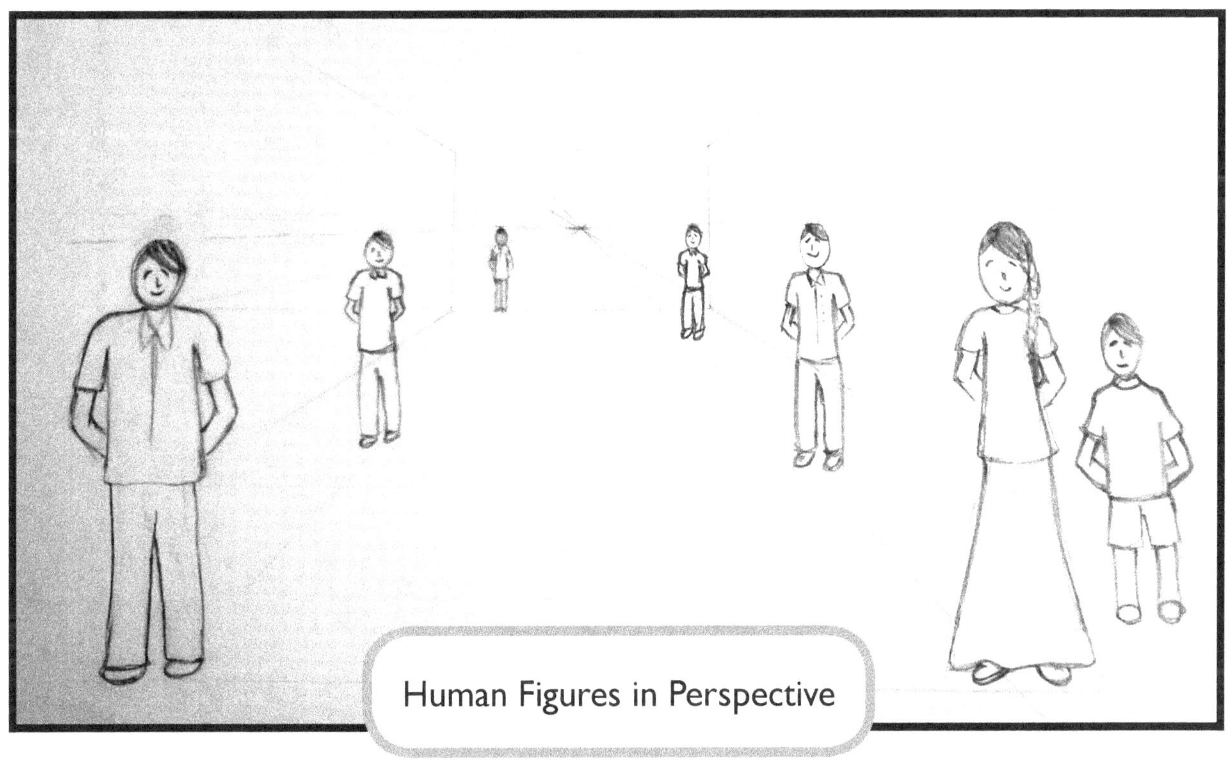
Human Figures in Perspective

You are watching an inter-school football match. You are seating on the ground just behind the goal post and net. Draw a pencil sketch of what you see from you seat.

Imagine you are standing in front of a coconut tree and a rose shrub in a garden. However, the coconut tree is shrunk to the size of the rose shrub and the rose shrub has enlarged to the size of the coconut tree. Draw the scene in pencil as you would see.

Students Sketches

Colour wheel

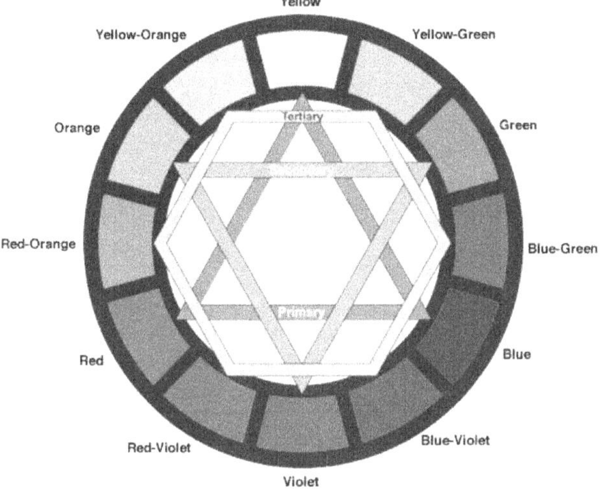

Tints and shades

Primary colours

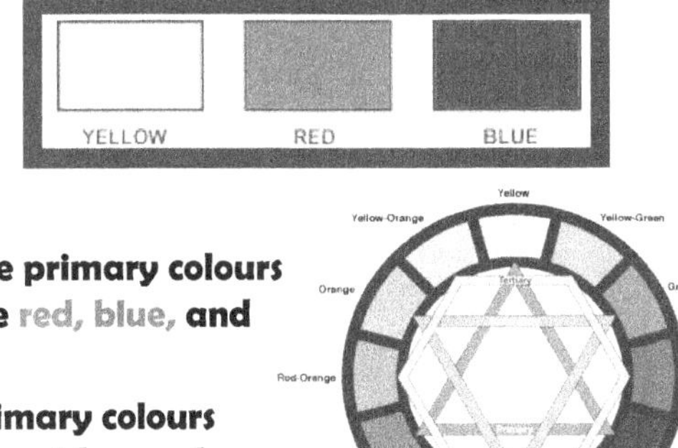

- **The primary colours are red, blue, and**

- **Primary colours cannot be made from other colours.**

Secondary colours

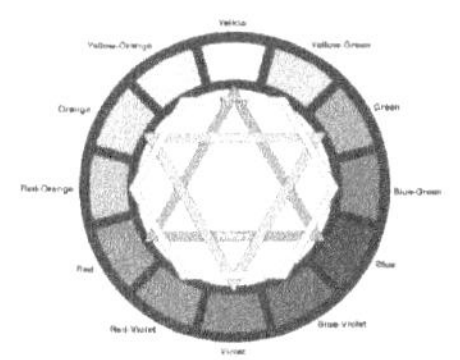

- **The secondary colours are green, and purple.**
- **Secondary colours are made from mixing the primary colours.**

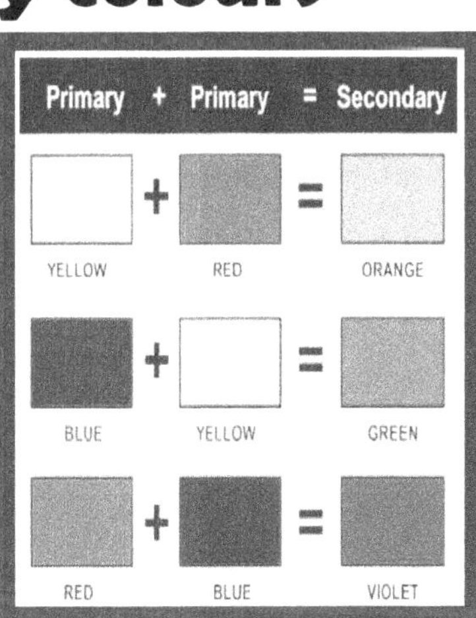

Compose and draw in given space a flooring pattern for center of the entrance lobby of a resort hotel on beach using circles of varying size and squares. You can use only primary colours.

Design a logo for Water polo Game to be used by national water polo players' association, using various shapes. Colour the logo using three colours of your choice.

Draw in the given space a poster for Bharat Jodo campaign. Colour it with suitable colours

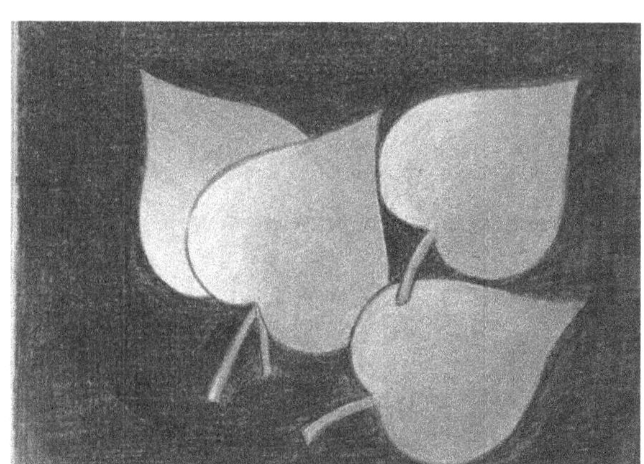

Draw a composition using form of a Peepal leaf (Use the form maximum 4 times) and colour it using warm colour scheme

Imagine you are studying in a School of Architecture. Design a suitable and attractive logo for the student Architect's bag. Colour your logo using primary colours only.

Design a logo for Hotel on a famous hill station. Colour your drawing with suitable colours.

Draw in the given space a poster for a Youth Festival to be held in your college shortly. Colour it with suitable colours

Design and draw in the given space a square graphic composition to be used on Tee Shirts for SAVE WATER Campaign. Colour the design using maximum four colours. The words (Save Water) should NOT be used.

Design and draw in the given space a square graphic composition to be used on Tee Shirts for SAVE WATER Campaign. Colour the design using maximum four colours. The words (Save Water) should NOT be used.

Design and draw in the given space a square graphic composition to be used on T-Shirts for Peace movement. Colour the design using maximum four colours.

Draw in the given space a poster for a Dance Academy which is going to open shortly in your neighbourhood. Colour it with suitable colours.

Design and draw in the given space a square graphic composition to be used on T-Shirts for Blood Donation Campaign. Colour the design using maximum four colours.

Famous Building's Photographs

LAXMAN JHULA

RISHIKESH

JAWAHAR KALA KENDRA, JAIPUR

Architect - Charles Correa

TAJ MAHAL, AGRA

NEEMRANA FORT PALACE, RAJASTHAN

MEENAKSHI TEMPLE, MADURAI, TAMIL NADU

MATRIMANDIR, AUROVILLE, PONDICHERRY

VIJAYA VITTALA TEMPLE, HAMPI, KARNATAKA

BARA IMAMBARA, LUCKNOW, UTTAR PRADESH

FATEHPUR MOSQUE, UTTAR PRADESH

AGRA FORT, UTTAR PRADESH

Fatehpur Sikri is a city in Agra district of UP, India. The historical city was constructed by Mughal emperor Akbar beginning in 1570 and served as the empire's capital from 1571 until 1585. Though the court took 15 years to build, it was abandoned after only 14 years because the water supply was unable to sustain the growing population. The surviving palace and mosque are a tourist attraction and a UNESCO World Heritage Site. All the buildings here were made of the red sandstone.

TOMB OF SALIM CHISTI, FATEHPUR SIKRI, U. P.

VIVEKANANDA ROCK MEMORIAL TAMIL NADU

RAMESHWARAM TMEPLE, TAMIL NADU

BADRINATH TEMPLE

NATRAJ TEMPLE, CHIDAMBARAM, TAMIL NADU

KEDARNATH TEMPLE UTTARANCHAL

BRAHMA TEMPLE, PUSHKAR

GOLCONDA FORT, ANDHRA PRADESH

HOWRAH BRIDGE, KOLKATA

SHERSHAH SURI TOMB, SASARAM

GOL GUMBAZ, KARNATAKA

SHRAVANABELAGOLA JAIN TEMPLE,

STATUE OF GOMATESHWARA, MYSORE, KARNATAKA

KERALA HOUSEBOAT

IIM BANGALORE	MAHABODHI TEMPLE, BODHGAYA, BIHAR
BHARAT BHAVAN BHOPAL Architect - Charles Correa	SALARJUNG MUSUEM, HYDERABAD
GWALIOR FORT, MADHYA PRADESH	JAHAZ MAHAL, MADHYA PRADESH

ELLORA TEMPLE, MAHARASHTRA

GATEWAY OF INDIA, MUMBAI

KEY MONASTERY SPITI,
HIMACHAL PRADESH

SANCHI STUPA, MADHYA PRADESH

CHHATRAPATI SHIVAJI TERMINUS

MUMBAI

VICTORIA MEMORIAL

KOLKATA

CAPITOL COMPLEX, CHANDIGARH

KANCHANJUNGA APARTMENTS

Architect - Charles Correa

SUN TEMPLE, KONARK, ORISSA

NEHRU CENTRE, MUMBAI

LINGARAJ TEMPLE, BHUBHANESHWAR

JAGANNATH TEMPLE, ORISSA

VICTORY TOWER, CHITTORGARH

BIRLA MANDIR, DELHI

JANTAR MANTAR, DELHI

CHAR MINAR, HYDERABAD

HUMAYUN'S TOMB, DELHI

HAWA MAHAL, JAIPUR

PARLIAMENT HOUSE
Architect - Herbert Baker
LOTUS TEMPLE
Architect - Fariburz Saabha
HALL OF NATIONS, PRAGATI MAIDAN
Architect - Raj Rewal
JEEVAN BHARATI BUILDING, DELHI
Architect - Charles Correa
AKSHARDHAM TEMPLE
BAPS, Pramukh Swami Maharaj
NDMC building, DELHI [Palika Kendra]
Architect - Kuldip Singh
ISKCON TEMPLE, DELHI
Architect - Achyut Kanvinde
BRITISH COUNCIL LIBRARY
Architect - Charles Correa
RASHTRAPATI BHAVAN
Architect - Edwin Landseer Lutyens
INDIA INTERNATIONAL CENTRE[IIC]
Architect - Joseph Allen Stein
IIT DELHI
Architect - Jugal Kishore Choudhary
INDIA HABITAT CENTRE
Architect - Joseph Allen Stein

DISNEY LAND , USA	FALLING WATERS, PENNSYLVANIA Architect - Frank Lloyd Wright	PENTAGON, USA
EMPIRE STATE BUILDING, NEW YORK, USA	BEIJING NATIONAL STADIUM [BIRD NEST]	MECCA, SAUDI ARABIA
GOLDEN GATE BRIDGE SAN FRANCISCO, USA	STATUE OF LIBERTY, NEW YORK, USA	BROOKLYN BRIDGE, NEW YORK, USA
WHITE HOUSE, WASHINGTON DC, USA	GUGGENHEIM MUSEUM, NEW YORK, USA	The **Guggenheim Museum** is a well-known museum located inManhattan in New York City, US. It is the permanent home to a renowned collection of Impressionist, Post-Impressionist, early Modern, and contemporary art and also features special exhibitions throughout the year. Designed by Frank Lloyd Wright, it is one of the 20th century's most important architectural landmarks. **GUGGENHEIM MUSEUM, NEW YORK, USA**

BURJ AL ARAB, DUBAI	ANGKOR WAT, CAMBODIA	GREAT WALL OF CHINA
BIG BEN AND HOUSE OF PARLIAMENT, LONDON	PETRONAS TOWERS, MALAYSIA	SUPREME COURT, USA
TOWER BRIDGE, LONDON	RONCHAMP, PARIS	PASHUPATINATH TEMPLE, NEPAL
STONEHENGE, UK	HAGIA SOPHIA, ISTANBUL	SYDNEY OPERA HOUSE SYDNEY, AUSTRALIA

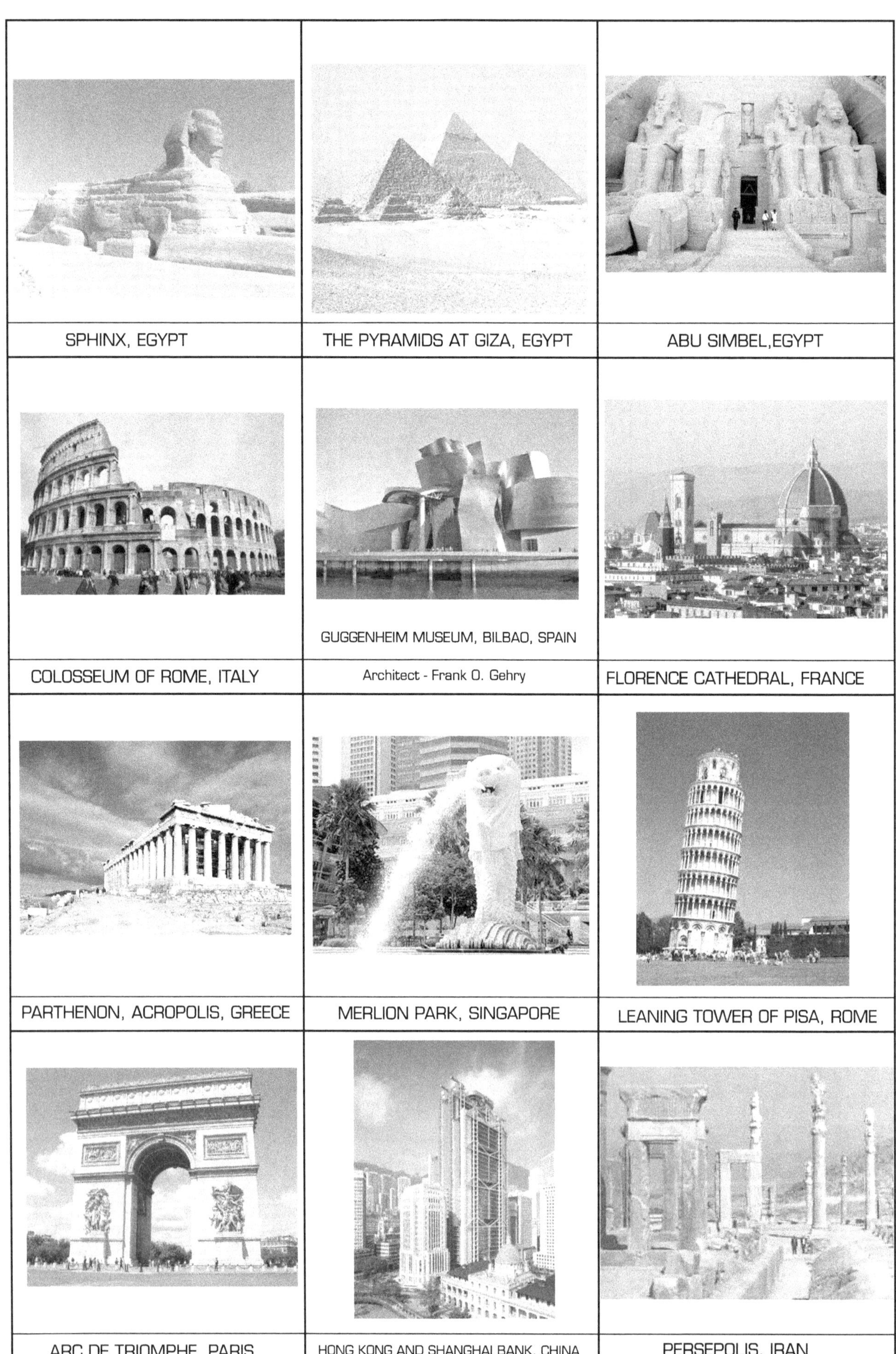

SPHINX, EGYPT	THE PYRAMIDS AT GIZA, EGYPT	ABU SIMBEL, EGYPT
COLOSSEUM OF ROME, ITALY	GUGGENHEIM MUSEUM, BILBAO, SPAIN Architect - Frank O. Gehry	FLORENCE CATHEDRAL, FRANCE
PARTHENON, ACROPOLIS, GREECE	MERLION PARK, SINGAPORE	LEANING TOWER OF PISA, ROME
ARC DE TRIOMPHE, PARIS	HONG KONG AND SHANGHAI BANK, CHINA	PERSEPOLIS, IRAN

NATA 2019 QUESTION PAPER (April 2019)

SECTION: MATHEMATICS

Q-1 If $a^2 - b^2 = 8$ and $a \times b = 2$, find $a^4 + b^4$.
   A. 4
   B. 8
   C. 72
   D. 64

Q-2 Find the value of $\log_y(x4)$ if $\log_x(y3) = 2$

   A. 6
   B. 4
   C. 12
   D. 3

Q-3 How many terms are in the Arithmetic Progression 20, 25, 30,..., 135, 140?
   A. 24
   B. 25
   C. 23
   D. 26

Q-4 If $\log_{10}10 = 1$, $\log_{10}100 = 2$, what is the value of $\log_5 125$?
   A. 5
   B. 25
   C. 1
   D. 3

Q-5 A and B together can do a piece of work in 30 days. A having worked for 16 days, B finishes the remaining work alone in 44 days. In how many days shall B finish the whole work alone?
   A. 30 days
   B. 40 days
   C. 60 days
   D. 70 days

Q6: If the side of a square increases by 30% then its area increases by:
   A. 56%
   B. 15%
   C. 30%
   D. 69%

Q7: **A** is two years older than **B** who is twice as old as **C**. If the total of the ages of **A**, **B** and **C** be 27, then how old is **B**?
   A. 6
   B. 10
   C. 7
   D. 5

Q8: Sarthak bought 7 new trading cards to add to his collection. The next day his dog ate half of his collection. There are now only 31 cards left. How many cards did Sarthak start with ?
   A. 38
   B. 55
   C. 35
   D. 62

Q9:A salesman has a 70% chance to sell a product to any customer. The behavior of successive customers is independent. If two customers **A** and **B** enter, what is the probability that the salesman will sell the product to customer **A** or **B**?
   A. 0.98
   B. 0.91
   C. 0.70
   D. 0.49

Q10: If the points (2a,a),(a,2a) and (a,a) enclose a triangle of area 18 square units. Then the centroid of the triangle is:
   A. (4,4)
   B. (8,8)
   C. (-4,-4)
   D. $(4\sqrt{2}, 4\sqrt{2})$

Q11: The sum of odd integers from 1 to 2001 is:

   A. $(1121)^2$
   B. $(1101)^2$
   C. $(1001)^2$
   D. $(1021)^2$

Q12: Everybody in a room shakes hands with everybody else. The total number of handshakes is 66. Then the total number of persons in the room is:

   A. 11
   B. 12
   C. 13
   D. 14

Q13: A circle of maximum possible size is cut from a square sheet. Subsequently, a square of maximum possible size is cut from the resultant circle. What will be area of the final square?

   A. 25% of the size of the original square
   B. 50% of the size of the original square
   C. 75% of the size of the original circle
   D. Double the size of the original circle

Q14: If log2 + log(x+3) - log(3x-5) = log3. The value of x= ?

   A. -6
   B. 5
   C. -3
   D. +3

Q15: Evaluate the integral $\int_{2}^{3} x^2 \, dx$

   A. $\dfrac{211}{5}$ B. $2\sqrt{3}$

   C. 5   D. $\dfrac{2}{5}$

Q16: The sum of the values of x satisfying $\tan\left(\dfrac{\pi}{4} + x\right) + \tan\left(\dfrac{\pi}{4} - x\right) = 2$ in the interval $[0, 2\pi]$ is:

    A. 6π
    B. 7π
    C. 4π
    D. 3π

Q17: A class has n students, we have to form a team of the students including at least two students and also excluding at least two students. The number of ways of forming the team is

    A. $2^n - 2n$
    B. $2^n - 2n - 2$
    C. $2^n - 2n - 4$
    D. $2^n - 2n - 6$

Q18: If a, b, c are odd positive integers, then number of integral solutions of a + b + c = 13, is
    A. 14
    B. 21
    C. 28
    D. 56

Q19: The function given by : $x^m y^n = (x + y)^{m+n}$ is:
    A. strictly increasing
    B. strictly decreasing
    C. constant
    D. neither increasing nor decreasing

Q20: The differential equation of all non vertical lines in a plane is:

    A. $\dfrac{d^2y}{dx^2} = 0$ B. $\dfrac{dy}{dx} = 0$

    C. $\dfrac{dx}{dy} = 0$ D. $\dfrac{dy}{dx} + x = 0$

Q21:Which of the following film was directed by Satyajit Ray.
A. Bhumika   B.   Shatranj ke khiladi
C. Nishant   D.   Ardhyasatya

Q22:How many surface does this model has?

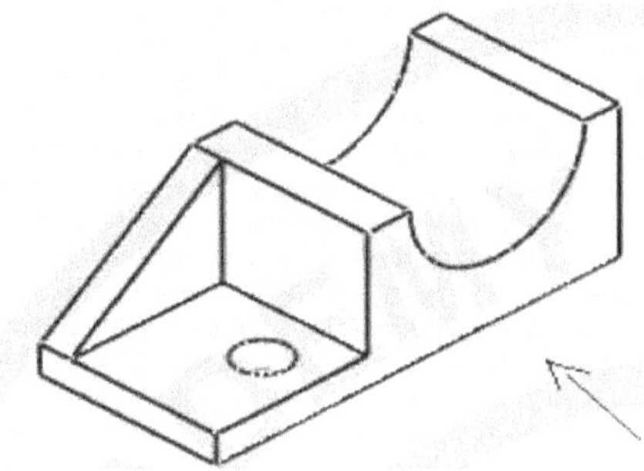

A. 12
B. 13
C. 11
D. 14

Q23:`A' starts his walk in north and turns left, similarly `B' starts his walk from the same point in east direction and then turns right, goes straight and then turns left. A & B faces are
A. In same direction
B. In opposite direction
C. Perpendicular to each other
D. None of above

Q24:Shown below are reflected images of a wall clock in mirror. Which one of the options shows 21:16 correctly.

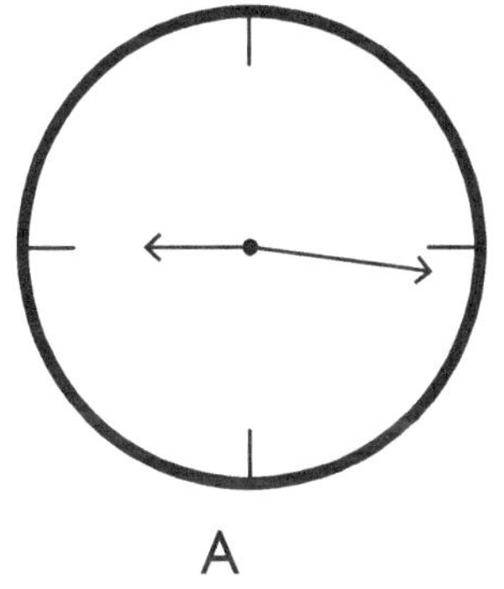

A

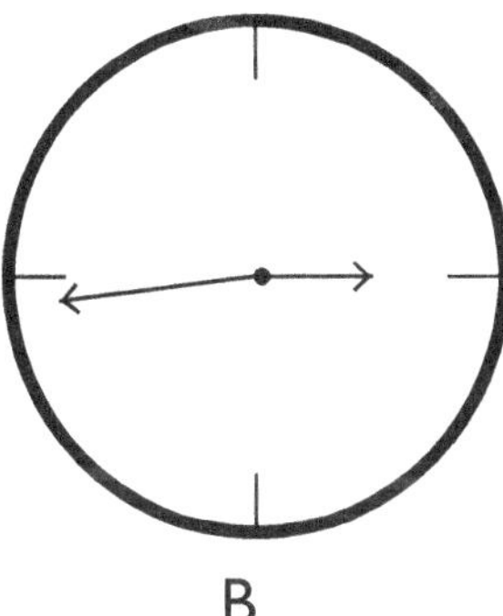

B

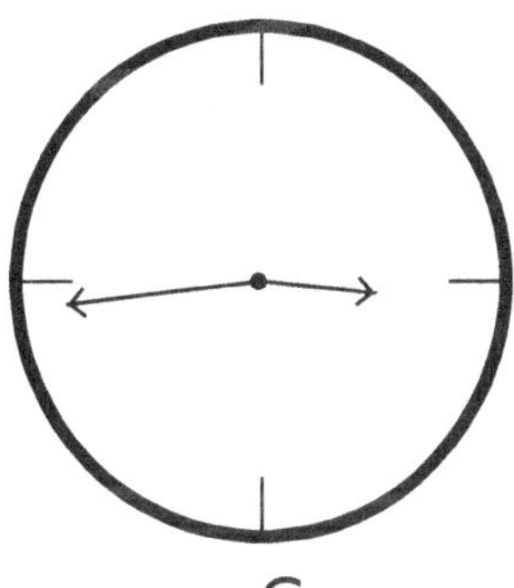

C

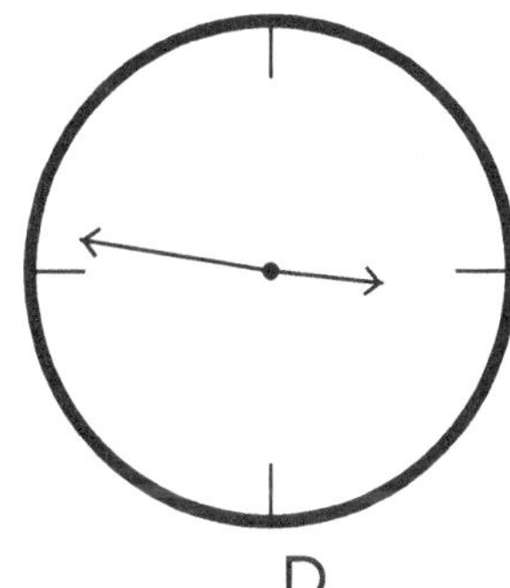

D

Q25:How many edges does a Tetrahedron has

    A. 4

    B. 8

    C. 3

    D. 6

Q26: Total number of circles in the given figure are

    A. 10

    B. 8

    C. 7

    D. 9

Q27:If a tank of the shape showed on the left contains 30 units of liquid , how much units would the shape on right approximately contain.

    A. 20

    B. 60

    C. 180

    D. 540

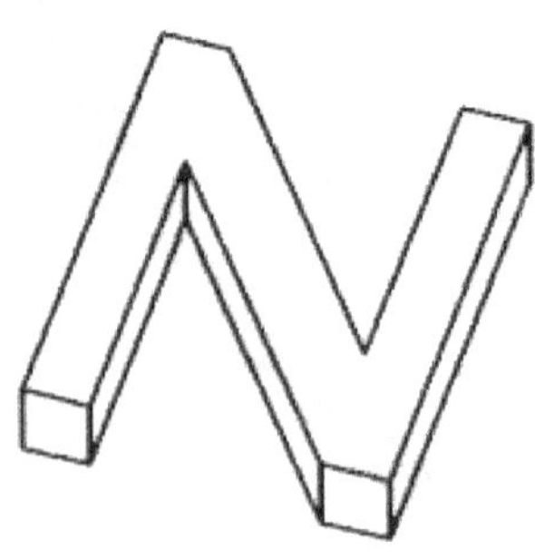

Q28:Ellora Temples in Maharashtra are executed,

    A. Left to Right   B.   Top to Bottom

    C. Bottom to Top   D.   None of above

Q29:A regular hexagonal pyramid is sliced by a plane such that it passes through the centre of its axis . How many additional edges shall be created.
- A. 12
- B. 11
- C. 9
- D. 24

Q30:Find the number of triangles in the given figure.
- A. 8
- B. 10
- C. 12
- D. 14

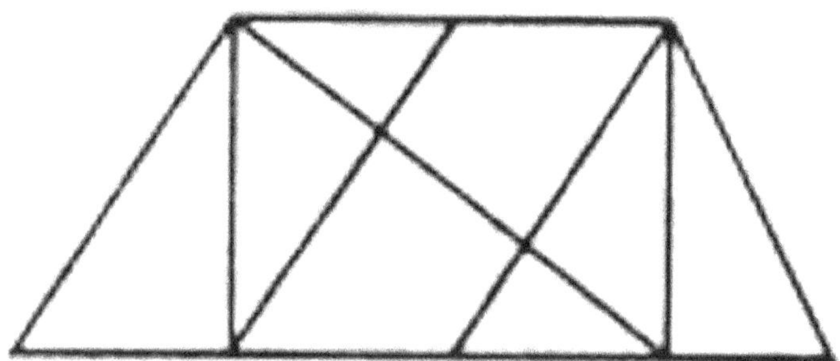

Q31:Find the minimum number of straight lines required to make the given figure.

- A. 13
- B. 15
- C. 17
- D. 19

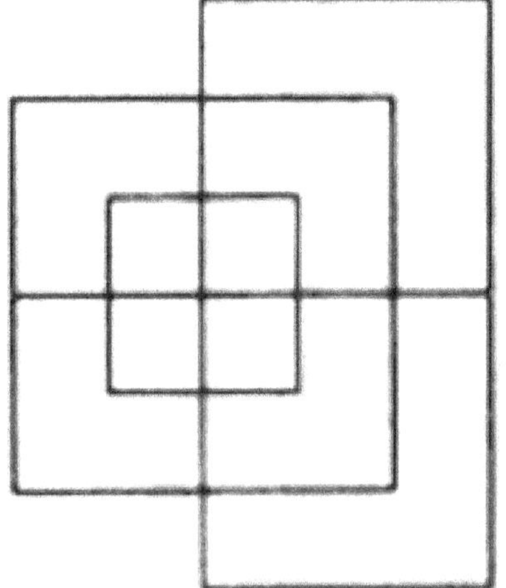

Q32:In a certain code language **COMPUTER** is written as **RFUVQNPC**. How will **MEDICINE** be written in that code language?
- A. MFEDJJOE
- B. EOJDEJFM
- C. MFEJDJOE
- D. EOJDJEFM

Q33: Which of the given options represents the front view of the given 3-D figure of a house?

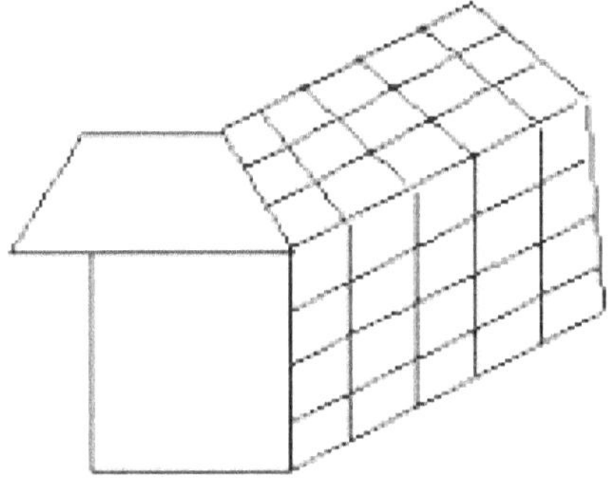

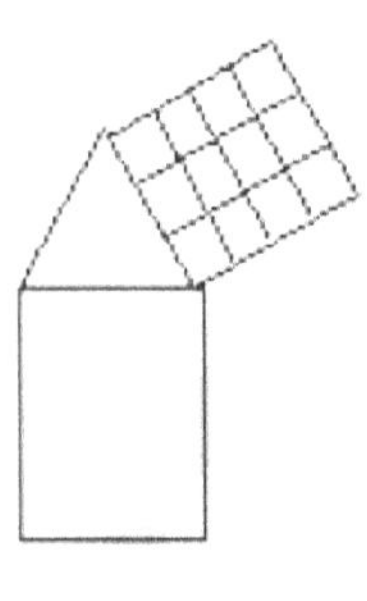

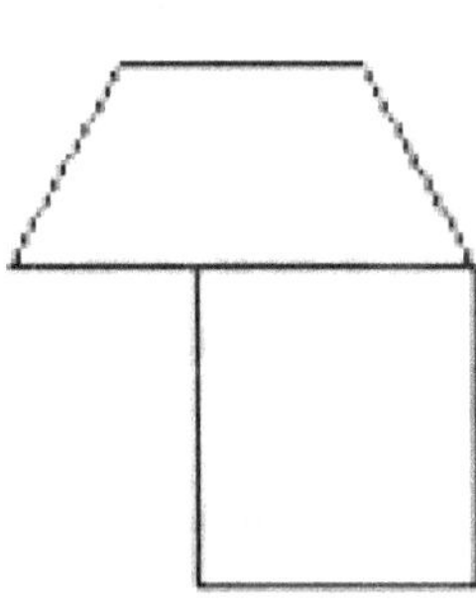

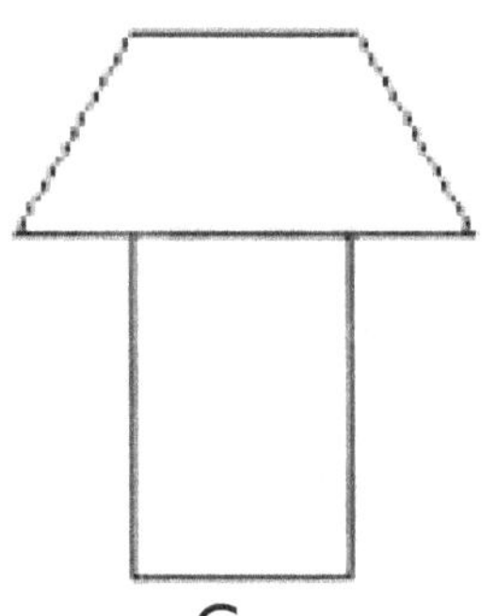

A.	B.	C.	D. None of these

Q34: Which city is known as PINK CITY
 A. Delhi
 B. Jaipur
 C. Udaipur
 D. Jodhpur

Q35: Which of the following does not form a part of Reinforced Cement Concrete?
 A. Steel
 B. Cement
 C. Sand
 D. Lime

Q36: If South-East becomes North, North-East becomes West and so on. What will West become?
 A. North-East
 B. North-West
 C. South-East
 D. South-West

Q37: One morning after sunrise, **Suresh** was standing facing a pole. The shadow of the pole fell exactly to his right. To which direction was he facing?
- A. East
- B. West
- C. South
- D. Data is insufficient

Q38: From the options provided, choose the 3-Dimensional drawing that best fits the side view shown:

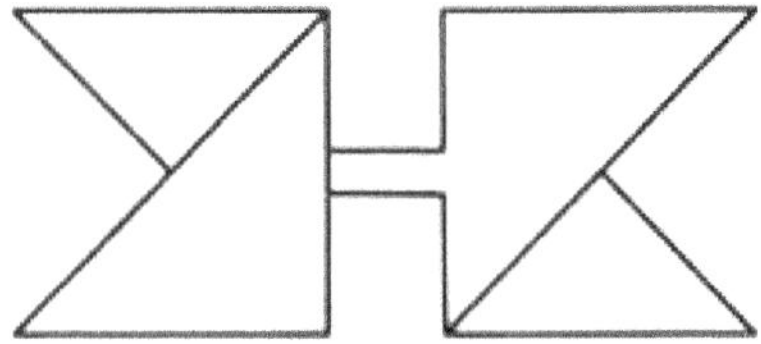

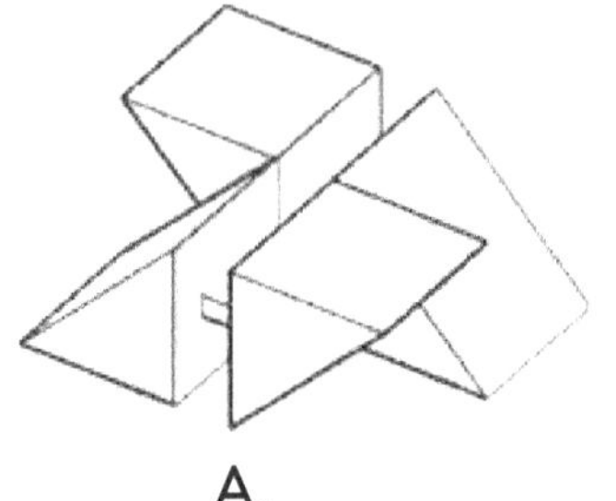
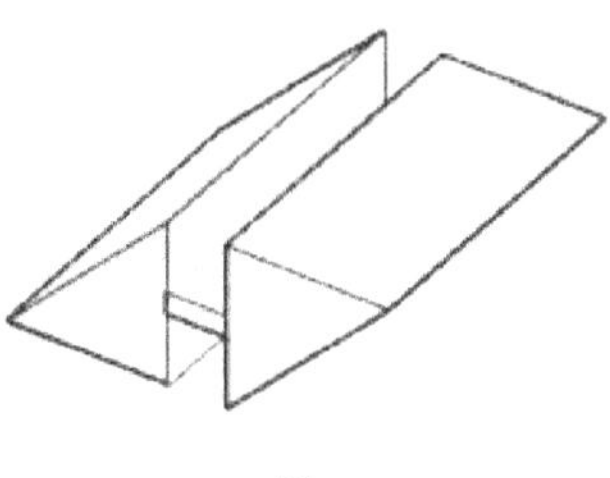
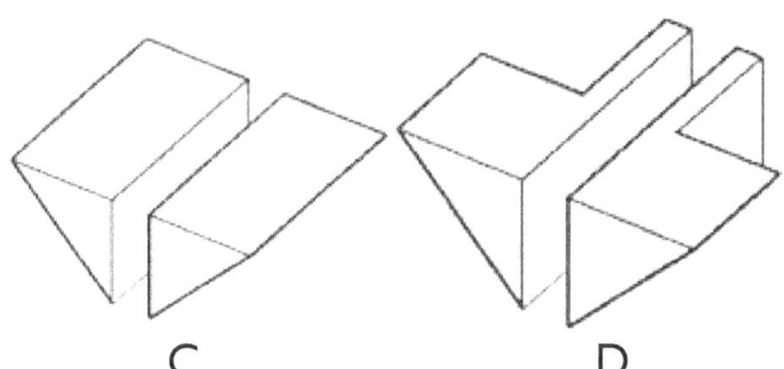

A.   B.   C.   D.

Q39: Which one is a truncated cone?

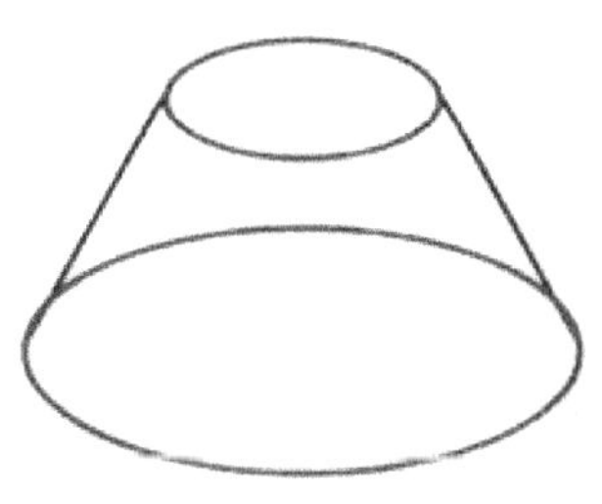
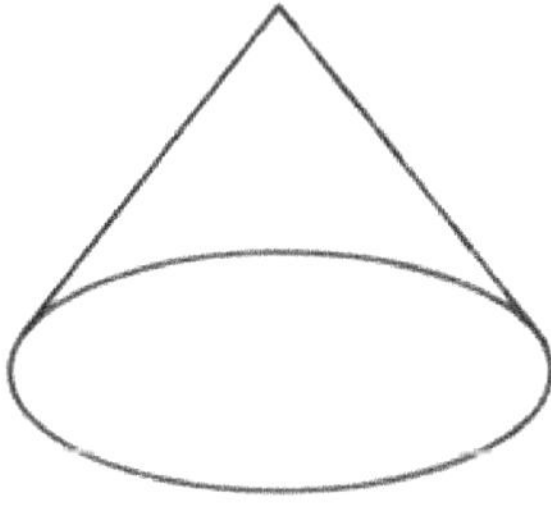
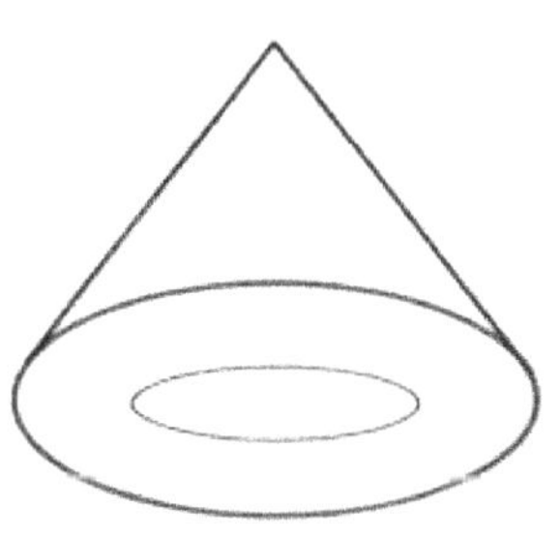
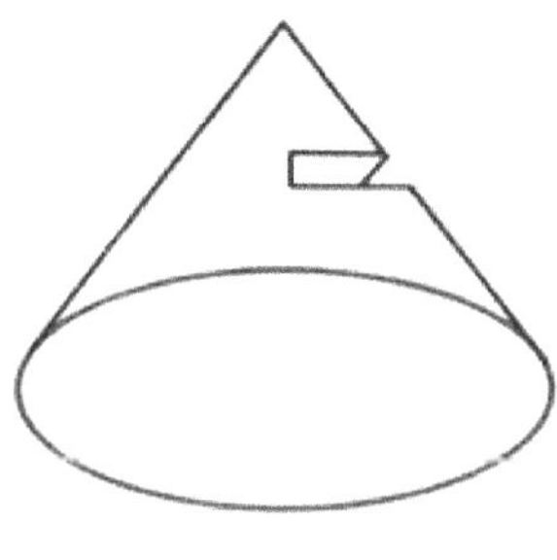

A.   B.   C.   D.

Q40: How many faces and edges does an octahedron have?
- A. 6 faces, 12 edges
- B. 12 faces, 8 edges
- C. 8 faces, 16 edges
- D. 8 faces, 12 edges

Q41: On which river does Guwahati stand?
- A. Gomti
- B. Godavari
- C. Brahmaputra
- D. Beas

Q42: Which is the largest brackish water lake in Asia?
- A. Loktak Lake
- B. Dal Lake
- C. Mansarovar
- D. Chilkha Lake

Q43:Ar. B V Doshi was awarded the Pritzker Architecture Prize in the field of Architecture, in the year.

    A. 2018   B. 2017   C.   2016   D. 2015

Q44:Which architect designed the Assembly Hall and High Court buildings in Chandigarh?

    A. Ar.Achyut Kanvinde   B. Ar. Charles Correa
    C. Ar. Le Corbusier   D. Ar. Raj Rewal

Q45:Name the largest single religious building in the world.

    A. Konark Sun Temple   B. Brihadishwara Temple
    C. Angkor Wat   D. Vatican City

Q46:What is a vertical load bearing component of a building called?

    A. Beam   B. Column
    C. Lintel   D. Sill

Q47:Granite is a __________ rock.

    A. Igneous   B. Sedimentary
    C. Calcareous   D. Metamorphic

Q48:Identify the below (in picture) structure.

    A. Colosseum
    B. Pantheon
    C. Agora
    D. Forum

Q49:The development of lateral surfaces of a pentagonal pyramid is __________

    A. Five rectangles
    B. Five squares
    C. Five triangles
    D. Five circles

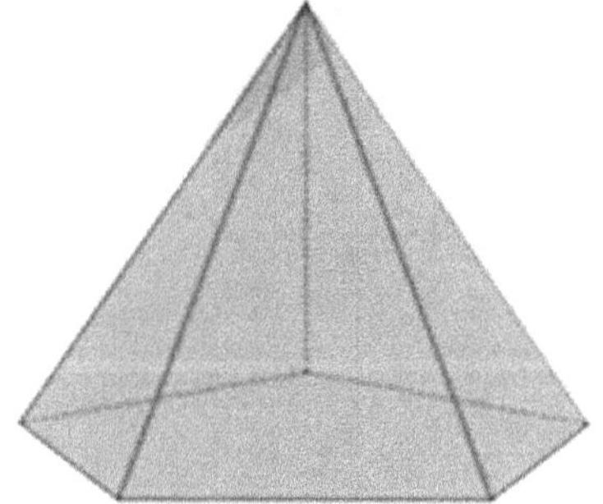

Q50: The figure shows a 3 dimensional view of an object.Identify the correct 2 dimensional top view from among the answers based on the direction of the arrow

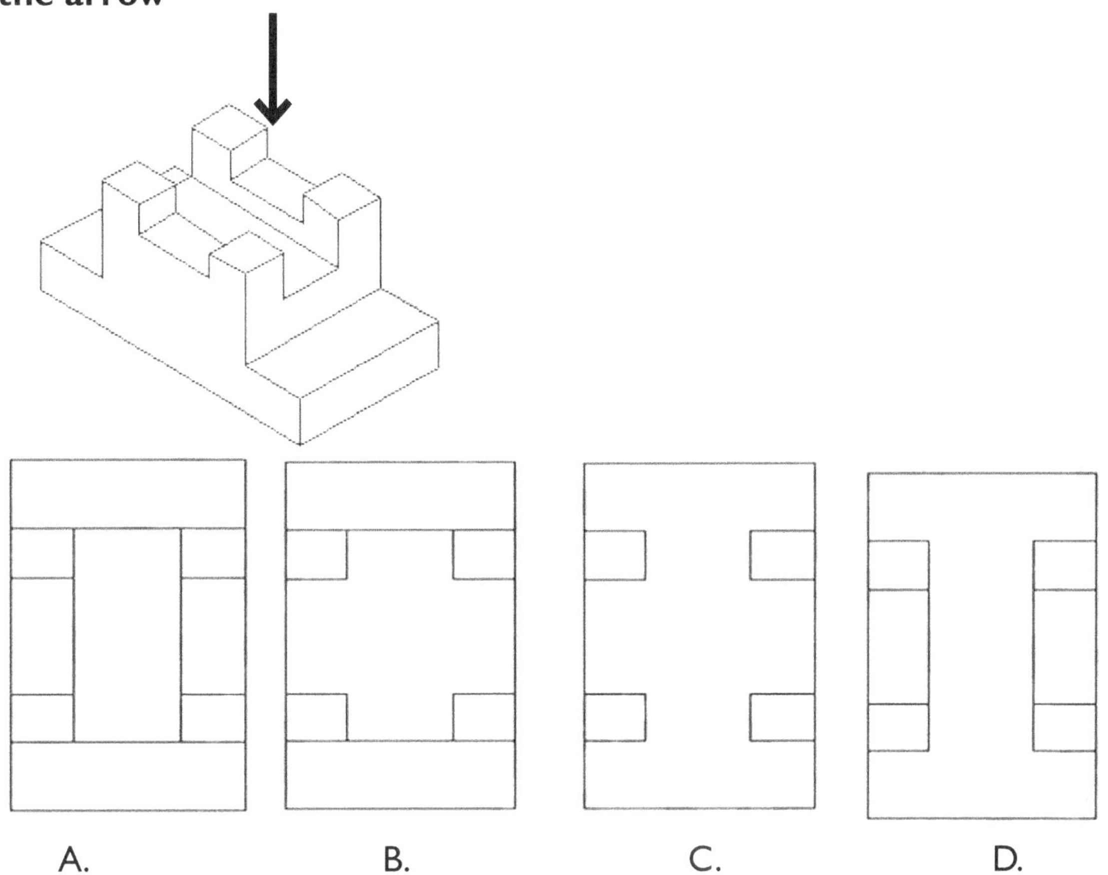

A.   B.   C.   D.

Q51: The figure shows a 3 dimensional view of an object.Identify the correct 2 dimensional side view from among the answers based on the direction of the arrow.

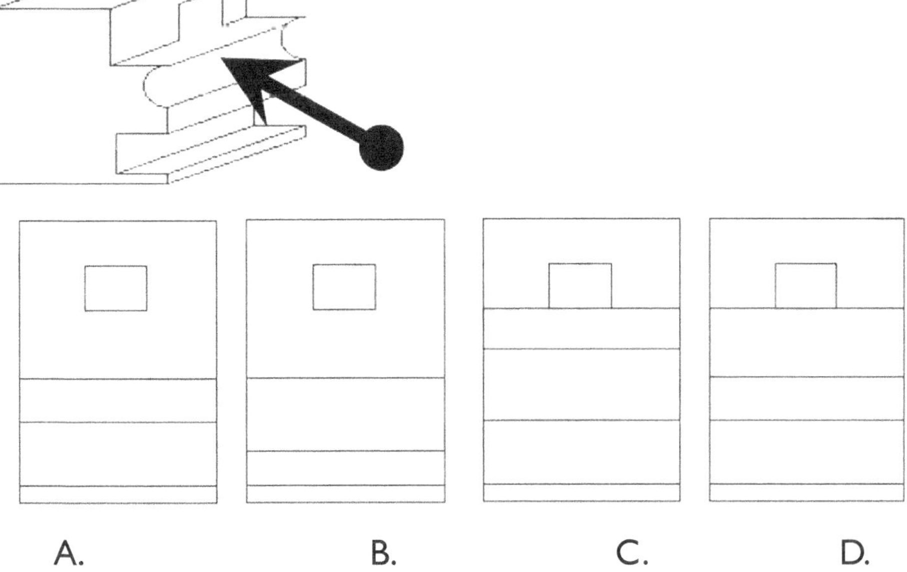

A.   B.   C.   D.

Q52:Identify the building in picture given below

- A. Lotus Temple, Delhi, India
- B. Sydney Opera house, Australia
- C. Guggenheim Museum, Bilbao, Spain
- D. St.Peter's Basilica, Vatican city

Q53:Sam ranked 9th from the top and 38th from the bottom in a class. How many students are there in the class?

- A. 45
- B. 47
- C. 46
- D. 48

Q54:Which unit does NOT belong to the same category?

- A. Inch
- B. Ounce
- C. Feet
- D. Yard

Q55:Identify the correct TOP view for the given 3D object.

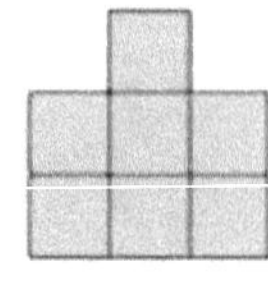

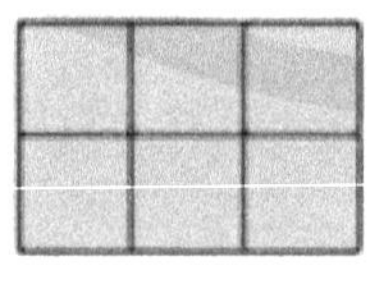

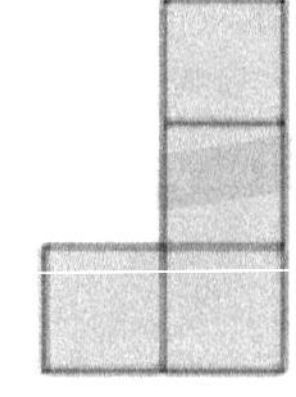

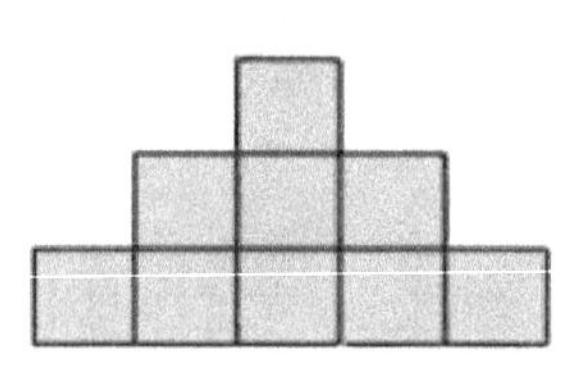

A.   B.   C.   D.

Q56: Vernacular refers to which of the following?
    A. Modern architecture
    B. Digital architecture
    C. Traditional architecture
    D. Contemporary architecture

Q57: Choose the alternative which resembles the water-image of the given combination.

NUCLEAR

(1) ᴚA∃ˌↃUᴎ   (2) ᴎ∩Ↄˌ∃Aᴚ
(3) ᴎ∩Ↄˌ∃Aᴚ   (4) ᴎ∩Ↄˌ∃Aᴚ

    A. 1
    B. 2
    C. 3
    D. 4

Q58: The type of roof suitable for the region where the rainfall is heaviest is
    A. Flat
    B. Pitched and Sloped
    C. Dome
    D. Vault

Q59: What time of the day is represented by the location of the Sun on the diagram?
    A. 6 AM
    B. 9 AM
    C. 12 PM
    D. 6 PM

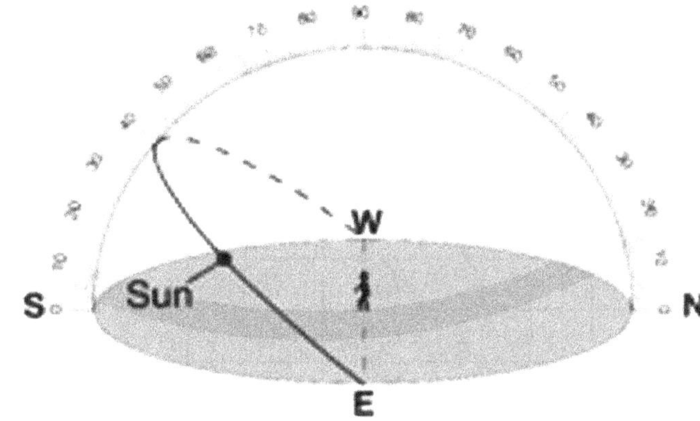

Q60:Identify the given structure.
  A. National War Memorial – Delhi
  B. National Soldier Memorial – Gwalior
  C. Indian Obilisk – Ahmedabad
  D. Amar Jyoti Memorial - Hyderabad

SECTION : DRAWING TEST

Q61:It is raining and you are looking out of a window from your living room. The window is a wooden panel window with horizontal grills. You can see a playground with play equipment. Some children are playing in the rain and some kids are playing with paper boats in puddles. Beyond the playground there is a tea shop and a hospital. Draw the view using your imagination.

Q62:Draw a composition with five geometric shapes such as circle, triangle, square, rectangle and hexagon. Each of the shapes is to be used at least once. The composition is to be coloured using a medium of your choice.

NATA 2019 ANSWERS									
MATHEMATICS									
1	2	3	4	5	6	7	8	9	10
C	A	B	D	C	D	B	B	B	B
11	12	13	14	15	16	17	18	19	20
C	B	B	D	A	D	B	B	A	A
APTITUDE TEST									
21	22	23	24	25	26	27	28	29	30
B	B	B	C	D	D	B	B	A	D
31	32	33	34	35	36	37	38	39	40
A	D	B	B	D	C	C	A	A	D
41	42	43	44	45	46	47	48	49	50
C	D	A	C	C	B	A	A	C	A
51	52	53	54	55	56	57	58	59	60
D	A	C	B	B	C	D	B	B	A

JEE (B.ARCH.) 2019 QUESTION PAPER (Day Shift)

Q-1 If the two lines $= \dfrac{x-2m}{2m+5} = \dfrac{y}{8m} = \dfrac{z-4}{2}$ and $\dfrac{x-2m}{m-2} = \dfrac{y}{-1} = \dfrac{z-2m}{1-3m}$ are parallel for some $m \in \mathbf{R}$, then the distance between them is:

1. $\sqrt{34}$
2. $\sqrt{10}$
3. $2\sqrt{5}$
4. $\sqrt{29}$

Q-2 $\displaystyle \lim_{x \to 3} \dfrac{\sqrt{x+6} - \sin(x-3) - 3}{(x-3)\cos(x-3)}$ is equal to

1. $-\dfrac{2}{3}$ 2. $\dfrac{5}{6}$

3. $\dfrac{1}{6}$ 4. $-\dfrac{5}{6}$

Q-3 If $6\cos^2\theta - 2\cos 2\theta - 3 = 0$, then $\tan^2 3\theta$ is equal to:

1. $\dfrac{1}{3}$ 2. $\dfrac{9}{2}$

3. 1 4. -3

Q-4 Let $f : \mathbf{R} - \{0\} \to \mathbf{R}$ be defined by $f(x) = a\log_e |x| + bx^3 + x^2$
If $x = -1$ and $x = 1$ are the critical points of $f\{x\}$ then :
    1. $f''(1) - f''(-1) = 4$
    2. both $x = 1$ and $x = -1$ are focal minima of $f(x)$
    3. $f''(1) - f''(-1) = 0$
    4. $x = 1$ is a local minima and $x = -1$ is
    a local maxima of $f(x)$

Q-5 If r is the remainder obtained on dividing $(98)^5$ by 12, then the coefficient of x^3 in the binomial expression of $\left(1+\dfrac{x}{2r}\right)^{2r}$ is given by

1. 102   2. $\dfrac{55}{2}$

3. 70   4. $\dfrac{91}{2}$

Q-6 The expression $\sim(p\leftrightarrow q)$ is equivalent to
1. $p \wedge \sim q$
2. $(\sim p \wedge q) \vee (\sim q \wedge p)$
3. $p \vee q$
4. $(p \wedge \sim q) \wedge (q \wedge \sim p)$

Q- 7 The value of $\displaystyle\int_{-3}^{3} \dfrac{5x^4 1}{1+e^{-x}}\, dx$ is:

1. $\dfrac{3^5}{5}$ 2. $2(3^5)$

3. 3^4 4. 3^5

Q-8 Let **P** be the point on the parabola $y^2 = 3x$ such that **OP** makes an angle of $\dfrac{\pi}{6}$ with the x-axis, where **O** is the origin. A normal is drawn to the parabola at **P** intersecting the axis of the parabola at **Q**. If S is the focus of the parabola, then **SQ** is equal to :

1. 9   2. $\dfrac{39}{4}$

3. $\dfrac{41}{4}$ 4. $\dfrac{39}{2}$

Q-9 If for two events **A** and **B**, in a random experiment, P(A | B)= $\dfrac{4}{5}$ and

P(B| A)= $\dfrac{1}{4}$, then P (A | A $\cup$ B) is equal to :

1. $\dfrac{5}{17}$ 2. $\dfrac{11}{16}$

3. $\dfrac{16}{17}$ 4. $\dfrac{5}{16}$

**Q-10 Let A be the set of all 3 digit natural numbers and
B= {x ∈ A: H.C.F. (x, 15) =1}. Then the number of elements in B is :**
    1. 240
    2. 360
    3. 480
    4. 420

Q-11 Let f: [0, 5] $\rightarrow$ **R be a continuous function such that |f(x)|** $\leq$ **3 for**

all x $\in$ [0, 5] and $\displaystyle\int_0^5 f(t)dt = 3$. Then the value of $\displaystyle\int_0^3 f(t)dt$ can be:

    1. 10
    2. – 4
    3. 12
    4. 6

**Q-12 Let R be a relation defined on Z x Z by (a, b) R (c, d) $\Leftrightarrow$ a – d = b – c,
where Z is the set of all integers, then R is :**
    1. transitive but neither reflexive nor symmetric.
    2. symmetric and transitive but not reflexive.
    3. symmetric but neither reflexive nor transitive.
    4. reflexive but n either symmetric nor transitive.

Q-13 If a, b and c (all distinct) are the sides of a triangle **A BC** opposite to the angles **A, B** and **C**, respectively, then $\dfrac{c\,\sin(A-B)}{a^2-b^2} - \dfrac{b\,\sin(C-A)}{c^2-a^2}$ is equal to :

    1. 0

    2. 2

    3. -1

    4. 1

Q-14 The set of all real values of α for which
the equation, $|x + 2| \cdot |x - 2| = \alpha^2 - 2\alpha$. has real solutions for x, is :

$$1.\ [1-\sqrt{5}],0]\cup[2,1+\sqrt{5}]$$
$$2.\ (-\infty,0]\cup[2,1+\sqrt{5}]$$
$$3.\ (-\infty,0]\cup[2,+\infty)$$
$$4.\ [-1-\sqrt{5},1-\sqrt{5}]\cup[1+\sqrt{5},\infty]$$

Q-15 The area (in sq. units) above the x-axis bounded by the parabola, $x^2 - y^2 - 1 = 0$ and the line $x - y = 0$ is :

    1. $\dfrac{8}{13}$ 2. $\dfrac{13}{3}$

    3. $\dfrac{10}{3}$ 4. $\ 4$

Q-16 Let $z\,(\neq -1)$ be any complex number such that $|z| = 1$. Then the imaginary part of $\dfrac{\bar{z}(1-z)}{z(1+\bar{z})}$ is : (Here $\theta = \arg z$)

    1. $-\tan\left(\dfrac{\theta}{2}\right)\cos\theta$ 2. $\tan\left(\dfrac{\theta}{2}\right)\cos\theta$

    3. $\tan\left(\dfrac{\theta}{2}\right)\sin\theta$ 4. $-\tan\left(\dfrac{\theta}{2}\right)\sin\theta$

Q – 17 If three vectors $\vec{V_1} = \alpha\hat{i} + \hat{j} + \hat{k}$, $\vec{V_2} = \hat{i} + \beta\hat{j} - 2\hat{k}$, and $\vec{V_3} = \hat{i} + \hat{j}$ are coplanar, and $\vec{V_1}$ and $\vec{V_3}$ are perpendicular, then the vector $\vec{V_1}$ x $\vec{V_2}$ is:

1. $-\hat{i} + \hat{j}$
2. $\hat{i} - \hat{j} + 2\hat{k}$,
3. $2\hat{i} - 2\hat{j} + \hat{k}$,
4. $-\hat{i} + \hat{j} + 2\hat{k}$

Q- 18 Let the tangent drawn at any point $P(x, y)$ on a curve intersect the x and y axes at two clistinct points A and B respectively. If $AP : PB = 5 : 1$ and the curve passes through the point $(2, 2)$ then an equation of the curve is:

1. $x^5y=2^6$
2. $xy^5=2^6$
3. $x^4y=2^5$
4. $xy^4=2^5$

Q-19 Let y be an implicit function of x defined by

$$\begin{vmatrix} x+y & 2 & 1 \\ 1 & x+y & 2 \\ 1 & 2 & x+y \end{vmatrix} + 12y = 0$$

If $y(0) = 1$, then $\dfrac{dy}{dx}$ a $x = 0$ is:

1. $-\dfrac{4}{5}$
2. $\dfrac{5}{4}$
3. $\dfrac{1}{2}$
4. $-\dfrac{1}{2}$

Q- 20 Let A be a 2 x 2 matrix such that $A^2 + A + I = 0$, where $I = I_2$. Then

$|\text{adj } (I-A)^6|$ is equal to:

1. 3^4
2. 3^9
3. 3^3
4. 3^6

Q-21 Let the ellipse $x^2 + 16y^2 = 16$ be inscribed in a rectangle whose sides are parallel to the coordinate axes. If the rectangle is inscribed in another ellipse that passes through the point $(16, 0)$, then the equation of the outer ellipse is :

1. $x^2 + 232y^2 = 16^2$
2. $x^2 + 248y^2 = 16^2$
3. $x^2 + 240y^2 = 16^2$
4. $x^2 + 256y^2 = 16^2$

Q-22 The sum of the infinite series

$$1 + 2 + \frac{2}{3} + \frac{6}{3^2} + \frac{10}{3^3} + \frac{14}{3^4} + \ldots\ldots\ldots \text{ is.}$$

1. 6
2. 4
3. $\dfrac{9}{2}$
4. 5

Q-23 Let f be a continuous function defined by

$$f(x) = \begin{cases} \dfrac{a\sin 2x - b\cos x}{\dfrac{\pi}{2} - x}, & x > \dfrac{\pi}{2} \\[3ex] 4, & x = \dfrac{\pi}{2} \\[3ex] \dfrac{2b\cos x}{\dfrac{\pi}{2} - x}, & x < \dfrac{\pi}{2} \end{cases}$$

Then the value of a + b is :

1. 1
2. 1
3. 4
4. 5

Q-24 If x_1, x_2 ... , x_n be the observed data such that

$$\sum_{i=1}^{n} x_i - 2n = 180 \quad \text{and}$$

$$\sum_{i=1}^{n} x_i - 7n = 30, \text{ then the mean of the}$$

data $(x_1 - 3), (x_2 - 3), \ldots, (x_n - 3)$ is equal to:

1. 5
2. $\dfrac{16}{3}$
3. 8
4. $\dfrac{13}{3}$

Q-25 Let A(1, 3) and C(5, 1) be two opposite vertices of a rectangle. The other two vertices B(a, b) and D(c, d) lie on the line y = 2x + k for some k. Then the value of (a + b) (c + d) is :

1. 16
2. 8
3. 24
4. 32

Q-26 Let the planes x – 2y kz = 0 and x + 5y – z= 0 be perpendicular. Then the plane through the point (2, – 2, – 2) and perpendicular to the given planes also passes through the point:

1. $(-1, 0, -7)$
2. $(1, 0, 7)$
3. $(0, 5, 8)$
4. $(0, 5, -8)$

Q-27 $\displaystyle \int \frac{\sec x}{\sqrt{\sin x . \cos^5 x}} dx$ is equal to: (where **C** is a constant of integration)

1. $2(\tan x)^{\frac{1}{2}} + \dfrac{1}{5}(\tan x)^{\frac{5}{2}} + C$

2. $2(\tan x)^{\frac{1}{2}} + \dfrac{2}{5}(\tan x)^{\frac{5}{2}} + C$

3. $(\tan x)^{\frac{1}{2}} + \dfrac{2}{5}(\tan x)^{\frac{5}{2}} + C$

4. $2(\tan x)^{\frac{1}{2}} - \dfrac{2}{5}(\tan x)^{\frac{5}{2}} + C$

Q-28 If the system of linear equations

x + 4y – 3z =2

2x +7y – 4z= α

– x – 5y + 5z = β

has infinitely many solutions, then the ordered pair (α,β) cannot take the value:

1. (3, –3)
2. (2, – 4)
3. (4, –2)
4. (–3 ,3)

Q-29 In an increasing geometric series, the sum of the first and the sixth term is **66** and the product of the second and the fifth terms is **128**. Then the sum of the first 6 terms of this series is :

1. 128
2. 129
3. 126
4. 127

Q-30 Let the abscissae of two points **A** and **B** on a circle be the roots of $x^2 + 2x - 4 = 0$ and the ordinates of **A** and **B** be the roots of $y^2 + 4y - 16 = 0$. If **AB** is a diameter of this circle, then the radius of this circle is :

1. $2\sqrt{10}$ 2. 6

3. 5   4. $2\sqrt{6}$

SECTION - APTITUDE TEST

Q-1 The Lotus Temple is located in which one of the following city ?
1. Lucknow
2. Kanpur
3. New Delhi
4. Nagpur

Q-2 Zaha Hadid was born in which country amongst the following ?
1. Iran
2. Iraq
3. Afghanistan
4. Turkistan

Q-3 An escalator moves in which of the following directions?
1. In steps
2. Only vertically
3. Vertically and Horizontally
4. Only horizontally

Q-4 Helical staircases are which one of the following?
1. Curving staircases
2. Dog leg staircases
3. Staircases with no railings
4. Straight flights

Q-5 Parquet flooring is usually made of which of the following ?
1. Wood
2. Cement
3. Granite
4. Marble

Q-6 The most famous temple in the Khajuraho group of temples is which one of the following?
1. Ganesh Temple
2. Kandariya Mahadev Temple
3. Krishna Temple
4. Shiva Temple

Q- 7 A small lift for carrying small loads only is known as which of the following ?
    1. A deaf bearer
    2. A jockey boy
    3. A dumb waiter
    4. A push upper

Q-8 Rooms with white painted walls appears to be which of the following ?
    1. Darker
    2. Smaller
    3. Narrower
    4. Larger

Q-9 The Sas Bahu Temple is located in which of the following ?
    1. Gwalior Fort
    2. Jaipur Fort
    3. Jhansi Fort
    4. Red Fort

Q-10 Which one of the following is a UNESCO World Heritage site?
    1. Bijapur
    2. Kochi
    3. Hampi
    4. Bijnor

Q-11 Which amongst the following is the city in Italy that is known for its leaning tower ?
    1. Rome
    2. Pisa
    3. Florence
    4. Venice

Q-12 Which one of the following is the tallest building in Bengaluru?
    1. World Trade Center
    2. Concord Tower
    3. Mantri Pinnacle
    4. UB Tower

Q-13 The fort in Hyderabad is known as which of the following ?
   1. Siladhari
   2. Golconda
   3. Virbanda
   4. Bahubali

Q-14 Hindustan and Parryware in the Indian market is known for which of the following product ?
   1. Wall tiles
   2. Pipes
   3. Sanitary ware
   4. Wooden tables

Q-15 Cement Plaster is used for which of the following?
   1. Covering walls
   2. Making roofs
   3. Making floors
   4. Making staircases

DIRECTIONS (Q-16 to Q-20) : One of the following answer figures is hidden in the problem figure in the same size and direction. Select the correct one.

Q-16

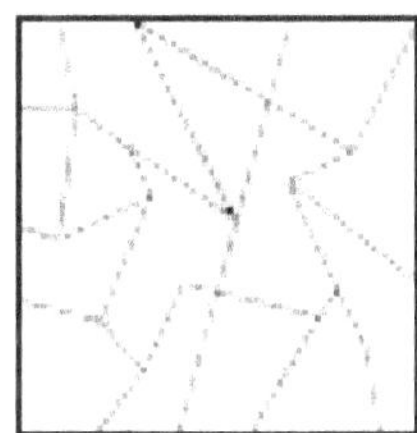

1.

3.

2.

4.

Q-17

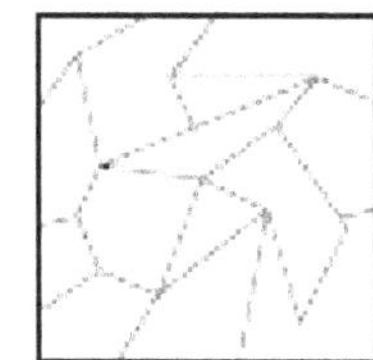

1.    3. 

2.    4.

Q-18

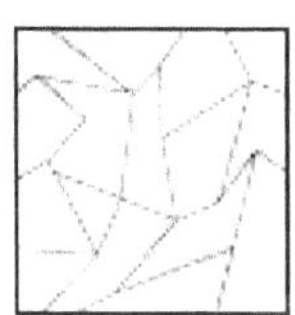

1.    3. 

2.    4. 

Q-19

1.    3. 

2.    4. 

Q-20 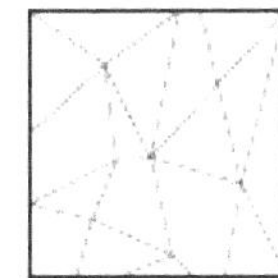

1.    3. 

2. 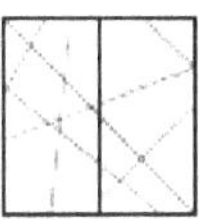   4. 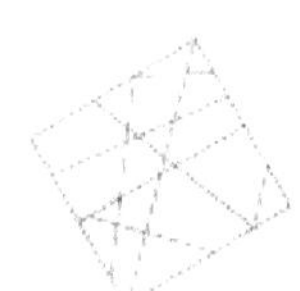

DIRECTIONS (Q-21 to Q-25) : Which one of the answer figure will complete the sequence of the three problem figures ?

Q-21 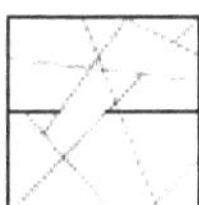 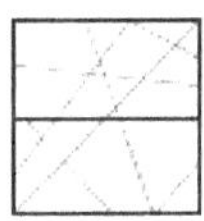 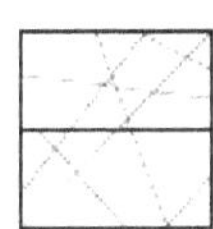 ?

1. 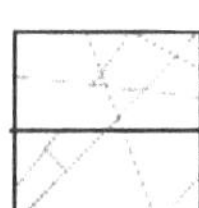   2.   3.   4.

Q-22   ?

1.    2.    3.    4.

Q-23 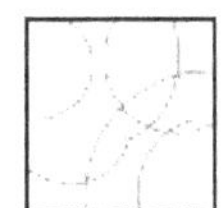 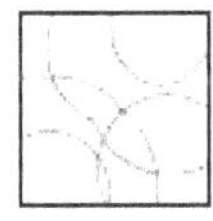 ?

1.    2.    3. 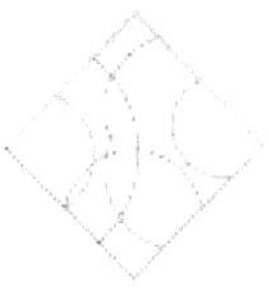   4. 

Q-24

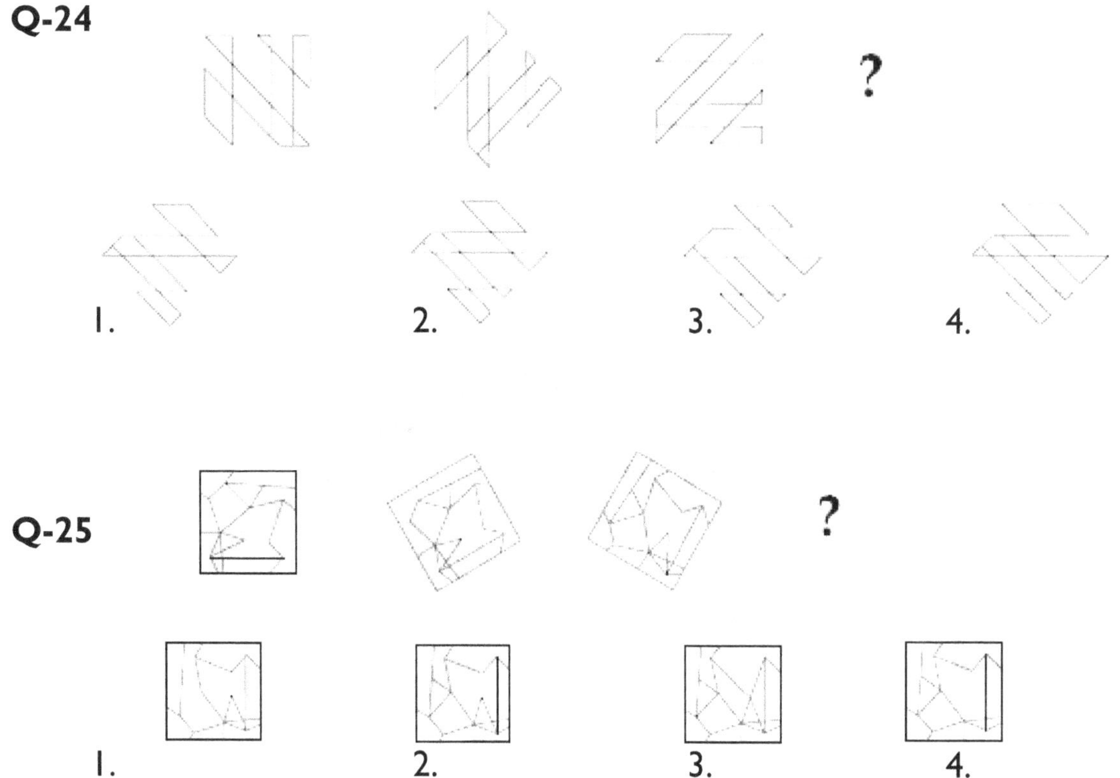

Q-25

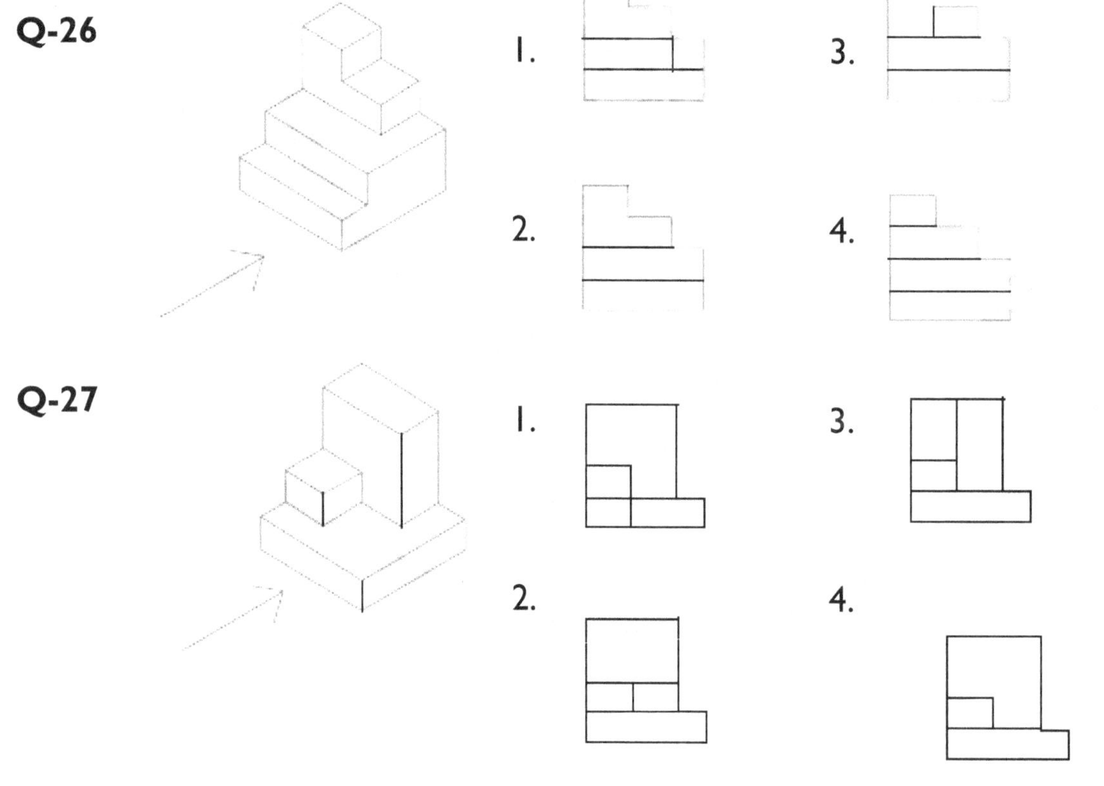

DIRECTIONS (Q-26 to Q-30) : The 3D figure shows the view of an object. Identify the correct front view looking in the direction of the arrow, from amongst the answer figures.

Q-26

Q-27

Q-28

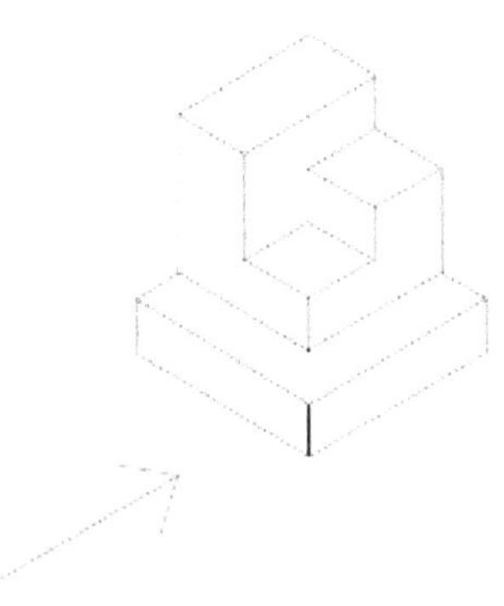

1. 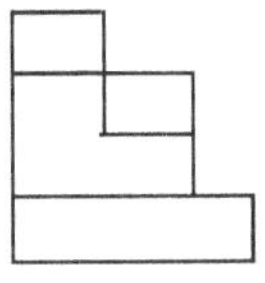

3. 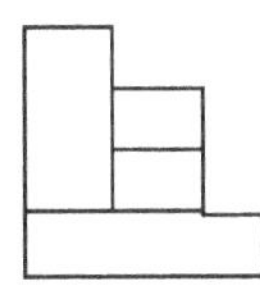

2. 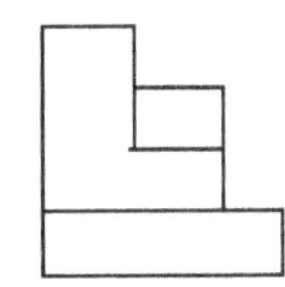

4. 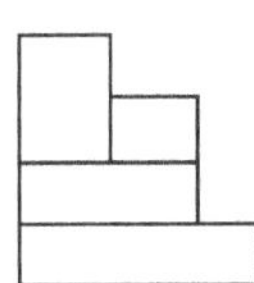

Q-29

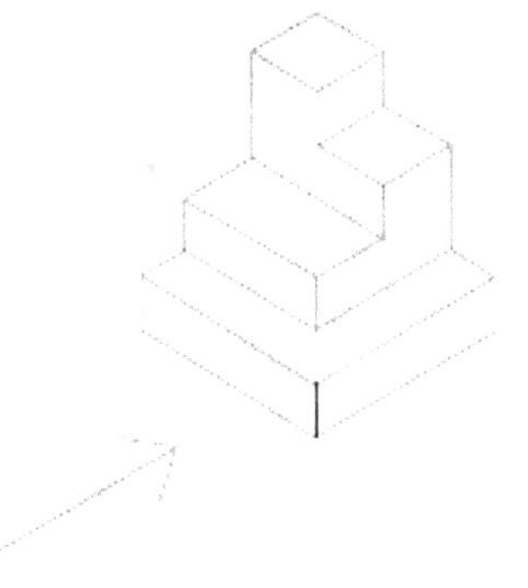

1. 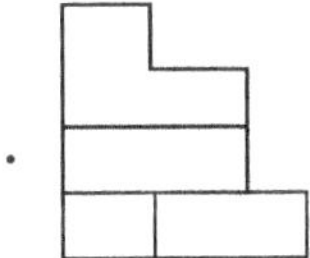

3. 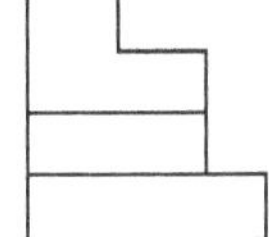

2. 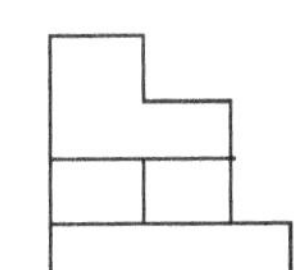

4. 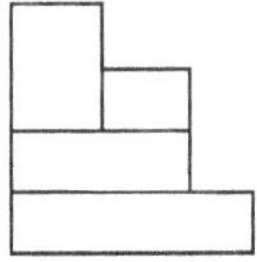

Q-30

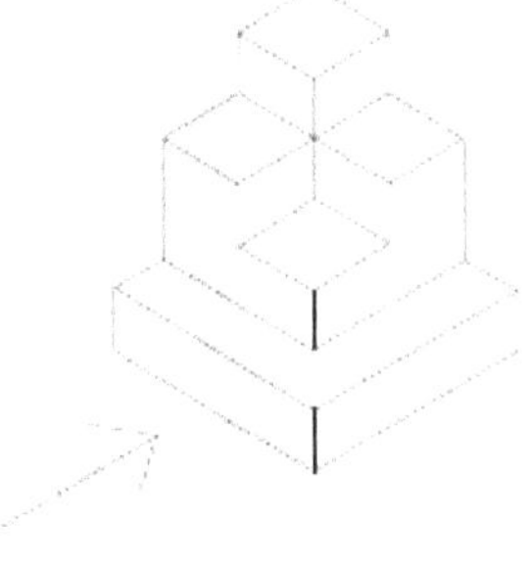

1. 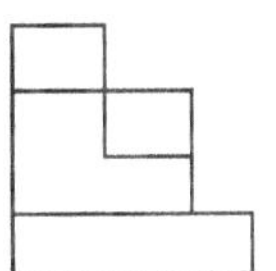

3. 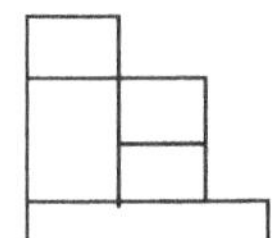

2. 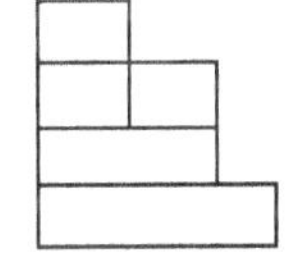

4. 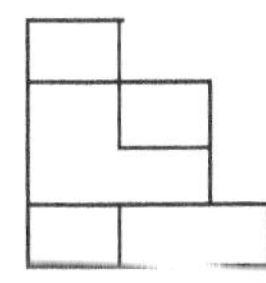

DIRECTIONS (Q-31 to Q-35) :Which one of the answer figures is the correct mirror image of the problem?

Q-31

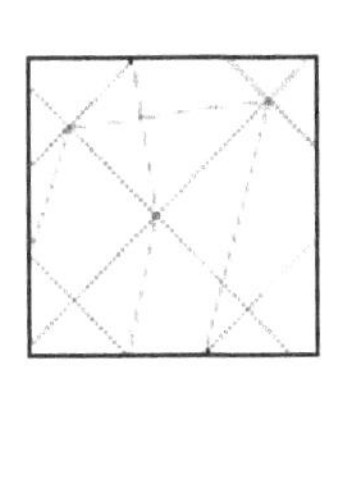

1. 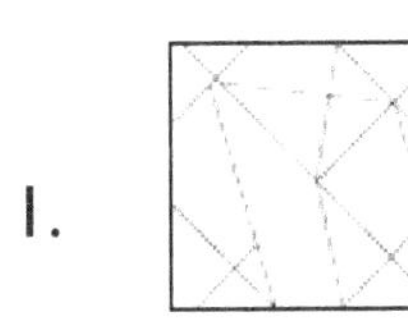

3. 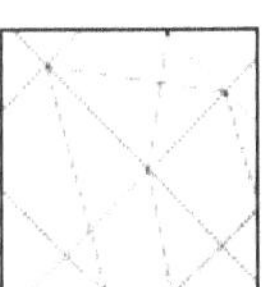

2. 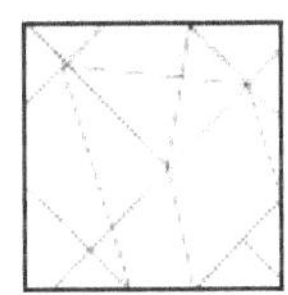

4. 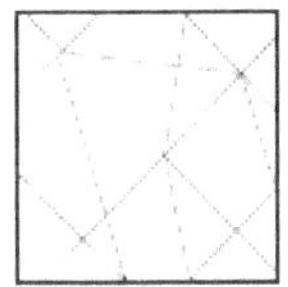

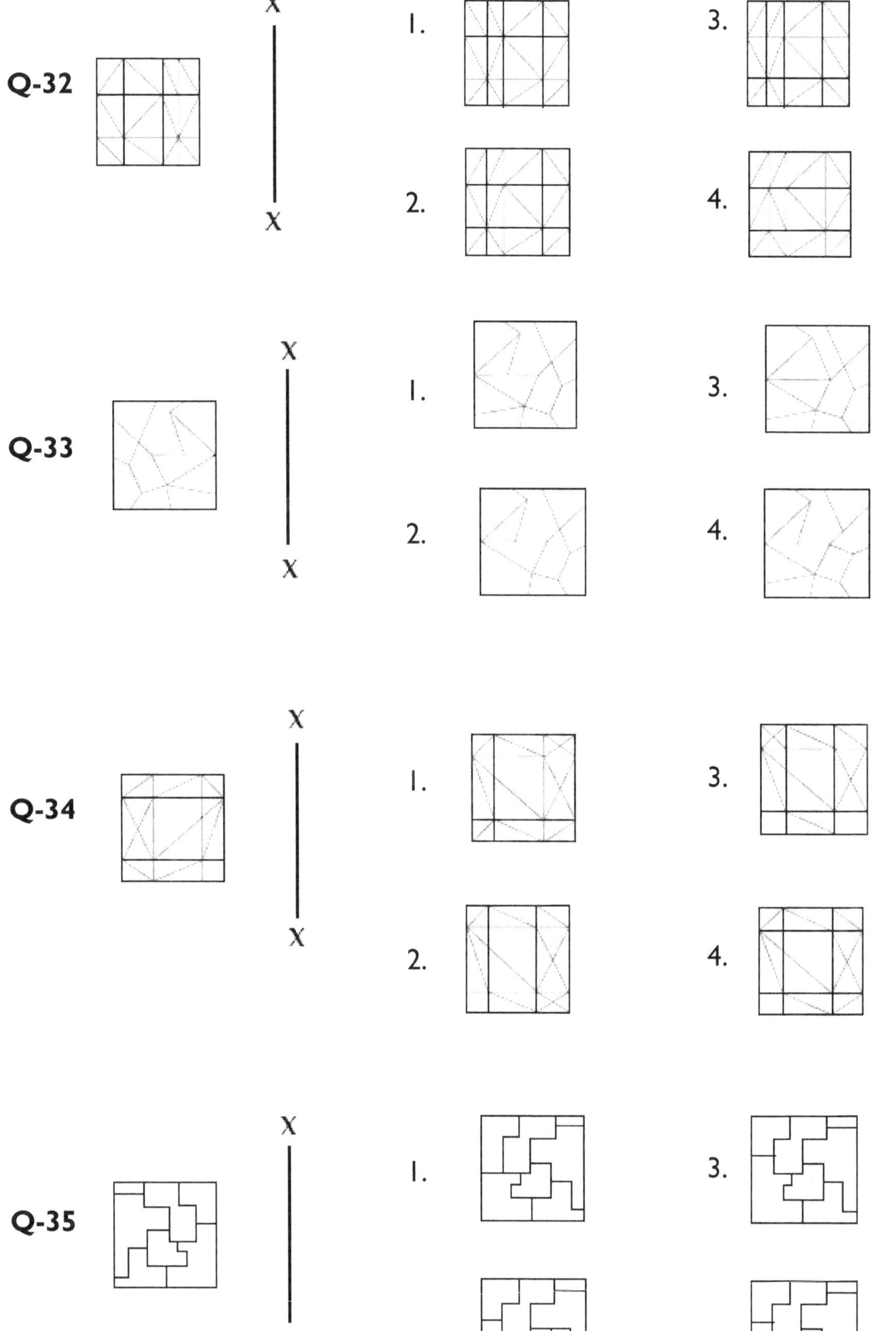

Q-32
X
X
1.
2.
3.
4.
Q-33
X
X
1.
2.
3.
4.
Q-34
X
X
1.
2.
3.
4.
Q-35
X
X
1.
2.
3.
4.

DIRECTIONS (Q-36 to Q-40) : The problem figure shows the top view of an object. Identify the correct elevation from amongst the answer figures looking in the direction of the arrow.

Q-36

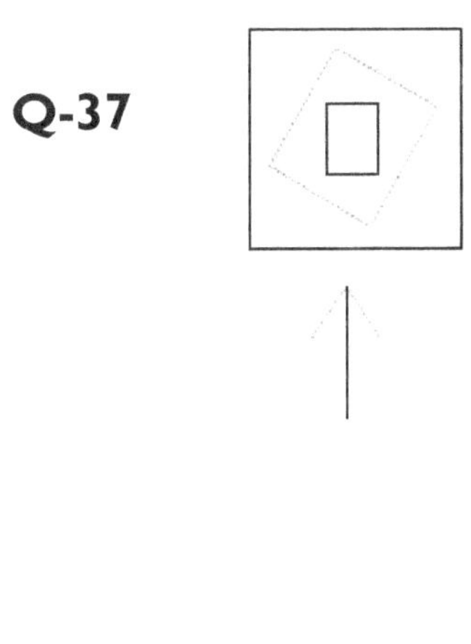

1. 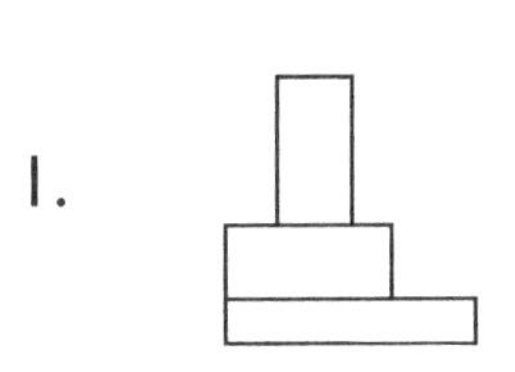   3. 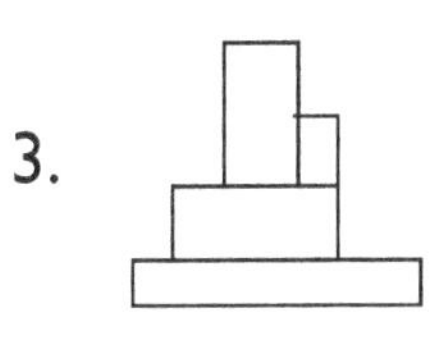

2.   4. 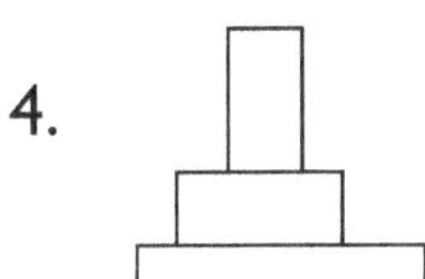

Q-37

1. 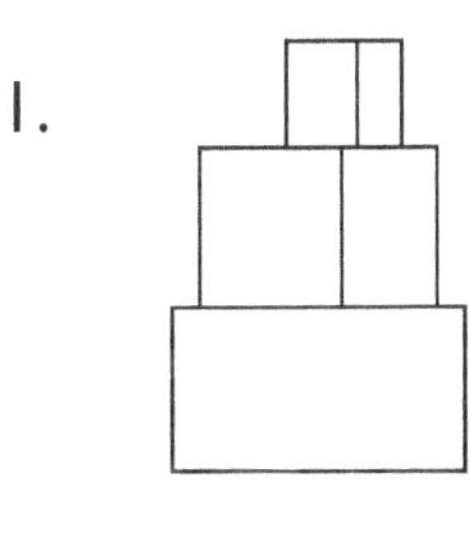   3. 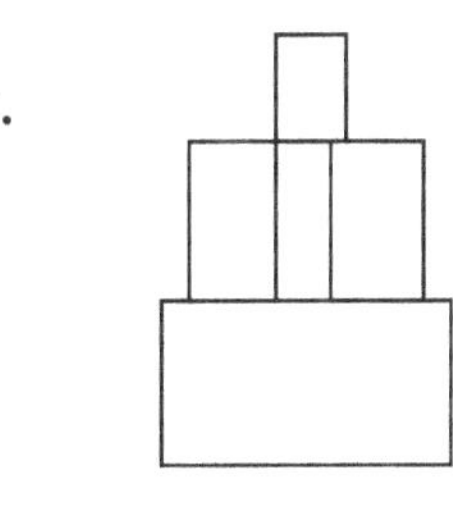

2. 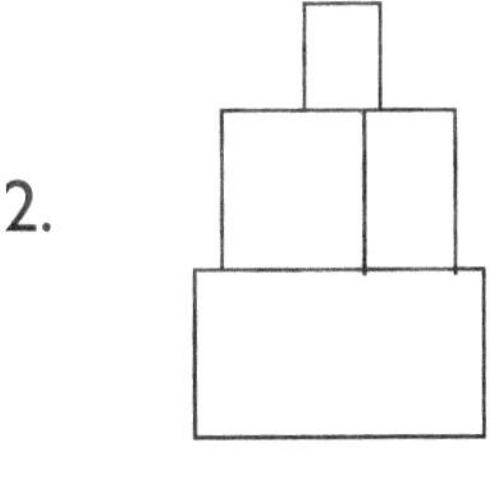   4. 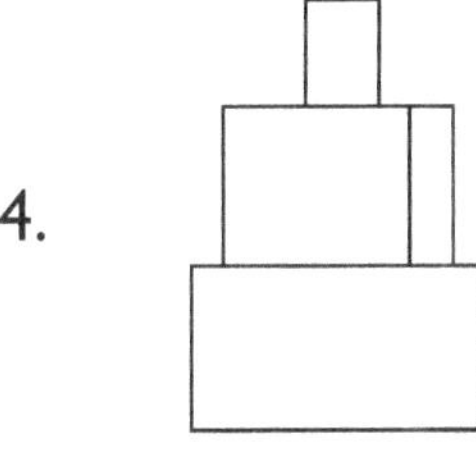

Q-38

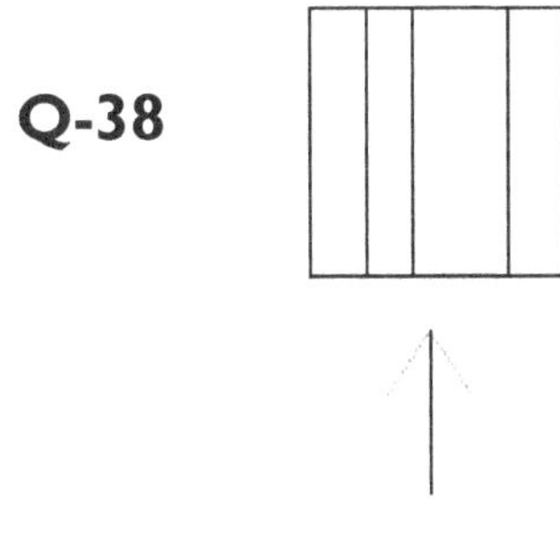

1.    3. 

2.   4. 

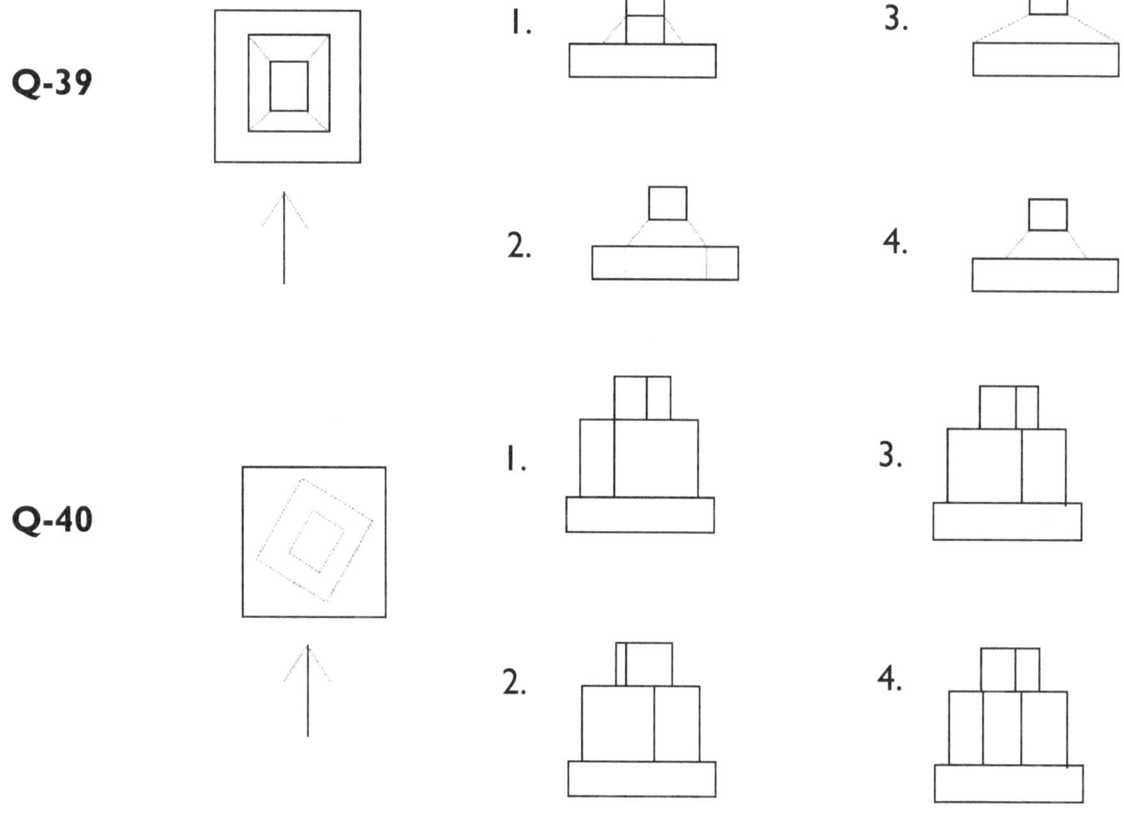

Q-39

Q-40

DIRECTIONS (Q-41 to Q-45) : The 3D figure shows the view of an object. Identify the correct top view from amongst the answer figures.

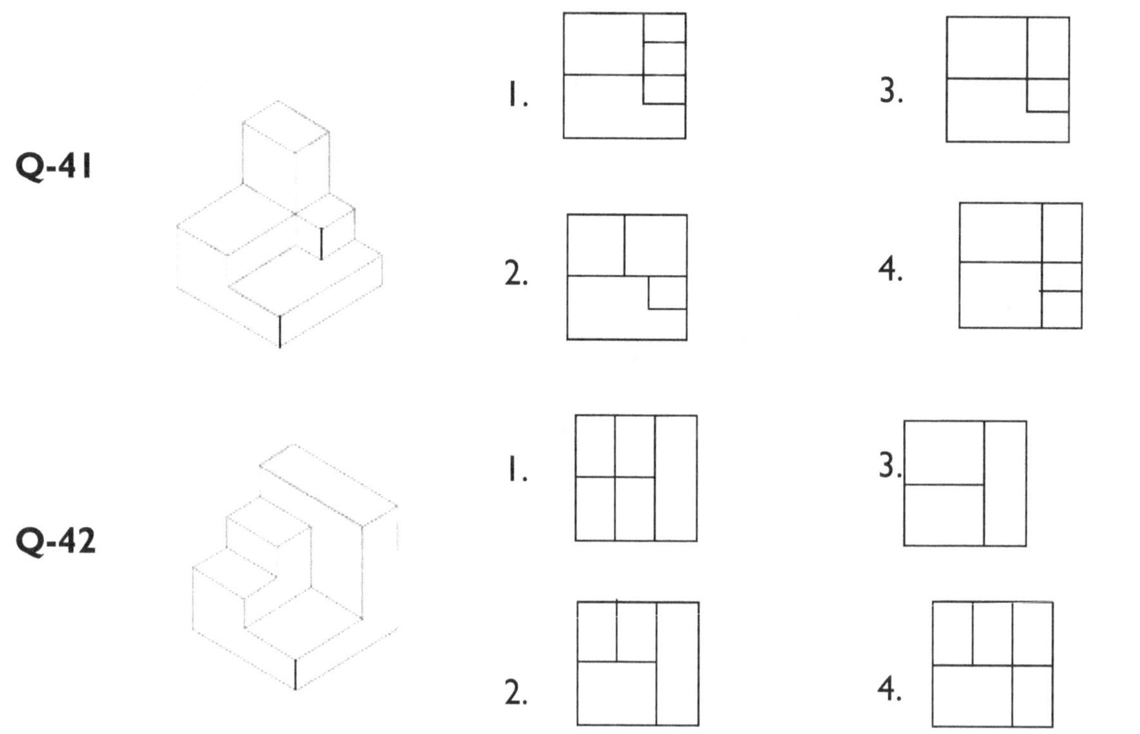

Q-41

Q-42

Q-43

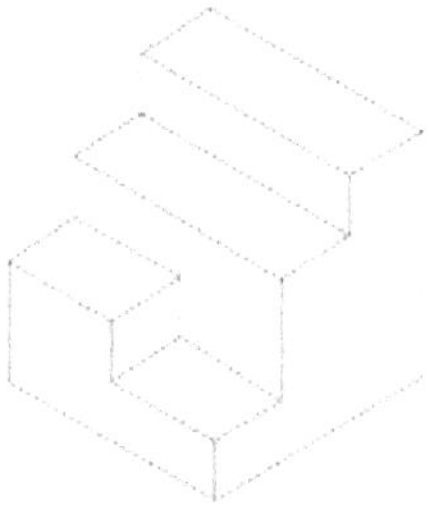

1.

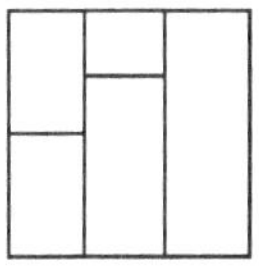

3.

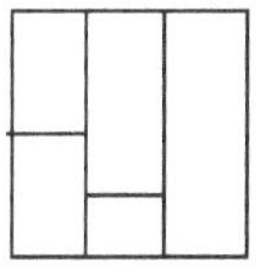

2.

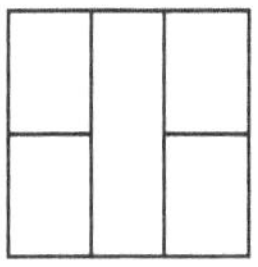

4.

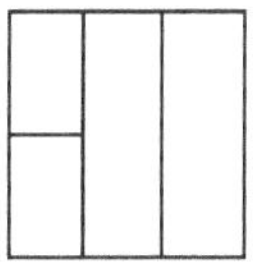

Q-44

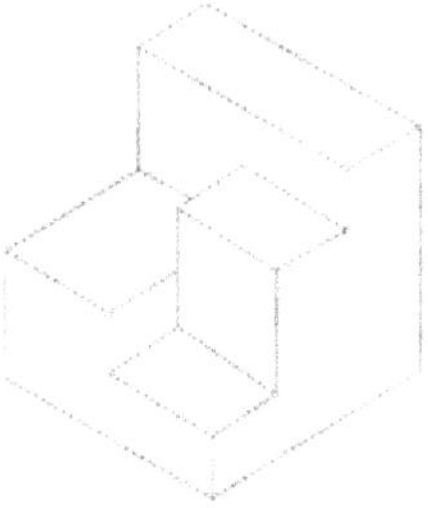

1.

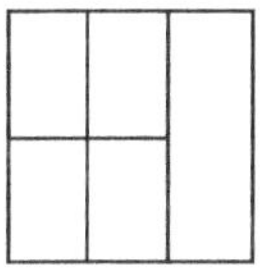

3.

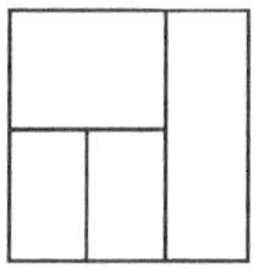

2.

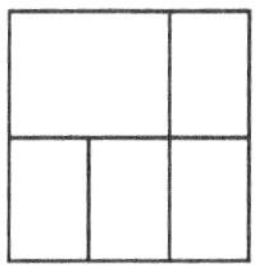

4.

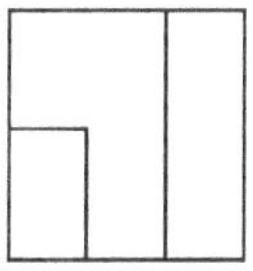

Q-45

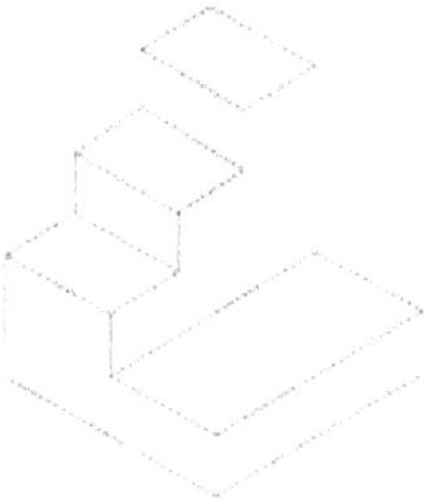

1.

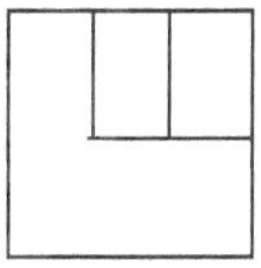

3.

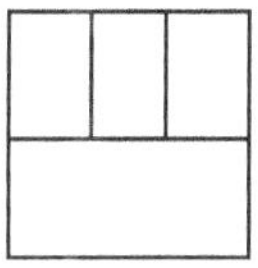

2.

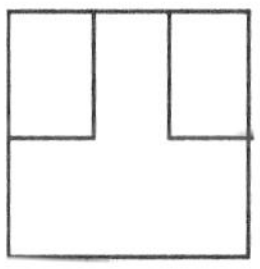

4.

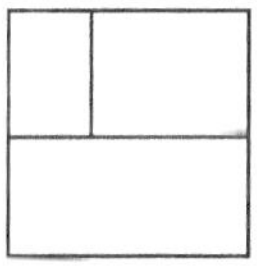

DIRECTIONS (Q-46 to Q-50) : The 3D figure shows the view of an object. Identify the correct side view looking in the direction of the arrow, from amongst the answer figures.

Q-46

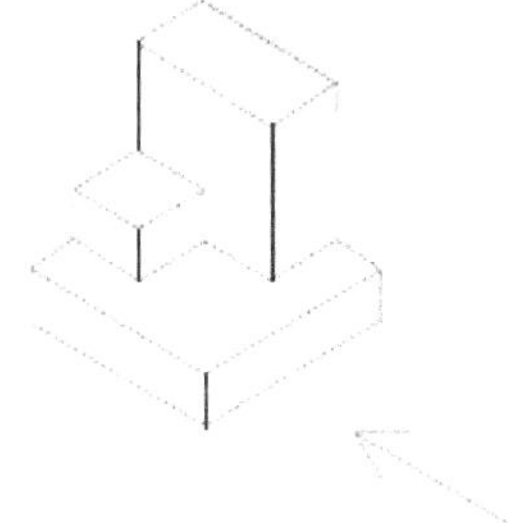

1.

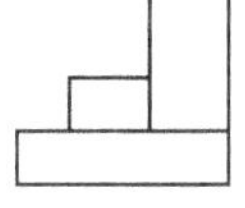

3.

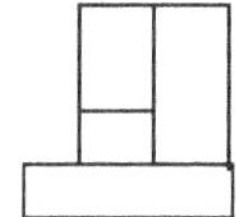

2.

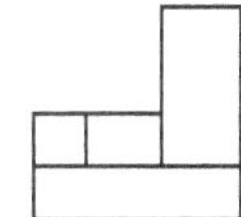

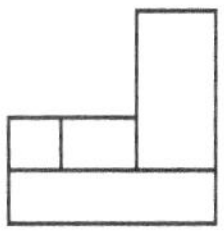

4.

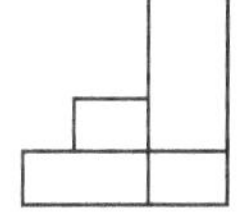

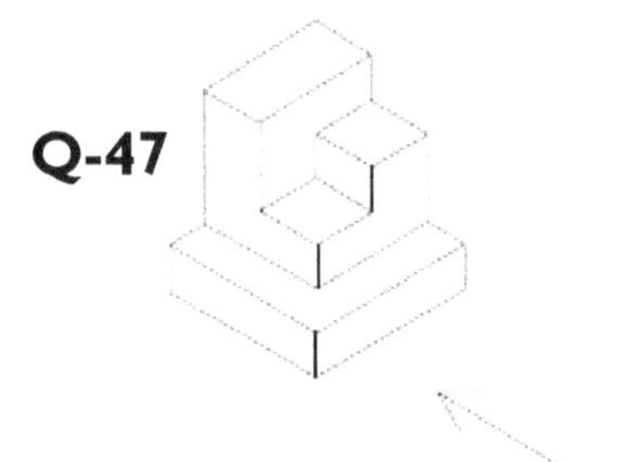

Q-47

1. 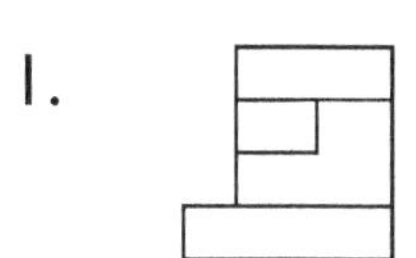
2. 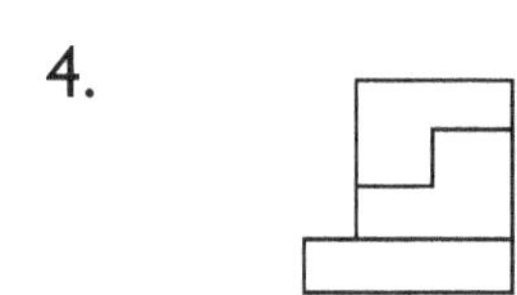
3. 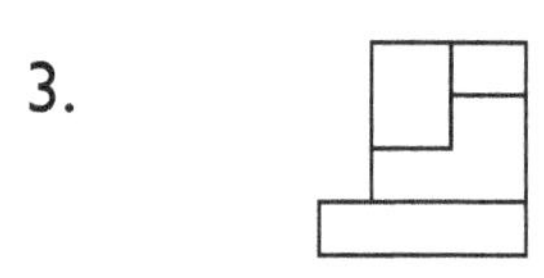

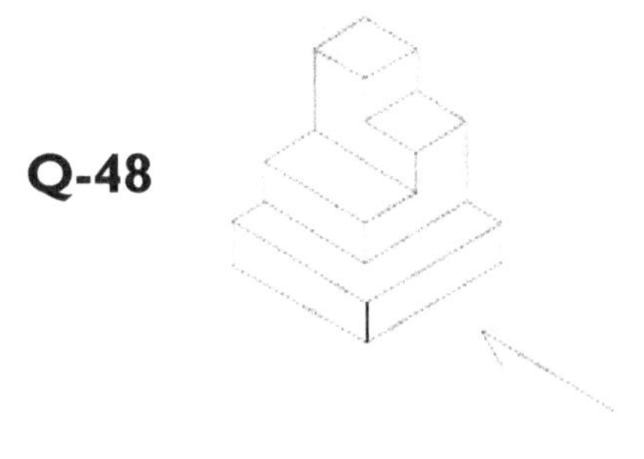

Q-48

1. 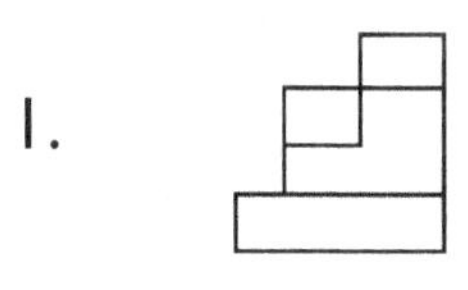
2. 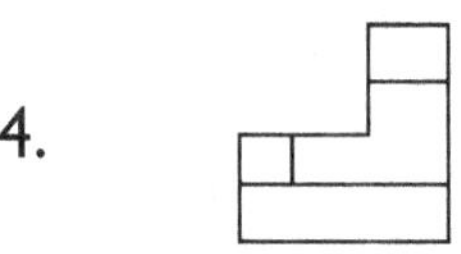
3. 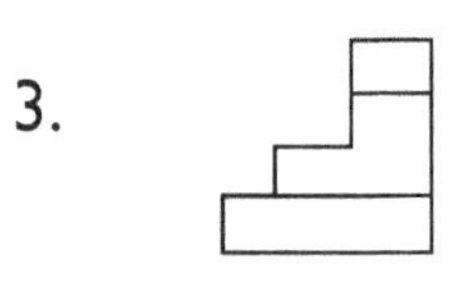
4.

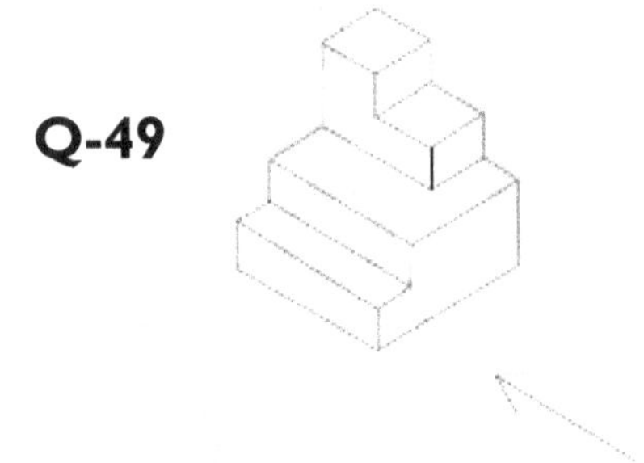

Q-49

1. 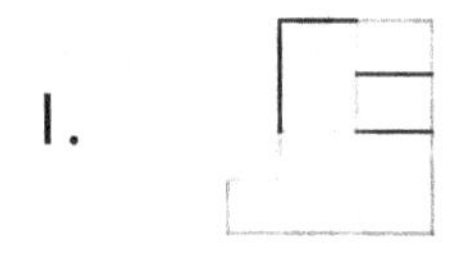
2. 
3. 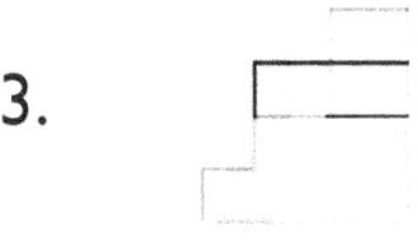
4.

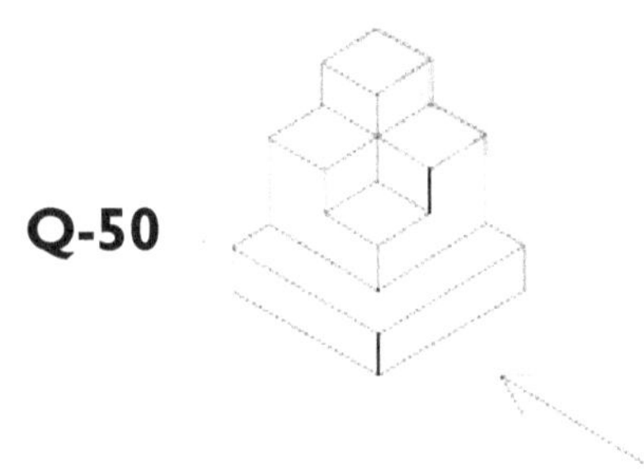

Q-50

1. 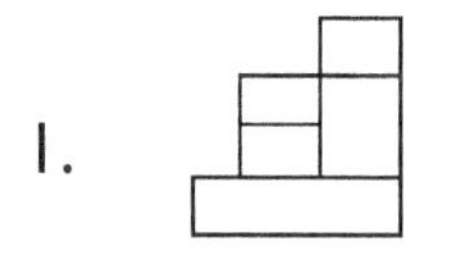
2.
3. 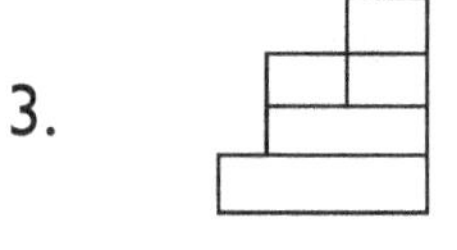
4.

<u>**SECTION - DRAWING**</u>

Q-1 In the space provided in the answer sheet for this question, draw margin lines to form a frame. In this frame create an aesthetic composition using only cubes. These can be of any size, and may be placed separate, overlapping or within each other. The idea is to produce an aesthetic and visually exciting composition of these shapes in the frame without making it represent any realistic form like house face etc. These shapes and the other spaces should be filled with some colors of your choice so that the visual quality of the composition is enhanced.

20 marks

Q-2 Copy the graphic image shown in he space provided for the answer of this question. Credit will be given to the exactness of our answer.

20 marks

Q-3 In the space provided for the answer of this question attempt any ONE of the following :

30 marks

Design and draw an appropriate pattern for a square table cloth. Color or shade it to enhance its visual quality .

OR

Draw a picture of a classroom looking towards the teacher from behind the students.

OR

Draw from imagination a picture of an officer sitting in his office.

Sketch of a view of a classroom looking towards the teacher from behind the students.

JEE 2019 ANSWERS

MATHEMATICS

1	2	3	4	5	6	7	8	9	10
2	4	3	2	3	2	4	2	3	3

11	12	13	14	15	16	17	18	19	20
6	3	1	1	3	1	2	2	3	4

21	22	23	24	25	26	27	28	29	30
3	4	4	1	1	2	2	4	3	3

APTITUDE TEST

1	2	3	4	5	6	7	8	9	10
3	2	3	1	1	2	3	4	1	3

11	12	13	14	15	16	17	18	19	20
2	3	2	3	1	1	4	1	1	4

21	22	23	24	25	26	27	28	29	30
3	3	3	2	2	2	4	2	3	1

31	32	33	34	35	36	37	38	39	40
3	2	1	4	3	4	2	3	4	3

41	42	43	44	45	46	47	48	49	50
3	2	4	3	3	1	4	3	4	4

PRESTIGIOUS ARCHITECTURE COLLEGES
OF
INDIA

There are more than 450 colleges of architecture in India. We are giving here names of some prestigious colleges. This list is not in the order of ranking.

1. School of Planning and Architecture, New Delhi
2. Chandigarh College of Architecture, Chandigarh
3. J.J. School of Architecture, Mumbai, Maharashtra
4. C.E.P.T., Ahmedabad, Gujarat
5. Faculty of Architecture & Ekistics, Jamia Millia Islamia, New Delhi
6. School of Planning and Architecture, Bhopal, Madhya Pradesh
7. Indian Institute of Technology, Kharagpur, West Bengal
8. Indian Institute of Technology, Roorkee, Uttarakhand
9. National Insitute of Technology (Various States)
10. Sushant School of Art and Architecture, Gurgaon, Haryana
11. D.C.R. University of Science and Technology, Murthal, Haryana
12. Birla Institute of Technology, Mesra, Ranchi, Jharkhand
13. Rizvi College of Architecture, Mumbai, Maharashtra
14. Anna University, Chennai, Tamil Nadu
15. State University of Performing and Visual Arts, Rohtak, Haryana

Ar. Ashok Goel with
Prof. A. P. Mittal, Member Secretary,
All India Council for Technical Education

Ar. Ashok Goel
with K.T. Ravindran, Former Chairman,
Delhi Urban Art Commission

Architect Ashok Goel with renowned architect Raj Rewal

Ar. Ashok Goel
Mr. Kapil Sibal, then HRD Minister, Govt. of India

Ar. Ashok Goel
Ar. Vijay Garg, Acting President,
Council of Architecture

Ar. Ashok Goel with Prof.K.K.Aggarwal,
Chairman, National Board of Accreditation

JEE (B.Arch.) 2020 QUESTION PAPER (January 2020)

PART I - MATHEMATICS

Q-1 If the roots α and β of the equation, $x^2 - \sqrt{2}x + c = 0$ are complex for some real number $c \neq 1$ and $\left|\dfrac{\alpha - \beta}{1 - \alpha\beta}\right| = 1$, then the value of c is

1. $2 + \sqrt{6}$ $4 + \sqrt{6}$

2. $3 + \sqrt{6}$ $1 + \sqrt{6}$

Q-2 If θ is the angle between the line $r = (\hat{i}+2\hat{j}-\hat{k})+(\hat{i}-2\hat{j}-\hat{k})$

1. $\dfrac{\sqrt{13}}{6}$ 3. $\dfrac{\sqrt{35}}{6}$

2. $\dfrac{\sqrt{11}}{6}$ 4. $\dfrac{\sqrt{7}}{3}$

Q-3 If an ellipse has centre at $(0,0)$, a focus at $(-3,0)$ and the corresponding directrix is $3x+25 =0$, then it passes through the point:

1. $(5,\ 4)$ 3. $\left(5,\ \dfrac{4}{\sqrt{2}}\right)$

2. $\left(\dfrac{5}{\sqrt{2}},\ \dfrac{4}{\sqrt{2}}\right)$ 4. $\left(\dfrac{3}{2},\ 4\right)$

Q-4 The area (in sq. units) of the region enclosed by the lines, $ax \pm by \pm c=0$ $(a,b,c \in R$ are positive and distinct$)$ is:

1. $\dfrac{2c^2}{ab}$ 2. $\dfrac{2b^2}{ac}$ 3. $\dfrac{2a^2}{bc}$ 4. $\dfrac{4c^2}{ab}$

Q-5 Let C be the circle concentric with the circle $2x^2+2y^2-6x-10y=183$ and having $\left(\dfrac{1}{10}\right)^{th}$ of the area of this circle. Then a tangent to C, parallel to the line, $3x+y = 0$ makes and interncept on the y-axis, which is equal to:

1. 17 3. 14

2. 10 4. 4

Q-6 If α and β are the coefficients of x^8 and x^{-24} respectively, in the expansion of $\left(x^4+2+\dfrac{1}{x^4}\right)^{10}$ in powers of x, then $\dfrac{\alpha}{\beta}$ is equal to:

1. 39 3. $\dfrac{13}{2}$

2. 26 4. $\dfrac{32}{3}$

Q-7 The value of $\cot \dfrac{\pi}{24}$ is:

1. $2 + \sqrt{2} + \sqrt{3} - \sqrt{6}$

2. $1 + \sqrt{2} + \sqrt{3} + \sqrt{6}$

3. $2 + \sqrt{2} + \sqrt{3} + \sqrt{6}$

4. $1 - \sqrt{2} + \sqrt{3} + \sqrt{6}$

Q-8 Let $S = 3+55+333+5555+33333+...$ upto 22 terms. If $9S +88 = A(10^{22} - 1)$ then A is equal to:

1. $\dfrac{630}{88}$

2. $\dfrac{530}{99}$

3. $\dfrac{350}{88}$

4. $\dfrac{450}{99}$

Q-9 If $f(x) = \begin{vmatrix} \sin x & \cos x & \tan x \\ x^3 & x^2 & x \\ 2x & 1 & x \end{vmatrix}$

$x \in \left(-\dfrac{\pi}{2}, \dfrac{\pi}{2} \right)$, then $\lim\limits_{x \to 0} \dfrac{f(x)}{x^2}$ is equal to:

1. 1

2. 2

3. 0

4. 3

Q-10 The integral $\int \dfrac{(2\sin\theta - 1)\cos\theta}{5 - \cos^2\theta - 4\sin\theta}\,d\theta$ is equal to: (where C is a constant of integration)

1. $2\log_e(2 + \sin\theta) + \dfrac{3}{2 - \cos\theta} + C$

2. $2\log_e(2 - \sin\theta) + \dfrac{3}{2 - \sin\theta} + C$

3. $3\log_e(2 - \cos\theta) + \dfrac{2}{2 - \sin\theta} + C$

4. $3\log_e(2 + \cos\theta) + \dfrac{2}{2 - \cos\theta} + C$

Q-11 For non-zero real numbers l, m, n and a, let $f(x) = lx^3 + mx + n$ and $f(a) = f(4a)$. Then the value $x \in [a, 4a]$, at which the tangent to the curve $y = f(x)$ is parallel to the x-axis, is:

1. $\sqrt{5}\,a$

2. $3a$

3. $\sqrt{7}\,a$

4. $2a$

Q-12 If the probability of a shooter A not hitting a target is 0.5 and that for the shooter B is 0.7, then the probability that either A or B fails to hit the target is :

1. 0.25   3. 0.20

2. 0.35   4. 0.85

Q-13 The area (in sq . units) of the region, $R = \{(x, y) : y \le x^2, y \le 2x + 3, x \le 1 \text{ and } y + 1 \ge 0\}$ is:

1. $\dfrac{13}{3}$ 3. $\dfrac{10}{3}$

2. $\dfrac{8}{3}$ 4. $\dfrac{11}{3}$

Q-14 The Boolean expression $\sim (p \vee q) \vee (\sim p \wedge q)$ is equivalent to:

1. $\sim p$ 2. $\sim q$ 3. q 4. p

Q-15 Let X be a random variable which takes values k with the probability kp, where k = 1, 2, 3, 4 and $p \in (0, 1)$. Then the standard deviation of X is:

1. 1   3. 3

2. $\sqrt{7}$ 4. $\sqrt{10}$

Q-16 Let P be the point of intersection of two lines

$\dfrac{x+10}{1} = \dfrac{y-21}{7} = \dfrac{z+11}{5}$ and $\dfrac{x-1}{5} = \dfrac{y-46}{9} = \dfrac{z}{3}$. If Q be the point (-10, 21, -11); then PQ is equal to:

1. 3   3. $5\sqrt{2}$

2. $5\sqrt{3}$ 4. 5

Q-17 If $x = e^t \sin t$ and $y = e^t \cos t$, t is a parameter, $\dfrac{d^2 y}{dx^2} + \dfrac{d^2 x}{dy^2}$ at t=0, is:

1. 2   3. 2

2. $\dfrac{1}{2}$ 4. 0

Q-18 Let A be a 2 x 2 matrix such that $3A^2 + 6A - 4I = 0$. Then a value of $|A+I|$ is:

1. $\dfrac{7}{\sqrt{3}}$ 2. $\dfrac{7}{3}$ 3. $\sqrt{\dfrac{7}{3}}$ 4. $\dfrac{3}{7}$

Q-19 In a certain town, 25 % families own a phone, 15 % families own a car, 65 % families own neither a phone nor a car and 2000 families own both a car and a phone.

Consider the following Statements (S)

(S_1) 35 % families own at least one of a car or a phone.

(S_2) 40,000 families live in the town.

Then -

Then :

1. (S_1) is true and (S_2) is false.
2. (S_1) is false and (S_2) is true.
3. Both (S_1) and (S_2) are false.
4. Both (S_1) and (S_2) are true.

Q-20 The set of all positive real values of k, for whIch the equation $x^3 - 9x^2 + 24x - k = 0$ has three distinct real roots, is the interval :

1. (18, 21)
2. (12, 16)
3. (14, 18)
4. (16, 20)

Q-21 If $S = \{z \in C : \bar{z} = iz^2\}$, then the maximum value of $\left|z - \sqrt{3} - i\right|^2$ on S is ___.

Q-22 $\displaystyle\lim_{y \to 0} \frac{(y-2) + 2\sqrt{1 + y + y^2}}{2y}$ is equal to__________

Q-23 If y=y(x) is the soution of the differential equation,

$$x\frac{dy}{dx} = y(\log_e y - \log_e x + 1), \text{when } y(1)=2, \text{then } y(2) \text{ is equal to}\underline{\hspace{3cm}}.$$

Q-24 The largest value of $n \in N$ for which

$$\frac{74}{^nP_n} > \frac{^{n+3}P_3}{^{n+1}P_{n+1}} \text{ is } \underline{\hspace{4cm}}.$$

Q-25 The interior angles of a polygon are all obtuse and are in A.P. If the smallest angle is 120° and common difference of this A.P. is 5°, then the number of sides of the polygon is ______ .

PART II - APTITUDE

Q.1 Which one of the answer figures is the correct mirror image of the problem figure with respect to X - X ?

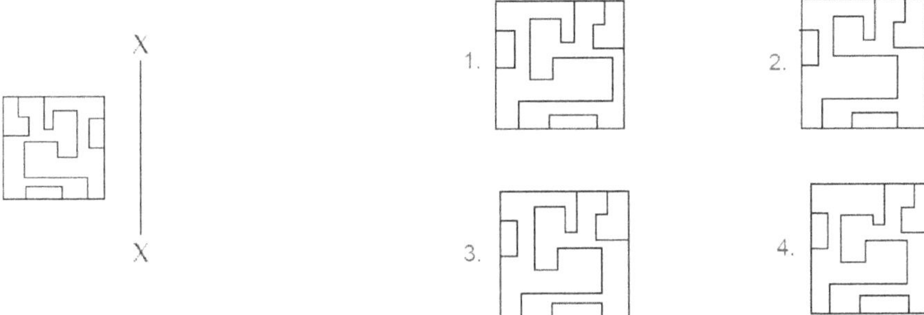

Q.2 Which one of the answer figures is the correct mirror image of the problem figure with respect to X - X ?

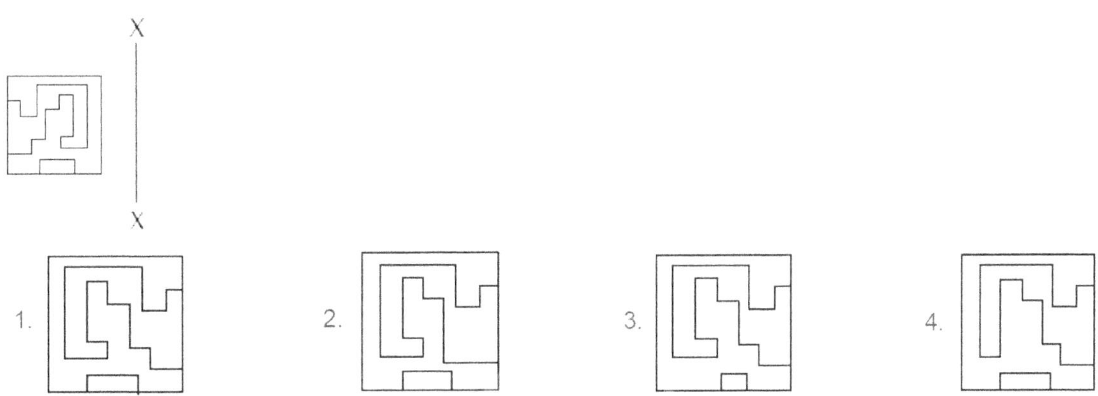

Q.3 The 3 - D figure shows the view of an object. Identify the correct top view from amongst the answer figures.

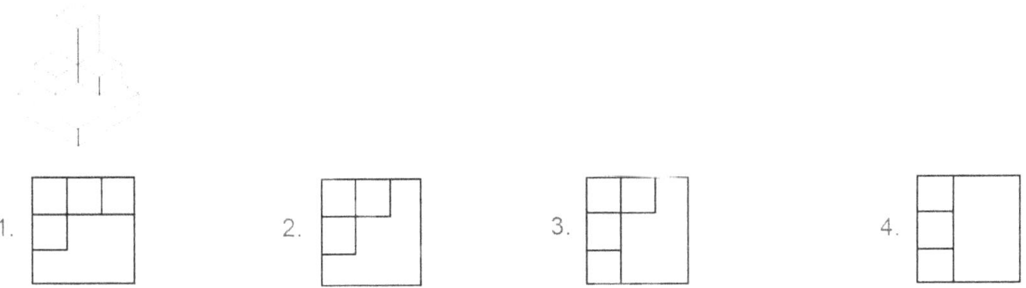

Q.4 The 3 - D figure shows the view of an object. Identify the correct view when the figure is opened up, from amongst the answer figures.

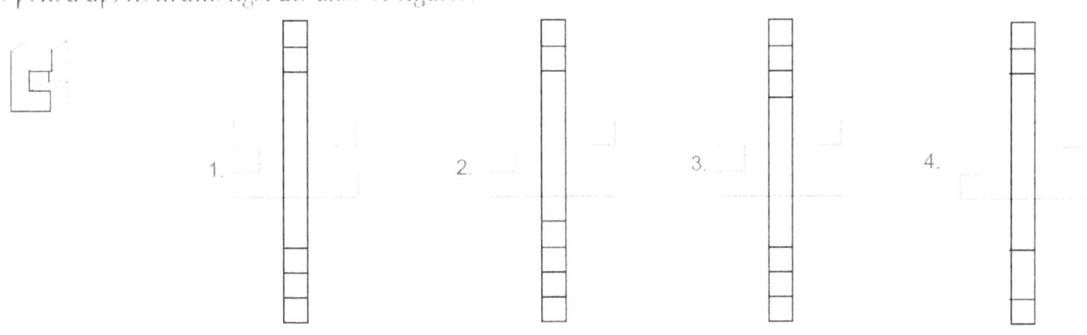

Q.5 In northern hemisphere, in summers, in which of the following directions does the sun set?

    1. South-west   2. North-east   3. North-west   4. South-east

Q.6 The 3 - D figure shows the view of an object. Identify the correct view in the direction of the arrow, from amongst the answer figures.

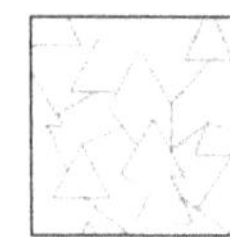
1. 
2. 
3.
4. 

Q.7 Which one of the following textures describes the surface of a mirror ?

1. Coarse   3. Grainy

2. Shiny   4. Wrinkled

Q.8 In which one of the following situations are trusses normally used in buildings ?

1. High Rise Buildings   3. Large Span Buildings

2. Buildings in Deserts   4. Under Water Buildings

Q.9 The problem figure is embedded in one of the answer figures given below in the same size and direction. Select, which one is correct.

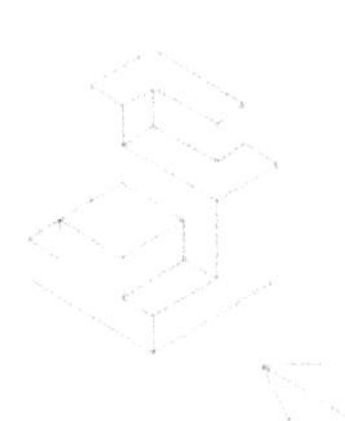
1.   2.   3.   4.

Q.10 The 3 - D figure shows the view of an object. Identify the correct view in the direction of the arrow, from amongst the answer figures.

1.   2.   3.   4.

Q.11 The 3 - D figure shows the view of an object. Identify the correct view when the figure is opened up, from amongst the answer figures.

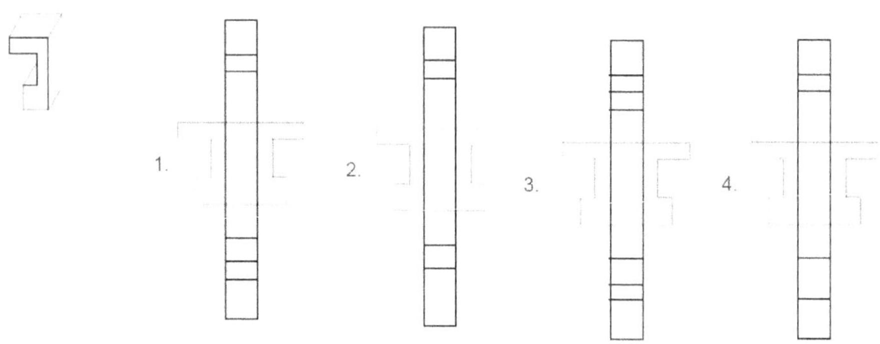
1.   2.   3.   4.

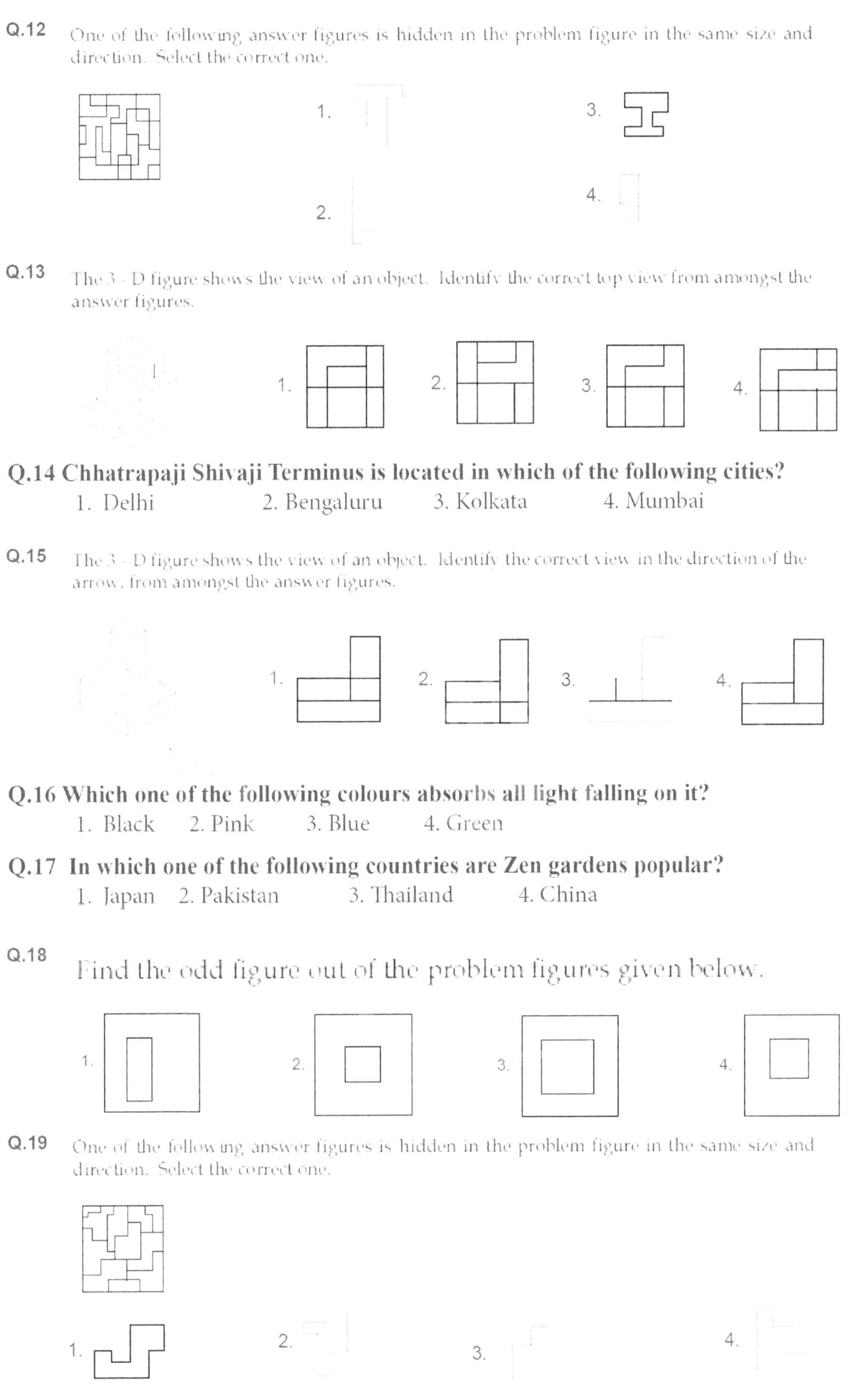

Q.12 One of the following answer figures is hidden in the problem figure in the same size and direction. Select the correct one.

1.

2.

3.

4.

Q.13 The 3 - D figure shows the view of an object. Identify the correct top view from amongst the answer figures.

1.   2.   3.   4.

Q.14 Chhatrapaji Shivaji Terminus is located in which of the following cities?

1. Delhi   2. Bengaluru   3. Kolkata   4. Mumbai

Q.15 The 3 - D figure shows the view of an object. Identify the correct view in the direction of the arrow, from amongst the answer figures.

1.   2.   3.   4.

Q.16 Which one of the following colours absorbs all light falling on it?

1. Black   2. Pink   3. Blue   4. Green

Q.17 In which one of the following countries are Zen gardens popular?

1. Japan   2. Pakistan   3. Thailand   4. China

Q.18 Find the odd figure out of the problem figures given below.

1.   2.   3.   4.

Q.19 One of the following answer figures is hidden in the problem figure in the same size and direction. Select the correct one.

1.   2.   3.   4.

Q.20 The 3 – D figure shows the view of an object. Identify the correct view when the figure is opened up, from amongst the answer figures.

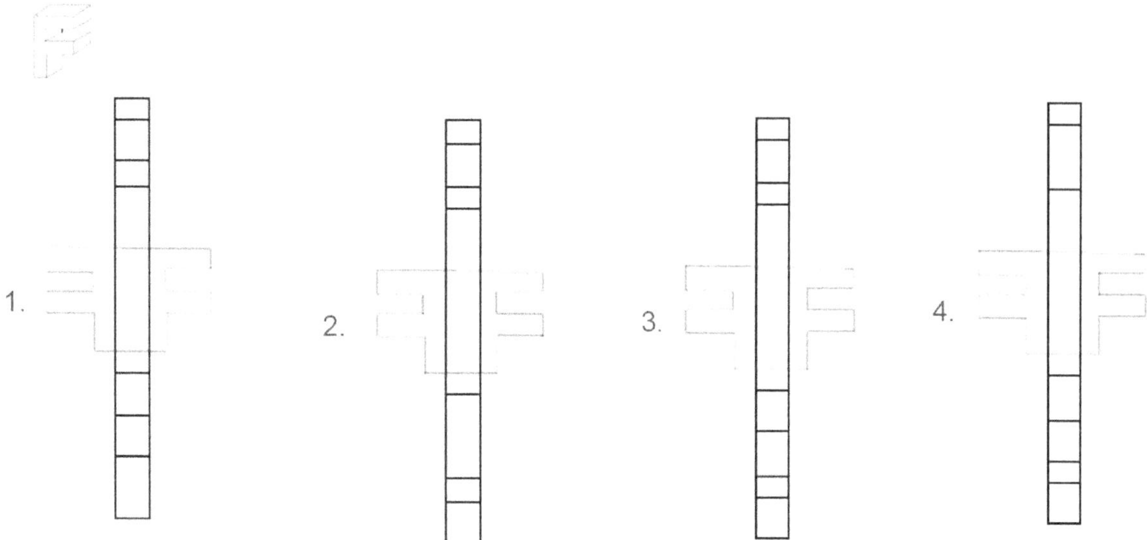

Q.21 Which one of the answer figures is the correct mirror image of the problem figure with respect to X - X ?

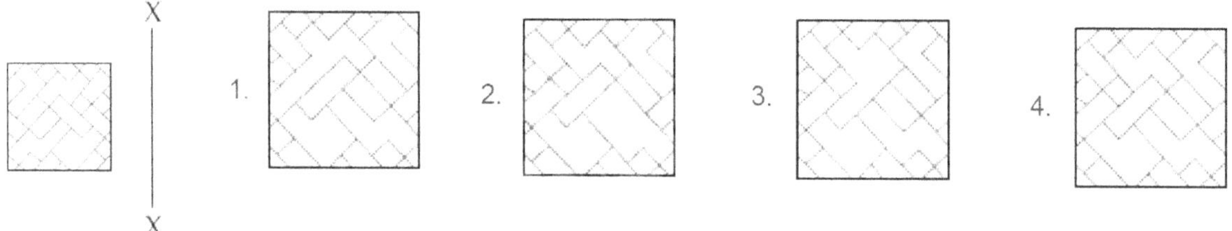

Q.22 The 3 – D figure shows the view of an object. Identify the correct view in the direction of the arrow, from amongst the answer figures.

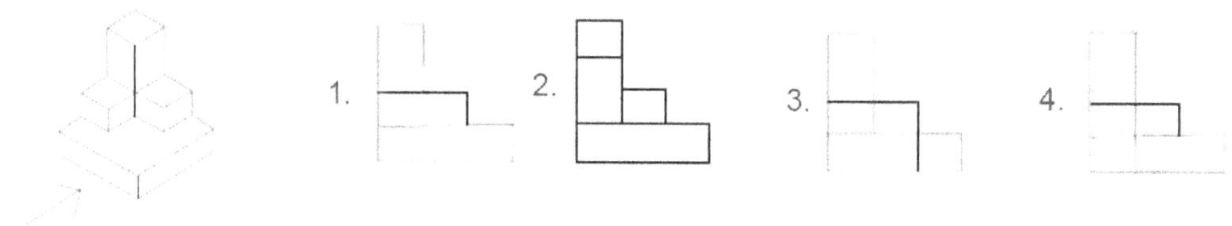

Q.23 The 3 – D figure shows the view of an object. Identify the correct view in the direction of the arrow, from amongst the answer figures.

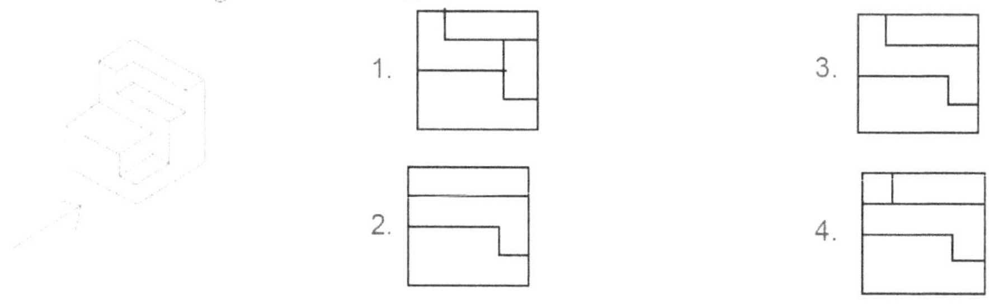

Q.24 One of the following answer figures is hidden in the problem figure in the same size and direction. Select the correct one.

1.

3.

2.

4.

Q.25 In which one of the following countries is Piazza San Marco located ?

1. Italy

2. Germany

3. England

4. France

Q.26 The 3 - D figure shows the view of an object. Identify the correct view in the direction of the arrow, from amongst the answer figures.

1.

3.

2.

4.

Q.27 Find the odd figure out of the problem figures given below.

1.

3.

2.

4.

Q.28 Which one of the answer figures is the correct mirror image of the problem figure with respect to X - X ?

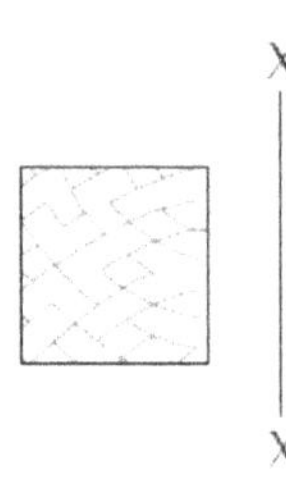

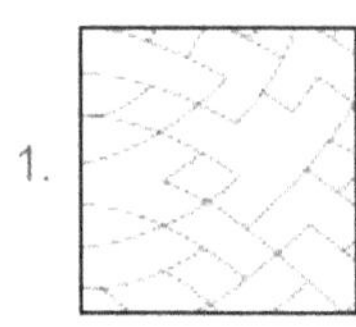

1.

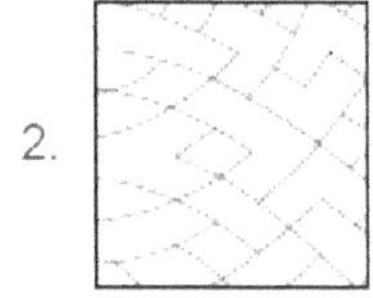

2.

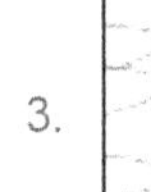

3.

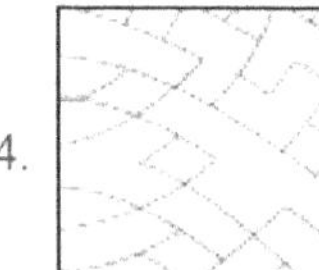

4.

Q.29 Which one of the following floorings is ideal for indoor badminton courts ?

1. Granite

2. Marble

3. Brick

4. Wood

Q.30 The 3 - D figure shows the view of an object. Identify the correct view in the direction of the arrow, from amongst the answer figures.

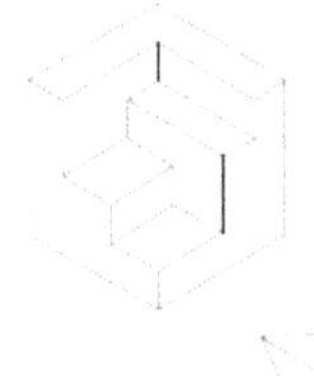

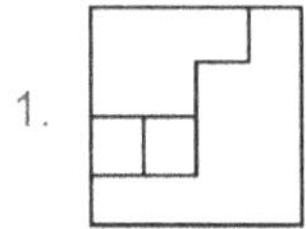

1.

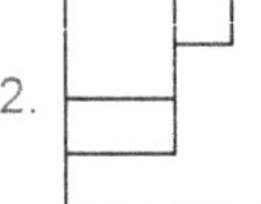

2.

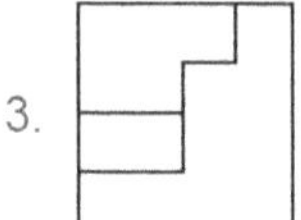

3.

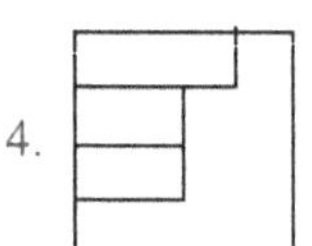

4.

Find the odd figure out of the problem figures given below.

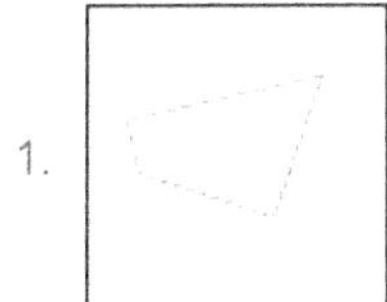

1.

2.   3.   4.

Q.32 In which one of the following States is the Konark Sun Temple ?

1. Karnataka

2. Haryana

3. Andhra Pradesh

4. Odisha

Q.33 The 3 - D figure shows the view of an object. Identify the correct top view from amongst the answer figures.

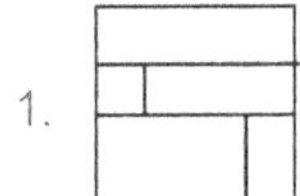

1.

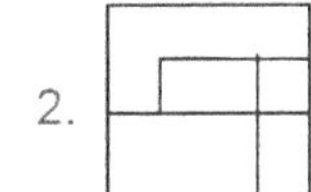

2.

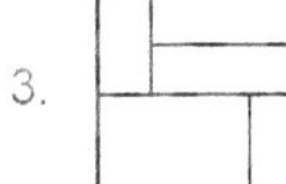

3.

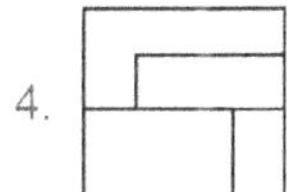

4.

Q.34 Which one of the answer figures is the correct mirror image of the problem figure with respect to X - X ?

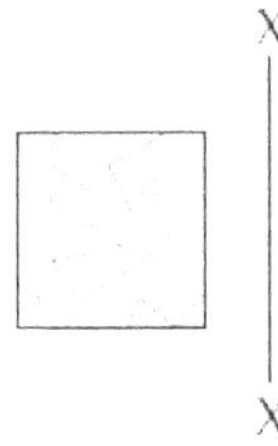

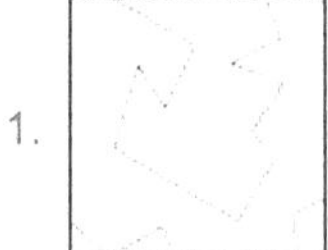

1.

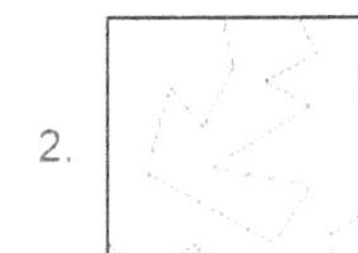

2.

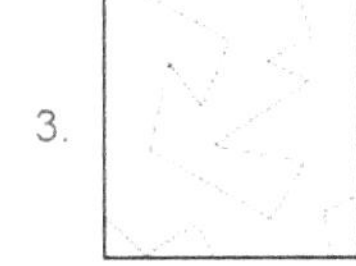

3.

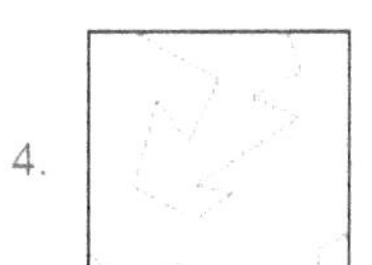

4.

Q.35 Which one of the following architects designed the Madhya Pradesh Assembly Building ?

1. B.V. Doshi
2. Raj Rewal
3. A.P. Kanvinde
4. Charles Correa

Q.36 Located in Paris, Louvre, is what type of building amongst the following?
1. A banquet hall   2. A museum   3. A dance hall   4. A residence

Q.37 What is the conventional height of doors of houses?
1. 2.5 metres   2. 2.1 metres   3. 1.5 metres   4. 2.8 metres

Q.38 Find the odd figure out of the problem figures given below.

1. 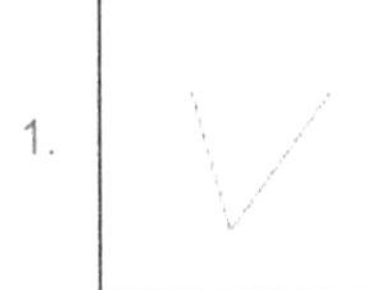   2. 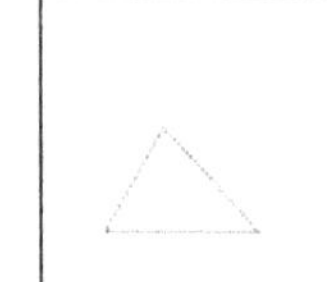   3.    4. 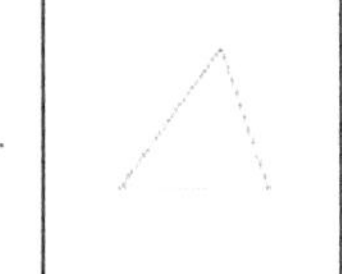

Q.39 One of the following answer figures is hidden in the problem figure in the same size and direction. Select the correct one.

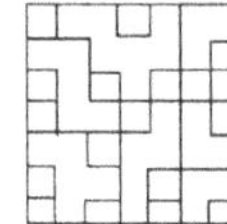

1. 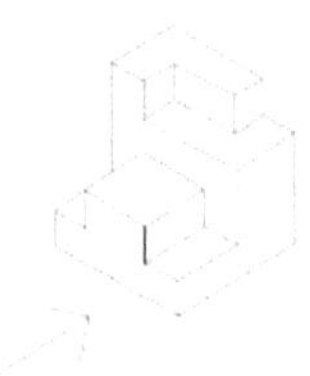   3. 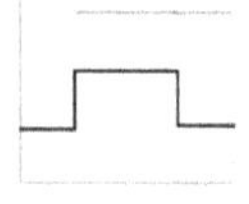

2.   4. 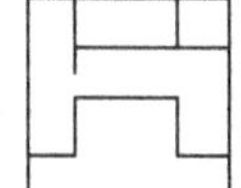

Q.40 The 3 – D figure shows the view of an object. Identify the correct view in the direction of the arrow, from amongst the answer figures.

Q.41 The 3 - D figure shows the view of an object. Identify the correct view in the direction of the arrow, from amongst the answer figures.

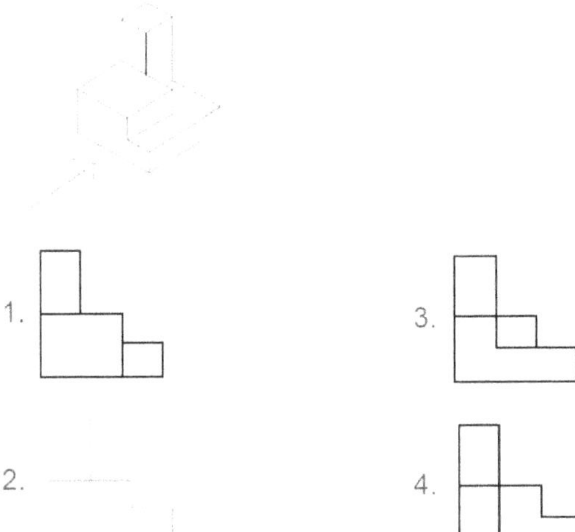

1.

2.

3.

4.

Q.42 The 3 - D figure shows the view of an object. Identify the correct top view from amongst the answer figures.

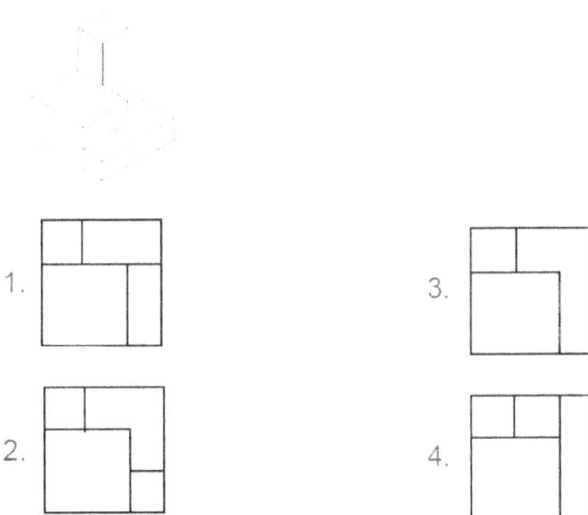

1.

2.

3.

4.

Q.43 The 3 - D figure shows the view of an object. Identify the correct view when the figure is opened up, from amongst the answer figures.

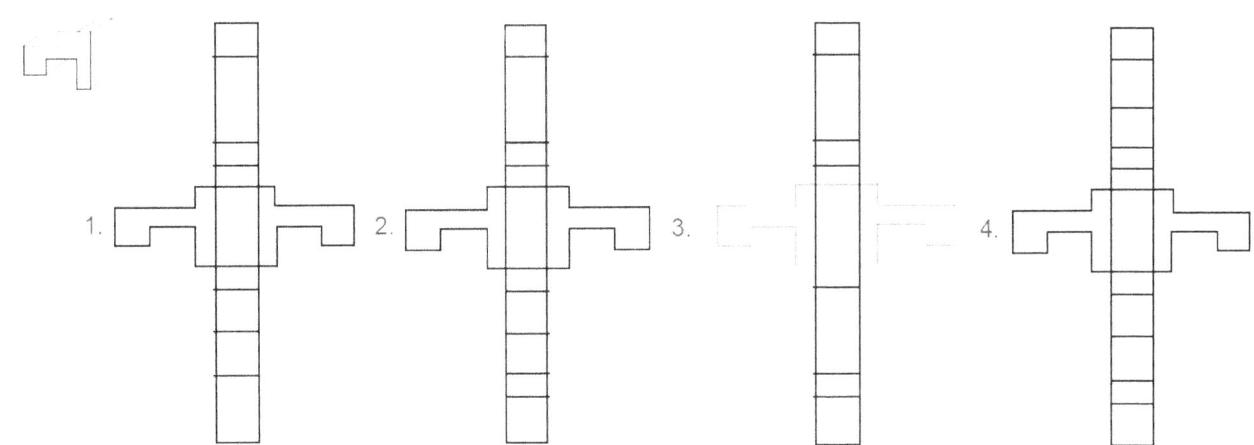

1.

2.

3.

4.

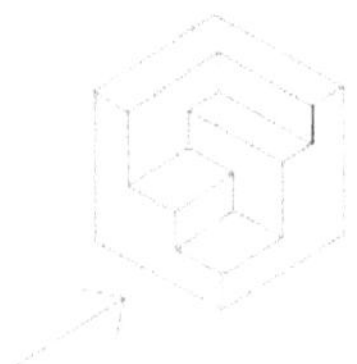

Q.44 The 3 - D figure shows the view of an object. Identify the correct view in the direction of the arrow, from amongst the answer figures.

1.

3.

2.

4.

Q.45 What is the thickness of a half brick thick wall?

1. 6"   2. 4.5"   3. 9"   4. 8"

Q.46 What is the purpose of louvers in buildings ?

1. To support buildings   3. As sun breakers

2. To hide something   4. To stop wind from entering

Q.47 Which one of the following colors is perceived as cowardice ?

1. Purple   3. Yellow

2. Orange   4. Pink

Q.48 The 3 - D figure shows the view of an object. Identify the correct top view from amongst the answer figures.

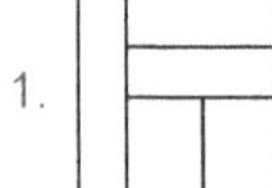

1.

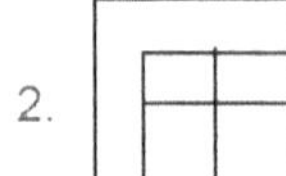

2.

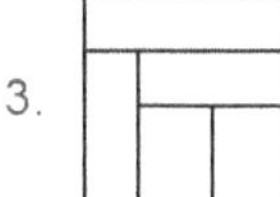

3.

4.

 Find the odd figure out of the problem figures given below.

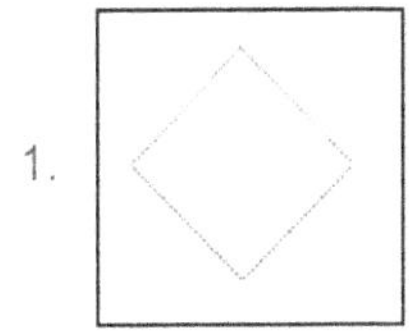

1.

2.

3.

4.

Q.50 The 3 – D figure shows the view of an object. Identify the correct view when the figure is opened up, from amongst the answer figures.

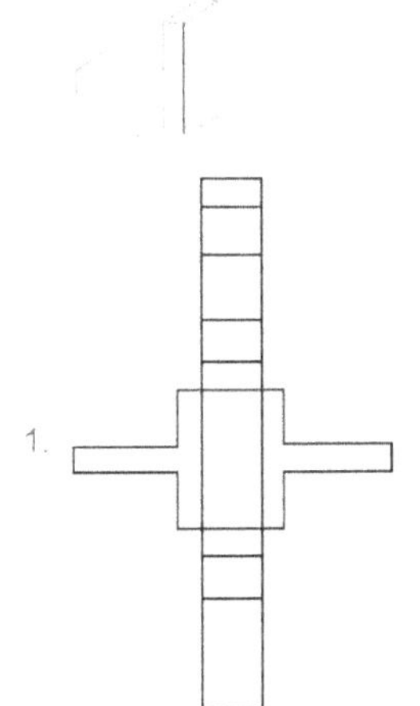

1.

2.

3.

4.

PART III - DRAWING

Q.1 Using various cylinders, create a beautiful composition. There is no restriction on number of cylinders, their sizes, placement, etc. Colour the drawing to make it more beautiful.

Q.2 Using your imagination, show a gymnast doing exercise.

OR

Imagine that some children are playing in the school playground. Draw their sketch.

OR

Draw the sketch of your grandfather or grandmother from your memory.

JEE 2020 ANSWERS

MATHEMATICS

1	2	3	4	5	6	7	8	9	10
2	2	2	1	1	2	3	2	1	2
11	12	13	14	15	16	17	18	19	20
3	4	4	1	1	2	4	2	4	4

21	22	23	24	25
9.0	1.00	8.00	6.00	9.00

APTITUDE TEST

1	2	3	4	5	6	7	8	9	10
3	1	2	1	3	2	2	3	3	3
11	12	13	14	15	16	17	18	19	20
1	4	3	4	4	1	1	1	3	3
21	22	23	24	25	26	27	28	29	30
4	1	3	1	1	1	2	2	4	3
31	32	33	34	35	36	37	38	39	40
3	4	4	3	4	2	2	1	4	1
41	42	43	44	45	46	47	48	49	50
2	3	2	3	2	3	3	4	1	2